Mark Potok, Paul Harsh
Marcelo Aparicio, María Unceta

Senior Series Writer
Tom Burns

Edited by
Erica Witschey

Everything Under the Sun Travel Guide Series
Other titles in the Series: Benidorm, Calvià (Majorca), Marbella, Maspalomas (Canary Islands), Palma (Majorca), Puerto de la Cruz (Canary Islands), Seville, Sitges (Costa Dorada), Toledo and Torremolinos

First published in the United States 1987
by NATIONAL TEXTBOOK COMPANY
4255 West Touhy Avenue, Lincolnwood, IL 60646

First published in Great Britain 1987
by HARRAP COLUMBUS
19-23 Ludgate Hill, London EC4M 7PD

First published in Spain 1987
by NOVATEX EDICIONES S.A.
Explanada, 16, 28040 Madrid

Collaborator: Lettice Small
Cover Design: Vitruvio 30
Cover Logo: Joan Miró
Drawings: Enrique Ortega
Field Research: Javier Ruiz
Maps: Javier Ruiz
Photographs: J. Dieuzaide, M. Esclusa, Photographic Archives of the Instituto Nacional de Promoción del Turismo, Salvat, W. Thorpe.
Senior Series Writer: Tom Burns
Series Editor: Erica Witschey

Colour Separation and Reproduction: Progreso Gráfico, S.A., Madrid
Electronic Editing: Isabel Balmaseda, software and interface by Protec, S.A.
Printed by: Gráficas Estella, S.A., Navarre
Typeset at: Pérez Díaz, S.A. Madrid

ISBN 0-8442-9203-6
D.L.: NA-468-1987

Printed in Spain

Published with the co-operation of the Spanish Ministry of Culture

CONTENTS

Introduction
5 Barcelona: A Sparkling Mediterranean Capital
6 How to Use this Guide
9 Basic Facts
11 Getting Ready for the Trip
The Guide
13 Beaches
15 City Itineraries
23 Consulates
24 Consumer Rights
25 Cuisine
31 Culture and History
32 Architecture
39 Cinema
40 Design, Crafts, Fashion and Decorative Arts
43 History
52 Literature
57 Music
60 Painting and Sculpture
64 Entertainment
72 Excursions
81 Fiestas and Festivals
85 Lodging
85 Apartments
86 Camping Sites
88 Hotels and Hostels
96 Mail
96 Mass Media
97 Organized Tours
98 Photography
99 Places of Interest
121 Police and Security
122 Restaurants
130 Shopping
140 Spanish Way of Life: Information for Foreigners
147 Sports
152 Useful Addresses
154 Wines
Maps and Street Index
158 Street Index
158 Maps

BARCELONA: A SPARKLING MEDITERRANEAN CAPITAL

It is a bit like London. With apologies to Dr. Johnson, if you tire of Barcelona, you tire of Life. Barcelona is that sort of place. It is a big, vibrant city where there is so much going on that you virtually have to run to stay in the same place. A visit to Barcelona is a completely enriching experience. The locals, naturally, claim it is the best city on the Mediterranean. They are almost certainly right.

Aptly, the high peak that rises up behind the city is called Tibidabo, from the Latin *I give to you*. That, explain the engaging people of the city, is because the Tempter took the Lord up to that mountain when He was in the wilderness and from that mountain peak the Tempter offered Him everything He could see (Tibi dabo) if He would fall down and adore him. Barcelona, according to that legend, is everything anyone could desire.

Like the few cities in the world that belong to the **top bracket** Barcelona is several things at the same time. It is a prosperous and busy commercial centre. It hums with activity be it financial or industrial. Barcelona has also got all the romance of a big seaport town. Like all the great port cities it is outward looking, inventive, varied and welcoming. Barcelona is, finally, a thriving haven for the arts and creativity. The people of Barcelona, immensely **wise, sophisticated and cultured** as they have always been, have traditionally channelled their wealth and prosperity towards beautifying the city.

Barcelona is at once **historic,** conserving lovingly past cultures, and yet, at the same time, **futuristic** and unfettered. The genius of Gaudí, Barcelona's artist *par excellence*, is emblematic of this all too difficult synthesis. In him you had the prime mover of Modernism, breaking every rule in the book as he soared in his architecture towards greater and greater heights of inspiration. And yet Gaudi's work is also rooted in a naturalism that has been with us since the world began. In Barcelona you can inmerse yourself in the Romanesque world and in the world of Picasso and of Miró. When you have visited the two worlds, centuries of experience apart, and then muse about them over a drink in the city's Gothic quarter, you wonder whether there is really a gap between the one and the other.

There are museums aplenty in Barcelona which take you through the **history of art** from the second century to Miró and Picasso in the 20C. But in a sense whole areas of the city, like the Gothic quarter, are museums. There is almost a surfeit, too, of art galleries for promising young painters converge on Barcelona like moths to a lamp. And there is **music** ranging from the grand productions of the Liceo opera season to the concerts of the Palau de la Musica. The world of letters is not forgotten: Barcelona is the centre of Spain's publishing industry. And the world of sports has modern facilities: in **1992** Barcelona will be home to the Summer **Olympics**.

Barcelona shows its civilisation in many other ways. It demonstrates it in the courtesy of its people, in the **excellence of its restaurants,** in the **elegance of its shops.** All of this and more is enveloped in a sense of enjoyment about life, a continual sparkle, that is properly Mediterranean. If you can drag yourself away from all the city's enchantments you have, in no time at all, a magnificent coast line, the breathtaking Pyrenees and a host of old towns and ancient monasteries that show how civilisation ran deep and spread wide.

HOW TO USE THIS GUIDE

This guide offers you **everything under the sun**, and everything under the moon and the stars as well, about enjoying yourself, travelling and living in this part of Spain. There's much more here than a listing of hotels and restaurants, monuments and museums: this book contains all the information, tips and advice a visitor will need. It includes suggestions on everything from shopping to sports, trips for the curious and energetic, detailed descriptions for the sedentary, maps and complete city plans, street guides and more.
You'll find an overall description of the city and region, accompanied by basic data, climatic conditions and other general information at the beginning of the guide. The rest of the book is organized **alphabetically** according to topics such as

LODGING

for instance, in a way that makes it easy to find what you're looking for. At the end of the guide's text there are general maps and city maps. A street directory follows.

Abbreviations

Only the most common abbreviations are used in the guide. Compass directions are given as N, S, E, and W (north, south, east, and west). Common abbreviations for weights and measures are also used.

When addresses are given, the abbreviation *c/* means *calle*, or street (as in c/ Huertas); avenue, *avenida*, is *Av*; highway, *carretera*, is *Ctra*; development, *urbanización*, is *Urb*; square, *plaza*, is *Pl* and building, *edificio*, is *Edif*. When an address doesn't have a street number, it usually is marked *s/n* for *sin número*, without a number.

Cross-References

The guide also incorporates a system of cross-references that refer the reader to other sections or pages where more information on the subject at hand is to be found. The references look like this: ▶ *page xx*. When sites or addresses can't be easily found by address, the guide refers the reader directly to notations in the maps at the back of the book, making getting there simple.

Highlighted Text and Classifications

Throughout the guide you will find words, symbols and complete sentences which are highlighted. The guide has five grades, or levels, of highlighting. The first, in black, indicates anything that is attractive or interesting for one reason or another. The second grade, highlighted in blue, refers to things the visitor should make every effort to see if in the area. The third, fourth and fifth levels correspond to the one, two and three **Miró suns**, which appear alongside the text and always beside an item highlighted in blue. The three grades indicate what the reader should make certain of seeing and experiencing before leaving the area. Their meaning is the following. ☉ : It's worth making a detour. ☉ ☉ : Spend a day on this one. ☉ ☉ ☉: This alone makes a trip to the area worthwhile.

Prices and Symbols

Generally speaking, this guide doesn't give prices. The reason is sensible enough: every price printed in any guide in the world is outdated. It makes more sense, and is more useful to the reader, to use a gradation of these symbols: from **$** to **$$$$$**.

Hotel equivalencies:	**Restaurant** equivalencies:
$: up to 2,000 ptas	**$**: up to 750 ptas
$$: from 2,000 to 4,000 ptas	**$$**: from 750 to 1,500 ptas
$$$: from 4,000 to 6,000 ptas	**$$$**: from 1,500 to 3,300 ptas
$$$$: from 6,000 to 8,000 ptas	**$$$$**: from 3,300 to 5,000 ptas
$$$$$: more than 8,000 ptas	**$$$$$**: more than 5,000 ptas

Symbols

In **Hotels**

- ★ category
- rating
- $ cost
- postal code
- telephone
- number of rooms
- bathroom
- hotel restaurant
- hotel bar
- ✂ hairdressing salon/beauty salon
- ♿ access and facilities for the handicapped
- safety deposit boxes
- medical aid
- baby sitting service
- TV television
- room phone
- P parking
- gardens
- ↕ lifts
- air-conditioned rooms
- meeting rooms
- dogs not allowed
- quiet/peaceful place
- swimming pool
- beach
- ♫ discotheque
- heated rooms
- sauna/workout facilities
- « view
- movie theatre/video
- children's playroom
- skin diving
- waterskiing
- sailing
- windsurfing
- tennis
- ♠ table games
- bowling/skittle
- golf
- horseback riding
- mini-golf
- fishing
- hunting
- AE American Express
- DC Diners Club
- V Visa
- EC Euro Card
- MC Mastercard
- CB Carte Blanche

In **Restaurants**:

- ☆ category
- rating
- $ cost
- postal code
- telephone

The guide carries a brief description and commentary on most hotels, restaurants, discotheques, clubs, bars and similar establishments that are worthy of note. Information on location is also included in these sections.

Up-dating the Guide

The book that you are holding in your hands contains more information than any other of its type. It is the product of a team of professionals working up to press time to make it accurate and up-to-date; but should the reader come across any error or outdated information, or have a new aspect or view of a certain topic, **help us to help you** in the next edition. Send any information or suggestions you have to:

Editors
Novatex Ediciones, S.A.
c/ Explanada, 16
28040 Madrid, Spain

Thank you for your confidence in the authors, the editors and the National Institute for the Promotion of Tourism. And now, a final suggestion: **enjoy yourself to the full.**

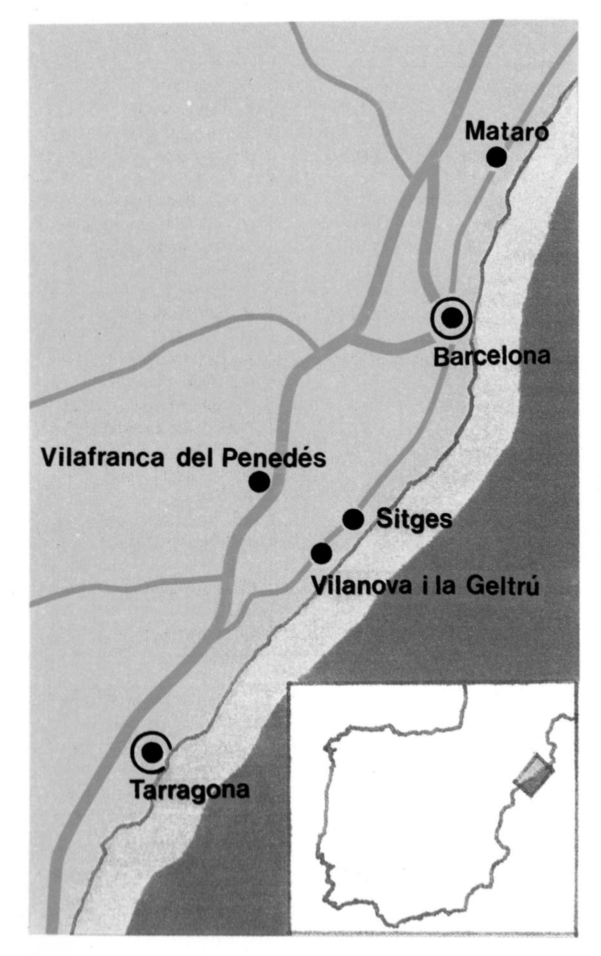

BASIC FACTS

Climate

The local weather is perhaps best described as Mediterranean, that is to say mild all year long. The Collserola mountain range, of which the *Tibidabo* forms part ▶ *page* 21, effectively protects Barcelona from the cold northerly winds. The weather is considerably more pleasant, particularly in winter, than it would be without this added shelter.

Autumn is very temperate as a rule, well into November. The *rains* normally come in October-November and February-March. Spring is usually brisk and cool, with beautiful sunny days, until the end of April.

The *mean air temperature* rarely goes below 12°C (54°F) in winter and 24°C (75°F) in summer. The region averages some 2,900 *hours of sunshine* per year.

How to Get There

By plane: The International Airport of El Prat de Llobregat, 14km from Barcelona, ☎ 370 10 11 and 325 43 04, is connected daily with almost all the capitals and major cities of Europe; it has an air shuttle service to Madrid with hourly departures and it is easy to make trans-Atlantic connections from here. Every 20 minutes a train connects the airport terminal with Sants Station in downtown Barcelona.

By road: Many international bus companies serve Barcelona. For those using their own car, the most direct route from France is the A17 motorway which joins the French B9 highway at the frontier of *Le Perthus-La Junquera*. From the border post of *Hendaye-Irún* and from *San Sebastián*, the quickest and easiest route is the A8 motorway, taking the Lasarte exit in the direction of Tolosa, and then the N420 highway followed by the A15 motorway —which leads to the A68 motorway— to Zaragoza; from there, take the A2 motorway to El Vendrell and then the A7 motorway to Barcelona. From *Santander* and *Bilbao*, the most direct route is the A68 motorway to Zaragoza followed by the A2 motorway to El Vendrell and from there the A7 motorway to Barcelona. Finally, from *Madrid* the easiest route is highway N2 to Zaragoza, then motorway A2 to El Vendrell, followed by the A7 motorway to Barcelona.

By highway, Barcelona is 620km from Madrid, 1,023km from Seville, 998km from Málaga, and 150km from La Junquera.

By sea: The large port of Barcelona is served by regular passenger lines that cater to three points in the Balearic Islands (Palma, Mahón and Ibiza) and the cities of Málaga, Cádiz, Algiers and Oran. There is also a ferry from Genoa. In addition, a great many cruise ships stop at Barcelona.

By train: Numerous trains connect Barcelona with the major cities and lines in Europe. The majority of both national and international trains arrive at Sants Station in downtown Barcelona, but some will come into Francia Station. Check at which station your train will arrive. In any case, there are frequent trains connecting both stations.

Language

The two official languages of Catalonia are Catalan and Castilian Spanish, both modern tongues that derive from vulgar Latin. Catalans passionately love their language for it has been the binding force of

Catalonia's identity, of its people and culture for centuries. Nevertheless, they will happily speak Spanish to other Spaniards or foreigners who do not know Catalan. Most signs and public notices are in Catalan, however, especially on highways, shops, and the various offices of the local autonomous government.

Location

Situated in the NE corner of Spain, Barcelona is the capital of the Autonomous Community of Catalonia and the seat of the autonomous government, the Generalitat ▶ *page* 52. Hugging the shores of the Mediterranean, it is a city with a long history as an industrial centre and its port is one of the most important and bustling in Europe. The city is an enclave within the Costa Dorada —it is a only a few kilometres from such busy tourist centres as Sitges, Arenys de Mar and Calella and some 100km from the furthest reaches of the Costa Brava.

Population

The population of Barcelona proper is more than 1.8 million people, and there are some 4 million in the greater metropolitan area. The city has been a great industrial centre since the mid-19C, giving rise to large-scale immigration from the poorer parts of Spain. Mixed with the Catalans, therefore, are numerous men and women from Andalusia, Castile, Galicia and Extremadura, each of whom brings something special to the collective life of the city.

The Catalans, and more pronouncedly the Barcelonans, share that joy of life that is peculiar to all Spaniards. Among the qualities history has given the Catalans are liberalism, a bourgeois aesthetic tradition that goes back to the Middle Ages, and a marked dedication to work. Enterprise is highly valued here, and Catalans are well-known throughout Spain for their openness to ideas from the rest of the world. Traditions are nevertheless jealously loved and guarded; the *sardana*, a Catalan dance, local music, cooking and customs all still thrive here. Catalans are peaceful, tenacious as businessmen, faithful to the soil —the hymn of Catalonia is *Els Segadors*, or The Harvesters— and their language. At the same time, these are the people who navigated the Mediterranean and sought their fortunes in America. They also helped bring the Industrial Revolution to Spain. All in all, they are the most European people of Spain, though the local hospitality is Spanish and conditioned by more than a century of dealing with tourists. The Catalan is at once gregarious and profoundly individualistic. He is sophisticated and elegant, imaginative and something of a dreamer, though with his feet always firmly planted on the ground.

Telephone

The telephone prefix for Barcelona and the province of Barcelona is **93**. The local phone system is fully automatic for calls to virtually the entire world.

Tourism Infrastructure

Barcelona has a hotel capacity for more than 14,000 visitors ▶ *page* 85. Most hotels are located at the *Eixample* —in Spanish, *Ensanche* or new district— and in the residential areas in the upper part of the city. There are also many more beds for visitors in both apartments and pensions. In the province of Barcelona there are more than 70 camping sites, most of them along the coast although nine of these camping sites are located within a 20km radius of the capital.

The city offers both tourist information services (see below) and a vast amount of tours to the visitor who wants to get to know it easily and comfortably.

Barcelona has anything you could want in the way of concerts and opera, excellent museums, a great variety of restaurants and night clubs for all tastes, shows, sports. It is certainly one of the most cosmopolitan places in Spain.

Tourist Information

Tourist Information Offices: El Prat Airport ☎ 325 58 29, open Monday through Saturday from 8.00 a.m. to 8.00 p.m.; on Sundays and holidays from 8.00 a.m. to 3.00 p.m. City Hall, Pl de Sant Jaume ☎ 318 25 25, open Monday through Friday from 9.00 a.m. to 9.00 p.m.; Saturdays from 9.00 a.m. to 2.00 p.m. Francia Station ☎ 319 27 91, open Monday through Staurday from 8.00 a.m. to 8.00 p.m. hours. Generalitat de Catalunya, Gran Vía de les Corts Catalanes, 658 ☎ 301 74 43, open Monday through Friday from 9.00 a.m. to 1.30 p.m. and from 4.30 to 8.30 p.m. Pablo Neruda Plaza, Av Diagonal and c/ Aragón ☎ 245 76 21, open daily March 15 to October 15 between 8.30 a.m. and 8.30 p.m. Barcelona port, Porta de la Pau, facing the monument to Christopher Columbus, open daily except Mondays between 10.00 a.m. and 8.00 p.m.
Municipal Tourism Office, Sants central station ☎ 250 25 94, open daily from 7.30 a.m. to 10.30 p.m., and also at the Spanish town or *Pueblo Español* of Montjuïc.

When to Go

It is always a good time to visit Barcelona. This is a city where every season of the year has its peculiar attractions. Aficionados of lyrical music may want to come for the opera season and lovers of the bullfight can attend the *fiestas* at La Merced. For those interested in the nearby beaches, the best time is naturally summer. But in general, the seasons are so pleasant, each in its own way, that it would be impossible to say which is the most attractive.

GETTING READY FOR THE TRIP

Baggage

If you are arriving by plane, it is important to keep in mind the weight limitations imposed by the airlines; more baggage will cost you money. Normally, one adult passenger in tourist class is allowed some 20kg. Over that weight, a supplement is charged. The number of handbags you can carry into the cabin is also limited.

Clothes: What to Bring

In Barcelona, as in the rest of Spain, *freedom and variety* are the norm when it comes to attire. Spain is Europe's second fashion leader and the fashion industry here is a modern one. Barcelona competes with

Milan as a world capital of design and fashion, and its middle classes dress accordingly —in style. Nothing is really considered shocking or far out in this city: the only rules are those you bring with yourself. Barcelonans have historically liberal attitudes towards such things and that, combined with the influence of tourists, helps make the eclectic fashion scene in the city a pleasure to watch.

The only exceptions to the general rule that you may dress as you like are in casinos, the Liceo (Opera House), and at formal events —gala dinners, official luncheons, luxury restaurants and so on—, where jackets might be required for men.

Barcelona's climate is generally mild and somewhat humid. During the summer it's advisable to bring clothes made of light cotton and linen. A light jacket for cooler evenings is a good idea. During the spring and fall, cotton or light wool clothes are the most suitable. In winter months you will need something heavier. Still, the temperature rarely drops below 10°C (50°F). One should be prepared for rain during the months of October, November, March and April, as well as during the entire winter, when rain is quite frequent.

Going Through Customs

Foreigners arriving in Spain must have a valid passport. Nationals of some countries are required to obtain a visa in advance of arrival; the visa can be obtained at the Spanish consulate in most large cities. The citizens of most European countries need only bring with them their valid identity card. In case of doubt, the best course is to consult your local Spanish consulate.

Tourists need pay no taxes or duties on personal effects like clothes and other articles needed for their stay. There are, however, limits to the amounts of tobacco, alcoholic beverages and perfumes that you can bring with you into Spain, which vary according to the country from which you are travelling.

You are also limited to 2 cameras and 10 rolls of film each, one 8mm or 16mm movie camera, one portable tape recorder, one portable typewriter, one bicycle, equipment for golf, tennis and fishing, and 2 firearms with 100 cartridges a piece for hunting.

To obtain a more detailed list of the articles that are restricted in some way, consult your local Spanish consulate.

Hunting and Fishing

It is helpful to contact the local hunting or fishing federation or association before coming to Spain; they provide a wealth of information about licences, seasons and permits, and also can give good advice about the locale and what to expect.

Insurance

Anything is possible on a trip, so it is wise to purchase health insurance valid for Spain or to make sure your existing policy covers you here. You may also want to consider insurance covering last minute cancellations of a holiday. You can consult the Spanish Tourism Office, a travel agent or your own insurance company: they will also be able to inform you about vehicle insurance. A visitor whose country has reciprocal medical agreements with Spain should not forget to bring his social security documentation.

BEACHES

The city of Barcelona is edged by more than 12km of beaches, divided into two main stretches. Approximately 7km, however, from the mouth of the Llobregat River to the beginning of the port breakwater, have been declared off-limits to bathers because of the risk of contamination from waters polluted by various industrial effluents. The second stretch, which reaches the eastern city limit of Barcelona in the Camp de la Bota, is 5,600m long and contains the city's two most popular beaches —Barceloneta beach and Mar Bella beach— visited by some 50,000 bathers at weekends and holidays.

Both beaches are equipped with every kind of service, notably cleaning and sanitation. **Barceloneta beach** is the best equipped beach in Catalonia, with *showers, bathrooms, 150 waste-Red Cross and local police posts, children's games, informative signs and an information service, megaphones for contacting bathers* and *notices giving the schedule for sand cleaning and sifting.* Beach officials also provide a daily analysis of the chemical and bacteriological purity of the sea water. This is the main urban beach, and it is frequented by children, families, teenagers and senior citizens; Barcelonans come to this stretch of sand to swim, sun-bathe and eat either on the beach or in the numerous bars, restaurants and *chiringuitos* (a type of outdoor bar) located nearby.

Mar Bella beach is perfect for those who prefer more energetic activities than just lying in the sun. It has a range of facilities for a variety of *water sports.* There is a *sailing school,* an area marked off for *windsurfing* and *equipment for canoeing.* On Sundays, a 5km long track is opened to the public for *jogging.*

Topless bathing has become quite common is Spain and the cosmopolitan beaches of Barcelona are no exception. That being said, however, tolerance does not go so far as to make total nudity acceptable on the city's beaches. Nevertheless, there are several beaches reserved for nude bathing, where naturists can feel quite at ease, both on the Costa Brava to the north and the Costa Dorada to the south.

Beaches of the Costa Dorada

Barcelona is situated in the centre of the Costa Dorada, which stretches from Calella and the Tordera River in the NE (next to neighbouring Gerona and the Costa Brava) to Sant Carles de la Rápita in the SW, in Tarragona, at the mouth of the Ebro River (bordering the province of Valencia). The visitor in search of a beach can take the highway toward France and the NE, or Ctra N-II that hugs the coast, to the numerous beaches that are found in nearby towns like Masnou, Premià de Mar, Canet de Mar, Pineda de Mar and Calella. Toward the SW, in the direction of Tarragona, just a few kilometres out of Barcelona and **Sitges, Castelldefels** offers excellent beaches that are very popular with Barcelonans (see *Sitges,* another title in the *Everything Under the Sun* travel guide series). There are also beaches in Vilanova i la Geltrú, Cunit, Calafell, **Salou** (a major tourist centre with a very international flavour; see the *Salou* guide in the *Everything Under the Sun* series) and **Cambrils**. See also the section on 'Excursions' ▶ *page* 72 for more information.

CITY ITINERARIES

Barcelona is a city made for walking. Despite its large size, the urban centre that visitors will most want to see comprises a relatively small area, and the buildings, museums and other areas of interest are also grouped quite closely together. Still, even the most rapid trip through all the itineraries given below will take the visitor a minimum of three days. One of those days should be given over to the **Ramblas**, the **Gothic quarter** and the numerous museums and interesting buildings that are located nearby. The **Modernist Barcelona** of the Ensanche also requires a full day to see its streets, admire the façades of its houses and enjoy the excellent shopping in the area. **Tibidabo** and **Pedralbes**, the area of **Montjuïc** that overlooks the city, and **Güell Park** make up another day's sightseeing for even the most hurried visitor.

To complement the Barcelonan itineraries given below, the reader will find in this guide a section on 'Places of Interest' —buildings, museums, churches, and so on— that will be seen on the tours.

Itinerary 1: Plaza de Cataluña and the Ramblas

Looking towards the sea, the city spreads outwards in concentric circles to the slopes of its two celebrated hills, Montjuïc and Tibidabo, which encircle it from north to south. Barcelona's charm owes much to its multiplicity. Prism-like, the city has many faces: exuberant and densely populated in the historical centre; middle-class in the Ensanche; residential and sophisticated along Diagonal, Bonanova and Sarriá; working-class in Sant Martí and Sant Andrés; and fun-loving with its parks and fun-fairs on Tibidabo and Montjuïc.

The city centre is **Plaza de Cataluña**. This is the focal point of all the city's major events: the *Diada*, Catalonia's national day, on September 11; the St. John's Day celebrations which are marked with bonfires and dancing on June 24; the week of festivals and celebrations in honour of La Mercé, Barcelona's patron saint, on September 27.

Up to the middle of the 19C, Barcelonans who wished to escape the narrowness and constraint of the city's medieval streets could leave the walls at the Porta dels Orts gate. A short walk would bring them to a small clearing, intersected by a flowing stream that was ideal for walking or for a family picnic. This field, where well-to-do citizens built summer villas and weekend retreats, is now the Pl de Cataluña. Today, with its fountains and gardens surrounded by department stores, travel agencies, cinemas, hotels, restaurants, shops and banks, it is the commercial hub of the new Barcelona.

So many boulevards and streets start and end in Pl de Cataluña that the plaza is popularly referred to as a lake that is constantly being replenished by the great rivers that course through the city, the Gran Vía, the Rambla de Cataluña, the Paseo de Gracia, and above all, the Ramblas.

Barcelona's internationally renowned **Ramblas** begin at the Pl de Cataluña and descend gradually towards the sea. The 1.5km walk is full of unique sights and sounds. Newspaper stands with periodicals from around the globe, flower sellers, kiosks crowded with birds and animals for sale, not to mention the throngs of people strolling up and down or sitting at the numerous tables on the pavement, day or night, all make it the most popular boulevard in the city. It is little wonder that this exciting promenade has been the heart of Barcelona for over a hundred years.

Originally the Ramblas boulevard was a stream that flowed towards the port alongside the outer city walls erected by James I in the 13C. At the time, this area beyond the town's western limit was an active commercial district. The stockyards, brimming with cattle, goats and sheep were located here and the daily chore of weighing, bundling and selling grain and straw was carried out in this zone. It was also the grim site of public executions. To the left, coming down from the Plaza de Cataluña, are the colleges and monasteries built in the 16-17C which now account for the name given to this particular stretch of the Ramblas, Rambla de Capuchinos.

To the uninformed visitor, the Ramblas may appear to be one continuous boulevard. But the astute observer will notice that there are five distinct sections, each with its own unique flavour, style and rhythm. Starting at the top (Pl de Cataluña) is **Canaletas**, a favourite with football supporters who gather here to comment on the fortunes or misfortunes of their beloved team, Barcelona F.C., the city's successful, world class football club, which is known simply as Barça.

Next comes **Rambla de los Estudios**, so called because there was once a university here which Philip V converted into army barracks for his troops. Later a thriving bird market developed here and this, together with the fact that there are thousands of sparrows perched in the trees of the Rambla gave rise to its popular name, *Rambla de los Pajaros*, literally the bird boulevard. Then comes **Rambla de las Flores** with its many colourful flower kiosks, constantly being portrayed on postcards and calendars. To the right is the Neoclassical **Vicereine's Palace** (*Palacio de la Virreina*, 1778), named after a Vicereine of Peru. Also to the right is the San José market, popularly known as the **Boquería**. In this market, laid out beneath a huge metal structure, there is a multitude of fruit, fish, meat, poultry and vegetable stands, all tastefully and harmoniously arranged. This is one of the most colourful and picturesque markets in Europe and the excellence and variety of the produce sold here is widely known, even beyond Spain's borders. This Mediterranean market is well worth visiting for aesthetic reasons alone, not to mention the surprises the shopper is likely to encounter in this incredible food bazaar ▶ *page* 119.

A few paces further along we come to **Rambla de los Capuchinos**. Two distinct worlds converge here: that of the well-off bourgeoisie and that of the working class inhabitants of the port district. Here stands Spain's world-famous opera house, the *Gran Teatro del Liceo*. Starting here, and branching out from **Rambla de Santa Mónica** lies the notorious and alluring *Barrio Chino* (China Town). This district, with its narrow winding streets and derelict buildings, is the true heart of the port district. Here, living side by side in precarious equilibrium, are Barcelona's poor but honourable citizens along with prostitutes, pimps, transvestites, thugs, immigrants with uncertain futures, pedlars, beggars, senior citizens subsisting on inadequate pensions, down and out artists, tourists, suspicious shopkeepers and sailors who come here in search of *drugs* and fast, cheap sex. The *Barrio Chino* is a grotesque yet integral part of Barcelona's port history.

About halfway down the Rambla de los Capuchinos and to the left is the Neoclassical **Pl Real**. Built in the last century, this plaza, with its palms, ornate façades and ochre coloured arcades, has a definite Italian flavour. It is also a meeting place for hang-abouts and young people who drift between the bars, cafes and benches in the square. The lamp posts were the work of the young Gaudí, Barcelona's internationally renowned architect.

Itinerary 2: The Gothic Quarter

To the left of the Ramblas (facing the sea) and to the right of Vía Layetana lies the *Barrio Gótico* or Gothic quarter, the old historical centre of the city. Peaceful by day and night, this *barrio* contains within its streets, houses and small palaces, the history of Barcelona's nobility between the 13-14C. With the exception of a few houses, the Gothic district is the same today as it was in those distant times. The entire zone is a living monument to the city's glorious past and the visitor who spends some time here will be aesthetically and spiritually rewarded. Every building is worthy of mention but a definite must for the visitor is **Pl Sant Jaume**, where the City Hall and the Palace of the Generalitat (Regional Government) sit facing each other across the square. On Sunday evenings the plaza is usually teeming with people dancing the ***sardanas***, a graceful and enchanting folkdance typical of Catalonia ▶ *page* 59.

The Palace of the Generalitat is a superb example of civic Gothic architecture. On the façade facing c/ Bisbe Irunita there is a beautiful medallion representing Saint George. An **upper gallery**, also Gothic, connects this building with the *Casa de los Canónigos* or **Prebendaries House**. Inside this 14C palace there is a wonderful patio with a splendid staircase and balustrade. Across the square, dating from the last century, stands the City Hall. Inside there is a room painted by Catalan artist J.M. Sert ▶ *page* 63. The façade facing c/ Ciutat dates from the 14C.

The Gothic Cathedral was erected on the site of an old Romanesque church. Begun in the 13C, work on the building continued until 1408. The steeple and façade, holding rigorously to the plans of 1408, were completed in the 19C. The interior, with three vaulted naves, is typical Catalan Gothic showing purity of line, sobriety (there are a few

Patio of Sant Jordi, Palace of the Generalitat

sculptures) and a taste for geometric spaces. The white marble grille is the work of Bartolomé Ordoñez, 16C, one of Spain's great Renaissance artists. Interesting wrought-iron work and magnificient retables can be seen in the side altars, especially in the Transfiguration retable, in the second chapel on the right. Walking toward the southern wall the visitor will encounter one of the most delightful and refreshing corners in the city, the cloister. This airy and expansive courtyard harmoniously blends the Gothic forms of the Cathedral's galleries with the venerable old trees standing in this green oasis.

Next to the Cathedral, on c/ Condes de Barcelona, is the interesting Frederic Marès Museum. This museum contains a very rich collection of Roman relics and wooden polychromatic sculptures from the Middle Ages (12-14C) as well as a fascinating mixture of antique objects and articles for personal use. Everything here was donated by the sculptor and collector after whom the museum is named.

From the Frederic Marès Museum, going down the c/ Condes de Barcelona and turning to the left, the visitor will come upon Pl del Rey. To the right of the plaza's entrance, on the corner, stands the Padellás Mansion. This building, an impressive example of 16C Renaissance architecture, houses the *Museo de la Historia de la Cuidad*, or City History Museum, with its collection of maps, objects and works of art that show the evolution of the city up to the 19C. Beside this building is the **Chapel of Santa Agueda**, an excellent example of 14C Catalan Gothic. Directly in front of the Padellás Mansion, on the NE side of the plaza is the *Palacio Real Mayor*, or Royal Palace, with its King Martin's Tower. For centuries this was the home of the Catalan monarchs. The building was erected in the 14C and was continuously enlarged and enriched by succeeding monarchs. Inside, the visitor can see the **Tinell Room**, the room where the Catholic Monarchs, Ferdinand and Isabel, received Christopher Columbus after his discovery of the New World. Completing the walk around the plaza, next to the Royal Palace, stands the Renaissance building known as the **Vicereine's Palace**. The archives of the Crown of Aragón are housed here.

Behind the plaza, in front of the buildings adjoining the Chapel of Santa Agueda and facing the Ramón Berenguer el Grande plaza, lie the remains of the Roman and Medieval walls.

Leaving the Barrio Gótico along Vía Layetana and taking c/ Platería from Pl del Angel, the visitor will encounter another of Barcelona's ancient treasures, the 4C walls that once surrounded the city's historic centre (*Barrio Gótico*). Too limiting to contain the young city's growth, urban expansion spread beyond the walls to form Barcelona's first suburbs. These districts were later encircled by a second wall erected by James I the Conqueror in the 13C. Between the 13-14C these new districts (Santa María del Mar and Bòria) grew spectacularly with the influx of sea-trade and commerce. The wide, straight c/ Montcada ran between the two neighbourhoods, contrasting sharply with the narrow, serpentine streets of the Gothic district. Luxurious palaces and mansions were built along this road by the city's nobility and well to do.

Each doorway along c/ Montcada opens onto a world of splendour and luxury. The Berenguer D'Aguilar Palace now houses the Picasso Museum, which contains hundreds of canvasses painted by the young artist between 1896 and 1917. Of special note are the *Manolas*, the *Harlequin*, and of course the widely known series *Las Meninas* (1959), donated to the museum by the artist in 1968. The Baroque Dalmases Palace is the headquarters of the Institute of Catalan Studies ▶ *page* 108. The Marqués de Llió Palace (14C) houses the impressive

Picasso Museum at the Berenguer D'Aguilar Palace

Rocamora collection of 18-20C garments and accessories in the *Museo de la Indumentaria* or Clothing Museum. The Cervelló Palace is also worth seeing.

At the end of c/ Platería —the old street that led to the sea— stands the Church of Santa María del Mar, a masterpiece of Catalan Gothic architecture. Built by James I in the 14C, this architectural jewel which so honestly expresses the purity and sobriety of the Catalan style should not be missed. The bare walls and unornamented buttresses blend harmoniously with the spacious interior of three high naves separated by slender prism-like pillars and crowned by a large rose window. The *barrio* of Santa María del Mar offers the visitor a contrasting mixture of splendour and poverty: abandoned streets bleakly contemplate the elegant palaces of c/ Montcada and the splendour of the Church of Santa María.

Other well-preserved monuments that illustrate Barcelona's golden Gothic age are the **Lonja** and the Atarazanas. The Atarazanas are unique in the world. This building complex, situated to the right of the port zone, was begun by Peter the Great and completed towards the end of the 14C. These vast naves supported by delicate arches have witnessed the construction of naval fleets and merchant vessels for more than five hundred years. Today, the Atarazanas house the Maritime Museum with its superb collection of sail and steamship models, navigational instruments, ships' figureheads, drawings and maps, including one drawn by Américo Vespucci, the explorer who gave his name to the New World. There is a full scale reproduction of the Royal Galleon used by Don Juan de Austria, the victor in the Battle of Lepanto ▶ *page* 49. It is interesting that the original was also built here in the Atarazanas.

Next to the port there are two monuments in honour of Christopher Columbus: the Columbus Monument, an impressive statue of the great explorer and navigator, and a reproduction of the Santa María, the ship in which he discovered the New World (docked in the port).

Turning left at the bottom of the Ramblas and walking along Paseo de Colón, the visitor will come across Barcelona's famous flea-market just before reaching the Post Office. Within this four block area with its eastern bazaarlike atmosphere one can find everything from buttons to electronic equipment. Gold, silver and objects of any value can be bought, sold and traded here.

Itinerary 3: Ciudadela Park, Montjuïc

The Ciudadela Park is situated at the end of Paseo de Colón. It takes its name from the park built here by Philip V ▶ *page* 44 in 1716. A Universal Exhibition was held on this site in 1888 and the present gardens were designed by J. Fontseré in the 20C. The chief attractions of the park are its well-equiped Zoo which includes a popular whale and dolphin show, a Zoological and Geological Museum and the Modern Art Museum. The Modern Art Museum contains excellent examples of modern Catalan painting with canvasses by Fortuny, Casas, Nonell, Regoyos, Zuloaga, Sert, Dalí, Miró and Tapiés.

Leaving the Paseo de Colón on the left and before reaching the Post Office building, the visitor can follow the port road to
a lively working class district with a multitude of restaurants that offer a full range of sea food dishes. During the summer the restaurants set out their tables on the beach and it is possible to dine with one's feet practically in the water.

A walk back from the port district by way of **Av Paralelo** brings the visitor to Barcelona's revue theatre, cabaret and stage area. Here you will always find a colourful mixture of *payeses* (country folk) in Sunday suits and fashionable urbanites wearing the latest evening dress. *El Molino*, the city's traditional and popular theatre, is located here. It offers spectacular stage shows and risqué comedy with the show girls bantering and joking with the audience.

Continuing along the Av Paralelo the visitor will come to Pl de España and Montjuïc, a 213m hill which offers breathtaking views of the city and harbour. Within the Montjuïc park area there are a number of interesting attractions: the beautiful gardens created in anticipation of the 1929 International Fair; the Barcelona Exhibition Grounds; the **Greek Theatre**, built in 1929; the **Ethnological Museum**; and atop Montjuïc, the **castle**. The *Parque de Atracciones* or Fun-Fair Park and the traditionally popular Lighted Fountains designed by the poetic and ingenious engineer Carlos Buigas are also located here. Nearby the stadium for the 1992 summer Olympic Games is presently being built.

The Joan Miró Foundation, also on Montjuïc, is housed in a modern building designed by the architect Sert. It contains an impressive collection of paintings and sculptures by this prolific and internationally renowned artist. In contrast, the *Museo de Arte de Cataluña*, or Museum of Catalonian Art, in the National Palace, has a number of splendid collections from earlier times. The most outstanding is the Roman and Gothic series. These pieces were gathered from the numerous small churches scattered throughout Catalonia. Of special note are the friezes of Pedret, Boí, Santa María and San Clemente de Taüll (12-13C) and the retables and Gothic paintings by such masters as Borrassà, Mur, Martorell, Huguet and Bermejo (15C), as well as paintings by El Greco, Zurbarán, Ribera and Viladomat. The *Museo de la Ceramica* or Ceramics Museum, situated on the first floor of the same building, has an excellent ceramic collection with primitive pieces from the Balearic Islands, glazed tiles from the 18C and recent contemporary examples.

The Archaeological Museum is also situated on Montjuïc. This museum displays relics from the Peninsula's prehistoric cultures such as the Megalithic peoples of Antequera (Málaga) and Menorca. In addition, there are some excellent Roman and Greek artefacts (Ampurias, Barcino, Badalona). The *Pueblo Español* or Spanish Town exhibition, built for the 1929 International Fair, shows a series of reconstructions of houses, streets and plazas typical of Spain's diverse regions.

Next to Montjuïc, rising 532m above sea-level, is Tibidabo, Barcelona's other hill. Situated in the NW, Tibidabo offers the visitor an impressive view of the Mediterranean, the city centre and the fields inland. Its summit can be reached by the *tranvía azul*, funicular or by car. The best time for viewing the landscape is between late afternoon and sundown. The *Parque de Atracciones* or **Fun-Fair Park** is located at the top as is the unique **Automats Museum** and a small church which, when illuminated in the evenings, can be seen from almost every part of the city.

The wealthy residential district of Pedralbes spreads out from the bottom of Tibidabo's southern slopes. This area can be reached by taking Av Pedralbes which branches to the right from Av Diagonal (heading in a SSE direction towards Tarragona). Here, on c/ Bajada del Monasterio, is the beautiful Santa María de Pedralbes Monastery: Founded in 1362 by Elisenda de Montcada, this monastery is a classic example of Catalan Gothic. Inside there is an attractive chapel, **murals** by Ferrer Bassa (1346) ▶ *page* 61, an alabaster tomb containing the remains of the founder, 14C stained-glass windows, impressive examples of 15-17C religious art, a collection of 16-17C Catalan furniture, and 14-18C ceramic work. Not far from the monastery stands the National Palace of Pedralbes. This Italian style palace was built by King Alfonso XIII in the 1920s. It houses the *Museo de Carruajes* or Carriages Museum, a splendid collection of carriages, coaches and berlines together with assorted objects related to this subject.

Itinerary 4: The Ensanche

Architecturally speaking, **Modernist Barcelona** is, along with the Romanesque and Gothic districts, one of the city's greatest attractions and the one that gives it its current image and personality. During the industrial expansion of the second half of the 19C ▶ *page* 51, Barcelona entered a period of rich cultural growth and nationalistic affirmation that was dubbed the *Renaixença*. In contrast, the rest of Spain, feeling the loss of its American colonies, sank into decadence. This Catalan Renaissance was centred on language, poetry, architecture and design.

The city's flourishing industrial middle class wanted a new city that would break with the medieval structures of the past. The engineer Cerdá took on the task of creating the **Ensanche** ▶ *page* 38 a modern grid-like pattern of streets and boulevards. As this new Barcelona was being born, **Modernism** ▶*page* 36 spread throúgh the city even before the *art nouveau* phenomenon was known in any other city of Europe. Barcelona's new rich, wanting to express their recently acquired power and aware of *avant garde* ideas, whole-heartedly supported this modernist tendency.

Architects, designers, craftsmen and graphic artists have left an enormous number of monuments, houses and commercial buildings throughout the city. There are umpteen commercial establishments built in this modernist style throughout Barcelona, especially along the Ramblas and its side streets. Domènech i Muntaner built the Palau de la Musica Catalana (a few paces from the Cathedral) in 1908 and during the same period Puig i Cadafalch constructed the Ametller House (Paseo de Gracia, 41).

But it is the unique, unclassifiable genius of one man, Gaudí, ▶ *page* 42, that has left an indelible mark upon the city. Architect, blacksmith, potter, cabinetmaker, sculptor and painter, this original and extremely gifted man, heir to centuries of Mediterranean tradition, mixed the Gothic richness of the past with the influence of his native soil. He blended architectural structures with natural forms thus creating a new and exciting language in the field of spatial arts. Some of Gaudí's impressive work are the houses of Batlló, covered in mosaics (Paseo de Gracia, 43) and Milá, with its voluptuously curved façade and unusual chimneys (Paseo de Gracia, 92); the **Güell** Palace (Pl del Teatro in the Rambla de Santa Mónica), the **Chapel of the Güell Neighbourhood** (in Santa Coloma de Cervelló), and the fantastic Güell Park (situated at the foot of the Tibidabo), an ideal Garden city project that came to a halt when the architect died.

It is the *Sagrada Familia* or Holy Family, however, that has made Gaudí's name familiar throughout the world. This church, to which the architect devoted 40 years of his life, has become an instantly recognisable symbol of Barcelona. The building was begun in 1882 by the architect F. del Villar, but in 1891 Gaudí was commissioned to continue its construction. Work stopped after his death in 1926 in a streetcar accident but was resumed in 1940 and still continues. Gaudí, an artist who received his inspiration daily while working on the building, left no plans. The power, uniqueness and mysticism of this church have an exhilarating effect on all who are fortunate enough to see it.

The Ensanche is the centre of life in the modern part of the city. Paseo de Gracia, the wide, tree-lined boulevard that stretches from the Pl de Cataluña to Av Diagonal used to be a green, open promenade in 1824. Today, this exciting commercial artery with its beautiful buildings and shops still preserves the distinguished elegance of the old boulevard. The Rambla de Cataluña also leads from the Pl de Cataluña to Av Diagonal. This street has a number of fine shops on either side of the terraced walkway ▶ *page* 131. The Av Diagonal, mentioned above, is a long, wide street that cuts through the Ensanche grid. The stretch that runs from Pl Juan Carlos I to Pl Francesc Macià is a high quality commercial district with numerous shops and boutiques (particularly the area around Pl Francesc Macià).

Barcelona is a dynamic and forward-looking city which has taken the Romanesque, the Gothic and, latterly, the Modernist worlds aboard and which continues to reflect architectural developments. There are many recently erected buildings around the city, some rationalist, such as Banca Catalana and *Banco Industrial de Bilbao*, both by Tous and Fargas (Paseo de Gracia), and other, such as the *Caja de Ahorros* by Busquets, with its dark glass façades (Av Diagonal), that are heirs to the ideas and influences generated by Mies Van der Rohe in the German Pavilion on Montjuïc (1929). Modest skyscrapers such as *Banco Atlántico* (Av Diagonal), the Football Stadium, by Mitjans, together with the peculiar forms of the Olivetti building and the open and airy rhythms of the Torres Trade, by Coderch, with their dark glass walls (Av de Carlos III at Av Diagonal) also add to the vigorous cityscape of modern Barcelona.

CONSULATES

Consulates provide a wide range of services for their nationals. They are there to provide assistance should one encounter difficulties with the Spanish legal system; to advise on local regulations; to act as public notaries for their own nationals; to help out in all emergencies. The very fact of being able to explain one's difficulties in one's own language can be a great relief if disaster strikes when one is abroad. Consulate staff are accustomed to dealing quickly and efficiently with all sorts of situations. A consulate can be especially useful in the following cases: **renewing passports** or obtaining other **documents** needed for travel; making **contact with family or friends** —this service can be a lifeline should you need money quickly; **advising** about transfer of funds and contacting next of kin at home in case of **sickness** or **death**.

In Barcelona you will find the following consulates:

Argentina, Gran Vía Corts Catalanes, 632 ☎ 317 58 82.
Austria, c/ Mallorca, 286 ☎ 257 36 14.
Belgium, c/ Córsega, 302 ☎ 218 07 58.
Bolivia, Pl Francesc Maciá, 8-9 ☎ 322 65 12.
Brazil, c/ Consell Cent, 357 ☎ 215 16 15.
Canada, Vía Augusta, 125 ☎ 209 06 34.
Chile, Gran Vía Corts Catalans, 591 ☎ 318 85 86.
Colombia, Pl Dr. Letamendi, 5 ☎ 254 02 48.
Costa Rica, Av Diagonal, 482 ☎ 217 73 92.
Cuba, Paseo de Gracia, 34 ☎ 318 19 36.
Denmark, Vía Layetana, 5 ☎ 310 20 91.
Ecuador, Pasaje Josep Llovera, 3 ☎ 209 57 31.
Finland, Gran Vía Corts Catalanes, 653 ☎ 318 18 38.
France, c/ Aribau, 200 ☎ 209 67 22; Paseo Gracia 11 ☎ 317 81 50; and c/ Sicilia, 137 ☎ 232 01 04.
Greece, c/ Nápols, 122 ☎ 246 22 90.
Guatemala, Gran Vía Carlos III, 82-98 and 94 ☎ 330 65 59 and 330 64 58.
Italy, c/ Mallorca, 270 ☎ 215 16 54.
Japan, Vía Layetana, 7 ☎ 310 20 97.
Mexico, Av Diagonal, 626 ☎ 201 18 22.
Morocco, Rambla de Cataluña, 78 ☎ 215 34 70.
Netherlands, Paseo de Gracia, 111 ☎ 217 33 58.
Nicaragua, c/ Aribau, 195 ☎ 201 90 59 and 201 31 27.

Panama, Av Diagonal, 435 ☎ 209 89 00.
Peru, Av Diagonal, 441 ☎ 250 38 33.
Philippines, Vía Layetana, 61 ☎ 318 84 36.
Portugal, Ronda Sant Pere, 7 ☎ 318 81 50.
Sweden, c/ Córsega, 289 ☎ 218 15 66.
Switzerland, Gran Vía Carlos III, 94 ☎ 330 92 11.
United Kingdom, Av Diagonal, 477 ☎ 322 21 51.
United States, Vía Layetana, 33 ☎ 319 95 50.
Uruguay, c/ Trafalgar, 4 ☎ 317 41 83.
Venezuela, c/ Praenza, 278 ☎ 215 01 12.
Venezuela, Paseo de Gracía, 111 ☎ 217 61 62 and 218 47 50.

CONSUMER RIGHTS

Spanish legislation protects the rights of consumers. Several agencies and groups can help the traveller in this regard; the National Consumer Institute; the relevant *Consejería*, or Ministry, of the regional government; the *Ayuntamientos*, or city halls themselves; and local consumer organizations. Use them if you think a product or service puts your health or safety in danger; if the quality or quantity of what you buy does not correspond to the price of the product or service; or if products or services do not live up to the basic norms of safety and quality.

Before making a claim, you should be quite sure of the facts, checking them carefully. Then decide on the best way to present your claim; personally (many times a simple personal request will solve the problem), by telephone, or by mail. Think specifically about what the problem is and what solution you are seeking.

How to present the claim? It is essential to provide clear facts: your name, address and telephone number; name, address and telephone number of the company or entity against whom you are filing a claim; why you are making a claim; and the solution that you are seeking. You should attach photocopies of all documents relating to the matter when filing claims. Make sure to keep a duplicate of your statement stamped by the office to which you present your complaint.

One particularly effective way of defending your rights in hotels, restaurants, bars, cafeterias, discotheques and so on, is the *libro de reclamaciones*, or complaints book. It is legally obligatory for all establishments to have such a book available to the customer. The simple act of asking for the complaints book —actually loose-leaf forms most of the time— is likely to take care of any problem. The complaint registered in the book is sent directly to local authorities, and the customer retains a copy.

Claims should be made as quickly as possible —if at all possible before you leave the locality; receipts for the object or service against which you are filing a claim should be included.

To obtain information or make a claim unrelated to tourism you may go to the *Servicio de Información al Consumidor* (Consumer Information Service). To consult a representative or make a claim, call ☎ 31,8 38 38. Another option is the Generalitat's *Departamento de Comercio, Consumo y Turismo* (Department of Commerce, Consumption and Tourism) located at Paseo de Gracia, 105 ☎ 237 24 42.

CUISINE

Catalan cooking is the most varied and sophisticated in Spain. Its supporters put it on a level with the most elaborate cuisine of France and with the best in Europe. Privileged by both history and geography, the cooking of the region embraces both the simplicity of Roman Spain ▶ *page* 45 and the elaborations of a wealthy middle class that flourished in the 19C. Variety stems from the great local diversity of land, climate and food products and to Catalonia's traditional openness to outside influences. Cooking as a local art has a long and unusually well-documented history (the first Spanish cookbook was written by Ruperto de Nola, who was Alfonso V's cook) and it remains enormously popular today. The people of Catalonia are true enthusiasts of fine cooking and eating, as is especially obvious during *fiesta* times.

It would require volumes to describe fully all Catalan gastronomy, but there are some basic features common to the region that should be explained, as well as some recipes specific to Barcelona.

Barcelona is a great international city, and that is just as true when speaking of food —the visitor will find a very wide range of restaurants offering cooking from other countries here, as well as Spanish and Catalan cuisine. Over the course of the 19C, Barcelona became a European restaurant capital, due principally to the tastes of the wealthy and flourishing middle classes. Since then the city has continued to grow as a restaurant centre and the taste for good eating has spread to all social classes. Barcelona daily receives its fine primary ingredients from surrounding Catalonia, the rest of Spain and the world over.

Cheeses

The perfect companion for a glass of wine is a slice of cheese. In Spain you can choose from among 500 local cheeses, each one peculiar to its region. The most popular cheese in Spain is ***Manchego*** which comes in three basic forms: fresh, semicured and cured. The better known cheeses include ***Cabrales***, made in Asturias, which is a *Roquefort* type blue cheese; the tasty ***Idiazabal*** that comes from the Basque country; the soft ***Tetilla*** of Galicia, and the tangy ***Mahón*** produced in Ibiza. There is always a local speciality, and you are unlikely to be disappointed.

Catalonia has a very long tradition of handmade cheese; to this there has been added in recent years the development of a modern industrial cheesemaking sector. With at least 14 varieties, the range should meet all tastes, especially if accompanied by the wines of Penedés, Alella, Ampurdán and other regions. Cava also makes a tasty accompaniment to a number of cheeses. ***Brossat*** is the cottage cheese made in Castile and the Basque country; it is a fresh cheese like ***Mató***, without salt, white and rindless. It is eaten alone, with honey (as the famous Catalan *mel i mató*) or with jam. Another similar cheese is ***Tendre***, also fresh and very well liked in central Catalonia. Goat cheeses like ***Garrotxa*** from Gerona and ***Nevat*** from Ampurdán have a very distinctive flavour. ***Llenguat***, with a very strong taste and pinkish in colour, is made from sheep's milk to which liqueur or oil has been added and fermented. The traditional ***Tupí*** cheese tastes similar, and comes from the Lérida and the Gerona areas. It is made with milk and mature goat's cheese and fermented with liqueur and anise in the same earthenware jars in which it is sold. It appears white and pasty and has a strong characteristic taste and smell.

Cuisine of Catalonia

Barcelona has adopted two Italian dishes with special gusto: ***cannelloni***, a pasta dish that, in accordance with local tradition, is on virtually every table in the city on December 26; and **rice *a la milanesa***, which Barcelona cooks have become truly expert at preparing from their own local recipes.

Sea food, both fish and shellfish, is a prime ingredient of Catalan cooking, and indeed hundreds of tasty local sea food dishes have developed in Barcelona and along the entire Costa Dorada. But there is much to Catalonia's cuisine: virgin **olive oil** from Lérida; fresh **vegetables** from the *huerta* (a richly irrigated plain) of Baix Llobregat; **rice** from the Ebro Delta; the **wines** of Penedés; the **fruits** that grow in the orchards of Gerona and Lérida; the **sausages** produced in Vic, Ampurdán and the interior (the pork sausages known as *chacinera* are rightly famous); and the local **small game** in winter. In order to understand and thus really appreciate Catalan cooking, one must know some of its fundamental elements.

The first such element is undoubtedly the use of **olive oil**. From time immemorial, olives have been the source of cooking oil for the populations of Mediterranean countries. Today, the experts report that the molecular structure and chemical composition of cooked olive oil makes it the easiest to digest and the least toxic of all vegetable oils. Some of the very best local olive oils are produced in the province of Lérida.

Olive oil is divided into two basic types: *virgin olive oil*, which has the most pronounced taste and is most used cold, as in salads; and *pure olive oil*, more neutral in taste and better for cooking. Olive oil is an important ingredient in the very popular ***pan con tomate*** (bread with tomato) dish, and is the essential basis of the famous ***allioli*** (garlic and oil, in Catalan) sauce, which is made by blending oil, garlic and salt. Local restaurateurs —a bit wary, perhaps, about alarming visitors from beyond the Pyrenees— will frequently add egg yolks to the *allioli*, effectively toning it down into a kind of mayonnaise that is not so heavy on garlic. Olive oil is also used in another local sea food sauce, the ***romesco*** of Tarragona. Naturally, olive oil mixed with *vinagre de cava*, or cava vinegar, a famous type of vinegar made in Penedés, makes excellent salad dressing.

The second basic element of Catalan cuisine is the **produce** of the *huerta*, the famous irrigated plains of the region that supply a wealth of **tomatoes, green peppers** and **eggplants** in the summer; **cabbage** and **cardoons**, in the winter; and **artichokes, fennel** and **broad beans** during the spring months. In addition, a true Catalan passion is **mushrooms**, particularly the type known as *rovellons* which grow in spring and fall. Try some of the local mushrooms: you will find that they taste of woods and sunshine. Another great favourite is **snails** (*caracoles* in Spanish); the fact that there are more than 30 good local snail recipes proves the point. ***Escalivada***, a cold dish of baked tomatoes, eggplant and green peppers dressed with olive oil and olives, is a first rate summer dish. ***Xanfaina***, a mixture of stuffed vegetables served with meat, is its wintertime equivalent.

Further inland in Catalonia, the pig is of special importance in local cuisine. Excellent **pork products** are made only in the foothills of the Pyrenees, mainly around the area of Vic. They include Ampurdán hams, Vic sausages or ***salchichones*** (a type of highly seasoned sausage), ***fuet*** (which is a thinner sausage), ***espetec***, black and white ***butifarras***

Pan con tomate and ham... a Catalan favourite

(a succulent type of Catalan sausage) and the blood sausage known as a ***bisbe***. Although these products are made inland, they are popular throughout the region, for they are a great complement to the products of the *huerta*. From northern Catalonia comes a recipe known as ***escudella de payes***, which literally means the peasant's cooking pot. It is made of white beans and cabbage with ham, bacon, ham and veal bone, and it is normally preceded by rice and noodle soup. Barcelona is the home of ***escudella i carn d'olla***, a Catalan version of Spanish stew. It includes a first dish of rice and noodle soup and another of meat, potatoes, white and black *butifarra* sausages which replace the *chorizo* and *morcilla* sausages used elsewhere in Spain— and a *pelota* or ball of lean meat chopped and mixed with bread crumbs, eggs and parsley. Another basic dish, ***mongetes amb botifarra***, is a mixture of white beans and *butifarra* sausages. No less popular is ***faves a la catalana***, broad beans with black *butifarra* sausage, bacon, loin and ham.

A third element of the Catalan diet is **sea food**, both fish and shellfish. The offerings in this area are innumerable, and so what is described below can only serve as a starting point for the reader.

Molluscs —principally **clams** (*almejas*), **cockles** (*berberechos*) and **date mussels** (*dátiles*)— are usually lightly grilled or steamed and served with an *allioli* or *romesco* sauce. They retain their natural flavour remarkably well when cooked in this manner. Also popular are **conch** (*caracoles*), served boiled, and **mussels** (*mejillones*), normally served in a marinera sauce. The relatively small spiny lobsters known as *langosta* are often grilled, and are more common in the north of the region on the Costa Brava. Also commonly grilled are **lobster** (*bogavante*), **Norway lobster** (*cigala*), **crayfish** (*langostino*) —the best crayfish come from S of Barcelona, around Tarragona and most especially in Sant

Carles de la Rápita— and **prawn** (*gamba*). Lobster and spiny lobster are also prepared in a number of ways besides grilling.

Rock-dwelling fish and shellfish such as the **spider crab** (*araña*) and **bream** (*boga*), used in Marseilles to make a very good bouillabaisse, are also prepared in soups in Catalonia, but are served grilled as well. ***Chopitos***, a kind of tiny squid, are succulent when cooked on the grill. The big fish of the Mediterranean —**sea bass, gilthead, corvina, turbot, sea bream, angler** and **hake** (*lubina, dorada, corvina, rodaballo, besugo, rape* and *merluza* respectively)— are prepared in many ways, but the full flavour of the fish is usually brought out by the simplest cooking method such as baking them in salt, *a la sal*. Small and medium sized **red mullet** are marvellous when grilled. A very little known, and cheap, local speciality that will be appreciated by *connoisseurs* is **manta ray** (*raya*). Dark fleshed fish which the Spanish call blue (*azul*) fish are especially cheap and good. They include **mackerel** (*caballa*), **sardines** (*sardina*) and **horse mackerel** (*jurel*), and are traditional fare at many rural *fiestas*, where they are cooked over wood fires or barbecue coals. **Tuna** and **tunny**, known as *bonito* and *atún* respectively, are delicious accompanied by sauces that balance their strong yet delicate flavour. **Anchovies** (*anchoas*) are fished off the coast near Gerona, and **codfish** (*bacalao*) is also very popular in the area.

Suquet de peix, also known as *dels pescadors*, is a typical Catalan sea food stew that has many variations but is always based on recently caught grouper, sea bass, gilthead, angler or other game fish. It is prepared in an earthenware casserole with oil, garlic, parsley, a little tomato, a lot of onions and fish broth. A second Catalan classic is the **shellfish *zarzuela*** (*zarzuela de mariscos*), a concoction that includes a variety of shellfish, almonds, and parsley boiled in an earthenware pot.

Barcelonans have their own special way of preparing fish in the oven. ***Bacalao a la llauma***, a cod dish, is probably the best example. It is made with chopped onions, garlic, tomatoes, parsley, paprika and grated bread, and topped with a beaten egg to give it a glaze in the oven. ***Xamfaina de bacalao*** is a sophisticated variant of the former, which began as a muleteer's meal. Cod is also prepared in a variety of other ways, with potatoes, hard-boiled eggs, spinach, raisins and pine nuts as common additional ingredients.

Finally, the last basic food source, after the products of the sea and of the *huerta*, is **rice**. Rice comes in a thousand forms in this country, especially along the coast S of Barcelona as you go toward Tarragona and the Ebro Delta bordering Valencia. A number of truly original rice dishes have developed here, including ***arròs Xat*** (rice cooked in a fish stew) and ***arròs de peix*** (rice with sea food). It is also easy to find rice dishes native to other Spanish regions in Barcelona and along the Costa Dorada. Examples are the popular ***arroz a banda, arroz negro*** and ***paella***. *Paella*, which is so well known and can be so badly cooked in touristy restaurants up and down the coast, is the native dish not of Barcelona, but of Valencia, some 300km away. *Paella* in fact originated not as a coastal sea food dish but as an inland meal mixing rice with rabbit, pork or chicken. Sea food *paella* is only a recent invention of the wealthier families on the Valencia coast. Unlike other Mediterranean rice dishes made with sea food, it is not swimming in broth. A note about *paella*: restaurants that offer to bring you a specially prepared *paella* in 20 minutes should be distrusted. Such a promise means that the dish will have been prepared earlier, with the rice done separately, and the result will be a miserable imitation of a fresh *paella*. A real individually prepared *paella* takes at least forty minutes to make.

Typical Catalan soups include ***fideos en cazuela***, a thick noodle soup with several kinds of sausage and pork ribs topped with grated cheese and a mixture of almonds and toasted hazelnuts. Another variant is ***sopa de pescado con fideos a la barcelonesa***, a fish and noodle soup typical of Barcelona.

Desserts and Pastries

In the area of **pastries**, Barcelona offers a rich assortment of local delights. Some of them are seasonal, like the ***bunyols***, a type of doughnut made all over Catalonia during Lent. ***Panallets***, made for All Saint's Day, and the expertly baked ***monas de Pascua*** and ***cocas de San Juan*** are also sold exclusively for religious festivals. Other desserts are all year specialties, like ***crema catalana***, a kind of custard made with toasted caramel and ***tortells***, a type of puff pastry doughnut that has become popular throughout Spain at breakfast time. Finally, ***mel i mató***, made of cottage cheese and honey, and ***menjar blanc***, a kind of almond paste that is cooked with milk and sprinkled with cinammon, both boasting Arab and Indian sweetmaking roots, are also found on menus frequently.

Wines, Cavas and Liqueurs

The visitor to Spain need only taste the wines of whatever area he happens to travel to in order to know that this country offers one of the greatest selections of wines in the world ▶ *page* 155. Catalonia holds a place of honour nationally, not only because it is the second largest producer in Spain but also because of the quality of the vineyards. And within Catalonia, Penedés is the most important and famous winemaking region. Several labels from this area have gained ground over French *champagne* in major markets like the United States, and many have won major international prizes previously only granted to Bordeaux wines. Thanks to the hard work of its traditional winemakers, the improved technological abilities of many wineries and the recent contributions of a new breed of entrepreneurial young wine-lovers, the wines of Penedés became the precursor and catalyst of the *new Spanish wines*. These now well-known wines are young and fresh, or well-aged and smooth, and are carefully controlled for quality. Many Spanish wines are now comparable to the great European labels.

Of the five *Denominaciones de Origen* or Officially Regulated Wine Regions, categories discussed in the 'Wines' section of this book ▶ *page* 154, the visitor should note that the wines of **Ampurdán** (NE of Catalonia, on the frontier with France) can be quite difficult to find outside the area in which they are produced; that the red wines of the year (*Vi novell*) can be very interesting; and that genuinely good whites are hard to find. Some selections to be tried are *Vi Novell* of the Cooperativa d'Espolla, *Tinto Cazador* and *Blanc de Blancs* of Perelada and *Gran Recosind* of Bodegas Santamaría. Some dry and semi-dry wines of **Alella** (a few kilometres N of Barcelona) are exceptional; try the *Alella Marfil* of Alella Vinícola and *Marqués de Alella* and *Chardonnay* of Atalella S.A.

The young and fruity whites of **Penedés** are exceptional, as are the older (2-3 year old) whites produced there. We suggest the *Blanc de Blancs* and *Blanc de Noirs* of Marqués de Monistrol; *Gran Viña Sol, Viña Esmeralda* and *Waltraud* of Bodegas Torres; *Chardonnay* of Jean

Leon; *Macabeo, Gran Blanc* and *Chardonnay* of Masía Vallformosa; *Xarelo* of Más Rabassa; *Gran Caus* of Can Rafols; *Bland Brut* of Cavas Hill; *Mont Marçal* of Mont Marçal; *Kraliner* of René Barbier; and *Vinya Teixidor* of Juan Llopart. Among the rosés, few of which are genuine, the visitor may want to sample *De Casta* of Bodegas Torres; *Rosado* of René Barbier and *Rosado* of Masía Bach. New Catalan reds are also produced with distinction in Penedés, above all cabernet-sauvignons and merlots. Try the famed *Gran Coronas Etiqueta Negra* or *Gran Coronas* of Bodegas Torres; *Viña Extrísima* of Masía Bach; *Cabernet-Sauvignon* of Jean Leon; *Gran Caus* of Can Rafols; *Vall Fort* and *Vall Reserva* of Masía Vallformosa: or *Cabernet-Sauvignon* of Segura Viudas. The **cavas**, or sparkling wines, of Penedés, are another topic altogether (see below).

In **Priorato**, we suggest you try *Cartoixa* from Scala Dei and *Priorato Joven* from Masía Barril.

Besides these, two more wine producing zones have been recognized by the local wine authority (INCAVI, *Instituto Catalán para la Vid y el Vino*, c/ Amalia Soler, 27, Vilafranca del Penedés ☎ 890 00 78) and, provisionally, by the national authority (INDO, *Instituto Nacional de Denominaciones de Origen*). They are the regions of **Conca de Barberá**, SW of Penedés, with good fresh whites (try *Blanco Perellada* and *Rosado Trepat*) and of **Terra Alta**, on the shores of the Ebro River. Terra Alta produces whites and clarets that are bubbly and have a bit too much body; but its reds are robust (suggested labels are *Vinya d'Hirto* and *Blanc de Belut* of Pedro Rovira). There are other wine growing areas in Catalonia, such as Raimat in the province of Lérida, that do not have the official *Denominación de Origen* designation. Of the Raimat wines, we suggest for reds *Clos Abadía* and *Cabernet-Sauvignon* and for whites *Clos Casal* and *Chardonnay*.

Cavas, officially categorized as a *Denominación Específica*, or Specific Denomination, are sparkling wines that are made rigorously in accordance with the *champenoise* method. Penedés and the surrounding areas make more than 100 million bottles of these bubbly wines a year, each of them according to the method of Dom Perignon, the Benedictine monk who invented the French method of making *champagne*, with results known today the world over.

Cavas have been made in Catalonia for more than 100 years. The pioneer was Codorniú, which today produces more sparkling wine made by the *champagne* method than any other winery in the world; and this vintner's example was quickly followed by others. One of the followers was Freixenet, which today has become very popular and successful in the United States. The capital of the cava country is Sant Sadurní d'Anoia: a visit to its wineries is an extraordinary experience (see 'Excursions' ▶ *page* 76). More than 50 *cavistas* —firms that make the cava sparkling wines— are jammed into this small and pleasant village. The quality of these wines, especially of the **brut** and the **brut nature**, is very high. But the wine-loving visitor should not try to compare these wines with those of the Marne, as local climate and varieties of grape give it a distinctive flavour. The international success of the Catalonian cavas is, in any case, proof of their intrinsic quality and their excellent value.

The visitor should forget the habit of drinking sparkling wine only at Christmas or when there is something important to celebrate. Bubbly, cava, is a good wine for all kinds of occasions, notably as a table wine during the summer, with aperitifs, or as a refreshing drink for mid-afternoon. Try it and judge for yourself.

CULTURE AND HISTORY

Here let the antiquarian pore over the stirring memorials of many thousand years, the vestiges of Phoenician enterprise, of Roman magnificence, of Moorish elegance, in that storehouse of ancient customs, that repository of all elsewhere long forgotten and passed by; here let him gaze upon those classical monuments, unequalled almost in Greece or Italy, and on those fairy Aladdin palaces, the creatures of Oriental gorgeousness and imagination, with which Spain alone can enchant the dull European; here let the man of feeling dwell on the poetry of her envy-disarming decay...; here let the lover of art feed his eyes with the mighty masterpieces of Italian art... or with the living nature of Velázquez and Murillo...; here let the artist sketch the lowly mosque of the Moor, the lofty cathedral of the Christian...; art and nature here offer subjects, from the feudal castle, the vast Escorial, the rock-built alcazar of imperial Toledo (to) the sunny towers of stately Seville...; let the botanist cull from the wild hothouse of nature plants unknown, unnumbered, matchless in colour, and breathing the aroma of the sweet south; let all, learned or unlearned, listen to the song, the guitar, the castanet; ...(For here,) as Don Quixote said, there are opportunities for what are called adventures elbow-deep.

RICHARD FORD *Hand-book for Spain*

Thus wrote one romantic English traveller in 1845. A century and a half later Spain remains that and much more. Spain's contribution to culture continues to be rich and diverse. Among the highlights are two major 19C novelists, Benito Pérez Galdos and Leopoldo Alas —Clarín—; two famous groups of writers, the *Generation of '98* and the *Generation of '27*, that included Nobel prize winners such as Vicente Aleixandre and Juan Ramón Jiménez, and other names no less universal —Valle-Inclán, Unamuno, Lorca, Machado, Alberti, Cela and Delibes; the philosophy of Ortega and the scientific research of Ramón y Cajal and Severo Ochoa, both of them Nobel Prize winners (Ochoa worked in the United States); the artistic genius of Goya and Picasso, of Dalí, Miró, Gris, and the more recent work of Tapiès, Saura, Ponç and Antonio López; the sculpture of Benlliure, Gargallo and Chillida; the internationally acclaimed architecture of Gaudí, and that of architects in the United States J.L. Sert and Moneo, the internationally known work of Bofill, the urbanism of Soria, precursor of Le Corbusier; the audacious engineering and the innovative technology of Torroja, Monturiol and Cierva; the work of famous musicians such as Pau (Pablo) Casals, Andrés Segovia, Plácido Domingo and Montserrat Caballé and composers like Falla and Luis de Pablo; the moviemaking of Buñuel, Berlanga and J.L. Garci (who won an Oscar in Hollywood); the recent fashion of Morago and Domínguez; the industrial design of Ricard and others; the songs of Julio Iglesias —heard today on five continents— and the youngest and hardest rock in Europe; the post-modern *movida*...

Barcelona, hugging the Mediterranean coast and looking towards France, is surely the most European city in Spain. Its intellectuals have for years travelled north to absorb the cultural life of the great European capitals beyond the Pyrenees, returning to enrich that of their own city. Today the movement is in many cases the reverse: Catalonia, and especially Barcelona, is famous for its contributions to European and world culture. Barcelona is a kind of moral centre of Catalonia, a concentration of the entire region's creative energies. This city not only participates in the life of Spain as a whole, but is a focal point in national cultural life. Consequently, arts and letters based on the

Catalan *language* form an exciting and vibrant part of local culture. As one author described it: Catalonia is a people united by a language.

The university of Barcelona, numerous cultural centres, an important publishing industry, intensive theatrical and musical life, a lively design and fashion industry —these are all evidence of the seemingly inexhaustible energies of the Catalan people. The cultural landscape here ranges from the earliest Roman works to the most advanced rationalism, something to be expected, perhaps, of such an eminently Mediterranean people.

Architecture and City Planning

The successive civilizations and empires that have swept across these lands have left an exceptional heritage. They mutually enriched each other by synthesis, first by destroying and then by building on what came before, by a dynamic interrelationship between the traditional and the new. Today, the traveller arriving in Barcelona will find Roman relics next to modern Miró sculptures, Gothic alleys and seigniorial 19C avenues, ochre-coloured stone buildings next to undulating, dark crystal façades, and impersonal housing blocks facing voluptuous, naturalist creations. Stop for a moment and see how, in this land that boasts more than 2,000 years of history and civilization, all this has its roots in a cultural legacy of continuity and continuous change.

Prehistoric Remains

Megalithic structures, more than 3,000 years old: the dolmens of Antequera (Málaga); the *talayots* and *navetas*, or tombs, of Menorca; the caves of Guadix (Granada). Remains of the Greek founders of Ampurias (Gerona) from the 4C BC and ruins of the walls of Ullastret from the Iberian period.

Roman (12C BC-4C AD) and Visigothic (5-7C AD) Heritage

Roman legacies include the great aqueducts of Segovia, Tarragona and Mérida (Badajoz); thermal baths (Badalona, Caldas de Montboy); mausoleums (Scipios brothers, Tarragona); theatres in Sagunto, Mérida, and Tarragona; bridges such as the ones at Alcántara (Cáceres) and Sant Sadurní d'Anoia: innumerable city walls (Tarragona, Barcelona) and triumphal arches (Bará in Tarragona and Martorell in Barcelona); the Itálica mosaics (Seville) and those of Ampurias (Tarragona), Tarragona, Barcelona and Bell-lloch (Gerona), the remains of which are being exhibited at the extraordinary Roman Art Museum in Mérida and the no less fascinating Archaeological Museum of Tarragona. Tarragona, the ancient imperial *Tarraco*, is in itself a goldmine of Roman ruins and relics. Next to the present day cathedral of Barcelona there are also important remains of a paleo-Christian basilica that was part of the old Roman city.

The Visigothic heritage comes across more clearly in ideas than in monuments. Two notable exceptions are the Centcelles mausoleum (Constanti, Tarragona) and the three Tarrasa shrines (Barcelona).

Moorish Architecture, of the Caliph of Córdoba (8-11C)

The arch of the Mosque (*Mezquita*) is in the classical Moorish horseshoe shape, with alternating elements of stone (white) and brick (red). The Mosque's stylised and abundant decoration includes caligraphic inscriptions, geometric drawings and plant motifs. In this area, the Caliph forms are mixed with Mozarabic and Carolingian patterns.

Pre-Romanesque Architecture (8-10C)

Using Visigothic architecture as a basis, Asturias developed a style of building that was a precursor of the Romanesque style: simple, austere churches, without ornaments and made of solid stone with semicircular arches. Santa María del Naranco and San Miguel de Lillo are two examples.

Moorish Architecture, of the Almojades of Seville (11-13C)

Almoravids and Almojades built mosques and minarets of austere brick, replaced the Moorish horseshoe arch with a more oriental version, a pointed arch, and introduced wooden coffered ceilings and those made of *azulejo* (a blue and white tile), as in the Giralda and the Torre del Oro of Seville.

Romanesque Architecture (11-13C)

The Christian kingdoms of the north consolidated their power as they faced their Arab neighbors to the south: the Christian architecture was solid and made of stone, as opposed to Moorish delicacy of form and of materials such as brick, wood and plaster. The earliest Romanesque, in Catalonia, is represented by sober churches with severe lines, barrel and ribbed vaults, flat walls, and narrow and elongated windows as in the monasteries of Ripoll and San Pedro de Roda. The religious fervour of the medieval world together with the flood of European pilgrims travelling the route to Santiago de Compostela were later responsible for a succession of churches that were marked by their softer lines, greater ornamentation, capitals, arches and religious medallions sculpted with absolute liberty by the artists. The cathedral of Santiago —which stands behind a Baroque façade that was added later— is the period's greatest work.

Roman Theatre, Mérida

Cathedral, Toledo

From the 10C, Catalonian Romanesque crowned churches with stone vaults, while in the rest of Europe naves continued to be covered with wood. The vigorous efforts of Abbot Oliva (11C) have left impressive examples of Romanesque architecture in Catalonia: the churches of Ripoll and San Vicente de Cardona; and in the 12C, churches of Besalú, of the monastery of Sant Joan de los Abadesses, of Santa María de Porqueres and of San Pablo del Campo (Barcelona), as well as the magnificent cloisters in Gerona and Sant Cugat.

In the province of Barcelona there are several other examples: the Church of Vilafranca del Penedés, the Chapel d'Espiells (Sant Sadurní d'Anoia), the hermitages of Mataró and Montserrat, the Church of Santa Cecilia (Montserrat), the chapel in the Olérdola mines and the 13C chapel of Santa Lucía attached to the cathedral of Barcelona.

Mozarabic and Mudejar Architecture (11-15C)

The Mozarabs —Christians who lived in Moslem territories— combined the architecture of the Visigoths with that of the Caliphate: an example is San Miguel de la Escalada (León). The Mudejars —Arabs who lived and worked under the Christians— prolonged the use of brick and refined ceiling work in wood and *azulejos*, an art that has lasted to the present: there are numerous examples in Aragón and the Alcázar of Seville.

Nasrid Architecture of Granada (14-15C)

The Alhambra in Granada is the great monument to Moorish architecture, the fruit of long and rich traditions of design, decoration

Modernist masterwork: Church of the Holy Family, Barcelona

and the arrangement of open spaces, delicate columns, sculpture and water.

Gothic Architecture (13-16C)

The Cistercian abbeys of Catalonia —Poblet, Santa Creus (Tarragona)— helped spread Gothic influences in Spain. Buttresses now became distinct flying buttresses that supported lofty barrel vaults. Ogival arches and fine stone carvings with filigree details became apparent; large columns rose toward the ceilings; enormous rose windows and others of multi-coloured glass lit church interiors: the cathedrals at Burgos, Toledo and León are three Gothic jewels. Later Gothic cathedrals (Seville) strove for immensity and returned to a strict floor plan in the shape of a cross that contrasted with the richer ornamentation of the Arab influence. The Castle of Coca and the Palace of the Generalitat (Barcelona) are Gothic examples of civic architecture. Examples of transition into the Gothic style can be seen in the cathedrals of Tarragona and Lérida. Fully Gothic are the cathedrals of Barcelona, Gerona, Tortosa and Manresa. The medieval splendour of Barcelona has left an abundant quantity of Gothic monuments: the Royal Chapel, Santa María del Mar (the masterwork of Berenguer de Montagut), the Pedralbes monastery, the Church and Cloister of Santa Ana, the churches of Santa María de Pino and Justo y Pastor, and the Chapel of Santa Ana in the Royal palace that contains an altarpiece by J. Huguet. Among the civic Gothic examples are the Tinell Room, the Consejo de Ciento, the Llotja, the Ataranzas, the Hospital of Santa Cruz, the Town Hall, the Chamber of Deputies and the house that lodges the Picasso Museum. Medieval Gothic centres of notable interest are the villages of Montblanc and Prades. Vilafranca del Penedés also has a Gothic district, the Chapel of San Juan and the Church of San Francisco.

Architecture of the Renaissance (16C)

The Isabeline style of the Catholic Monarchs embraced the Gothic —adding sculptured details to Gothic façades— in a new style known as the *plateresque*. This form, which took its name from the work of silversmiths, featured profusely ornamented surfaces as in the university of Salamanca. Another, more classical, tendency was seen in the works of Gil de Hontañón at the university of Alcalá (Madrid), of Siloe at the university of Granada and of Machuca in the palace of Charles V (Granada). Also important was the style known as *herreriano*, named after Herrera, the architect who built the Escorial for Philip II. This palace was built with the austerity of a monastery and the functionality of a royal residence, a monument of rectilineal severity and a spiritual ally of Spanish religious orthodoxy during the Counter-reformation. It was an emblem of the imperial psychology of Spain. During this period, Barcelona and Catalonia were no longer the dominant political and commercial nuclei of the country. This accounts for the shortage and relative lack of importance of the region's Renaissance architecture. One exception is the façade of the Palace of the Generalitat (Barcelona).

Baroque Architecture (17-18C)

In the middle of the *Siglo de Oro*, Spain's Golden Age, there was an exuberant explosion of voluptuous lines and curves, of exaggerated reliefs and motifs drawn from nature. Architecture, sculpture and painting blended together to decorate façades, retables and retrochoirs. The style at its most sumptuous may be seen in the wreathed columns of the ornate *churrigueresco* fashion initiated by the Churriguera brothers —as in the Plaza Mayor of Salamanca and the *Transparente* of the cathedral in Toledo. But Baroque architecture was different in every Spanish province as seen in the façades of the cathedral of Santiago, and those of the palaces in Ecija (Seville), of the grand houses in Jerez (Cádiz), of the palace of San Telmo (Seville) and of the sanctuary of the Cartuja (Granada). Examples in Catalonia are the Dalmases Palace and the Church of Belén in Barcelona, the façade of the cathedral of Gerona and the parochial church of San Bartolomé and Santa Tecla in Sitges.

Neoclassical Architecture (18-19C)

Coexisting with the Baroque, the classicism of Herrera was continued by Gómez de Mora (Plaza Mayor, Madrid) and Herrera the Younger (Basílica del Pilar, Zaragoza). As a reaction to the excesses of the Baroque period, there was also a return to the Greco-Roman classical world of columns, cupolas and similar features. Charles III promoted the new style and neoclassical landmarks in Madrid such as the Prado Museum, the Botanical Gardens, the Cibeles fountain and the Alcalá arch were built in his reign.

In Barcelona, the French military engineer Verboom built the Ciudadela (18C). The Church of La Merced and the Palace of the Vicereine are Neoclassic in design. In the 18C, before the Modernist explosion, the Plaza Real was constructed, the Liceo (1848) was built and iron was used in the construction of the Mercado del Borne.

Modernism and Contemporary Tendencies (19-20C)

Gaudí was a leading representative of the extravagant *Modernist* style, a singular combination of Catalonian Romanticism and the pre-Raphaelite world of John Ruskin: Gaudí used curved forms, plant motifs and earth colours, his lintels appeared to flow over doors and windows and his towers and balconies melted into heavy curves (houses of Batlló and Milá, Güell park and neighbourhood, Church of the Holy Family, Barcelona) ▶ *page* 100.

In Barcelona, Domènech i Muntaner built the Palau de la Música Catalana and Puig i Cadafalch constructed the Ametller House, while near Sitges he constructed the Novella Palace and in Sant Sadurní d'Anoia he built the Codorniú wine cellars ▶ *page* 76.

On the outskirts of Barcelona, numerous Modernist residences and mansions were built for the local bourgeoisie, as in Sitges.

Rationalism, in line with Le Corbusier, was propounded by the GATEPAC group of architects; García Mercadal in Madrid, and Subirana —apartment block in San Andrés, Antitubercular Clinic in Barcelona— and Sert (dean of the Harvard University architecture faculty since 1958) in Barcelona —as in the Fundación Miró. As dean at Harvard, Sert was succeeded by another Spaniard, Rafael Moneo, whose most recent work, integrating classicism and the most advanced present-day architecture, is the Roman Art Museum in Mérida. During the 1960s, realism was advocated by many (Bohigas, Correa and Milá). The latest *avant garde* tendencies crystallize in Bofill: Les Halles (Paris) as well as various works in Barcelona.

Popular and Traditional Architecture in Catalonia

The typical rural dwelling in Catalonia is the **masía**. This building

Masía, typical rural Catalonian dwelling

style was consolidated in the 16C and achieved its greatest development in the 18C. The styles vary greatly throughout Catalonia, but they tend to be smaller in the south than in the north, where the stables were larger. The coastal *masías* were more open, with porches, huge windows, and Mediterranean style galleries, while those further inland were more Romanesque, closed and solid. The *masías* usually had two floors and an attic based on a rectangular floor plan and a gable roof, although in Tarragona mansard roofs were frequently used. On the ground floor, behind the flagstoned porch, was the necessarily large kitchen, and beyond this were the storage rooms for farm tools and equipment. The bedrooms and living room were located on the upper floors and directly above these were the attic or lofts used for grain, hay and straw storage. The coastal *masías* frequently had adjoining watchtowers used for defensive purposes. The Barcelonan habit of calling gardened suburban homes *torres* (literally, towers) springs from this building custom.

City Planning

The evolution of Barcelona as a city extends from the first Iberian settlements on the site until today, something like 3,000 years of urban development. In the 1C the city the Romans called Barcino ▶ *page* 43 was the unwalled site of important civic and religious buildings. The city actually decreased in size during the early part of the Christian era (4C), when it was first enclosed by walls measuring over 9m high, 3.63m thick and 1,122m long. Some time after the year 1000 these walls ceased to contain all of the town's population, as several new districts began to grow around San Pedro de las Puellas, on both sides of the Vallés road, next to the church of Santa María and between the walls and sands of the Rambla.

During the first half of the 13C a new set of walls was built, known as the Rambla walls —5,096m long— to protect the neighbourhoods that had developed outside the original city walls. Over the 14C and the 15C, however, the area of the city doubled, and new walls had to be added. These stretched out towards the suburbs that had developed, and they had the effect of making the Ramblas the principal artery of what was by then a large city. Barcelona's port and sea walls were constructed during the 16C. Shortly after Philip V put an end to the political autonomy of Catalonia ▶ *page* 49, the military engineer Verboom —acting on orders from the monarch— drew up the first city plans for the district of Barceloneta. Then, during the mid-19C, the last remaining walls of the city's Gothic nucleus were torn down to assimilate the expansion of a flourishing commercial and industrial centre, a new and prosperous Barcelona ▶ *page* 51.

The 19C brought to Spain's great cities (Madrid, Barcelona) the process of widening narrow streets: the *Ensanche.* A new urban space, Cartesian in its geometry, grew up, based on grid patterns, great blocks, and systems of intersecting boulevards and major arteries.

The engineer and urbanist Ildefonso Cerdá was the man chosen in 1858 to plan the *Ensanche* of Barcelona in response to the new needs of the prospering middle classes. The so-called *Cerdá Plan* was the first grid plan for the city, with one set of streets running parallel to the sea and a second set running at right angles to those. The right angle corners of every intersection were bevelled back to create larger open spaces. Two great diagonal avenues crossed the new districts of the city from end to end. Unfortunately, the high quality of Cerda's planning did not fully come to fruition, due principally to the opposition of many landowners. Buildings have been allowed to rise much higher than the engineer foresaw, and the green spaces and public buildings he planned have not been completed.

Even more advanced was the work of Arturo Soria, who at the beginning of the 20C anticipated present day environmental concern with inner cities with his Ciudad Lineal (Madrid) project.

The 1950s were years of great speculation among the landlords of Barcelona. The result was a spread of chaotic urban development, which authorities later tried to correct. Today, in Barcelona as in all Spanish cities, there remains a tension between the traditional and the new —the saving of old quarters, rehabilitation of houses and the reclamation of space for pedestrians— and the demands of modern day life —highways, commercial centres and green areas.

A new surge of urban development is already taking place in anticipation of the 1992 Olympic Games, led by a number of public works projects that will transform important aspects of the city ▶ *page* 52.

Cinema

The burst of Spanish cultural activity over the last ten years is perhaps most obvious, and has the most markedly individual features, in the cinema. The mass market Spanish film-makers serve an audience which is largely between 25 and 45 years old, and the viewers' attitudes seem to mirror closely those of the directors. It is a happy situation for those behind the camera. The film-makers and their audience are both attentive to the changes shaping and reshaping Spanish society.

Spanish **cinema** is basking in the warmth of heightened popularity inside the country and increased prestige in international film circles. Luis Buñuel —*The Exterminating Angel, Viridiana, Belle de Jour*— is a landmark in the history of Spanish cinema, and he strongly influenced film-makers like Carlos Saura —*La Caza, Blood Wedding, Carmen*—, scriptwriters like Rafael Azcona and producers like Elias Querejeta.

Juan Antonio Bardem —*Death of a Cyclist*—, Luis Berlanga —*La Escopeta Nacional*— and Victor Erice —*The Spirit of the Beehive*— have completed a body of work that lies somewhere between political commitment, social satire and poetic metaphor. This line of work and Spanish film in general achieved a new dimension of international fame culminating with the Oscar awarded for *Volver a Empezar*, a film by José Luis Garci, and the two Golden Bear awards, given at the Berlin Film Festival, awarded to Manuel Gutiérrez Aragón for *Habla Mudita* and *Camada Negra*.

A different view of life is reflected in the work of Pedro Almodovar —*What Have I Done to Deserve This?, Matador*— which constitutes at once an exercise in black storytelling and a sardonic comedy of manners determined to *épater les bourgeois*.

Barcelona holds a film festival every year in June. Since 1986, the *Setmana de Cine de Barcelona* has come to substitute the already well known *Setmana de Cine en Color*, or Colour Film Festival of Barcelona.

Visitors can also take advantage of the *International Horror Film Festival* which has been taking place in October in Sitges ▶ *page* 84 during the last two decades.

Finally, the *Filmoteca*, c/ Travesera de Gracia, 63 ☎ 201 19 06, offers a variety of film cycles over the course of the year, typically grouped by director, country, and so on. Along with the wide variety of commercial cinemas, this film theatre completes the cinematographic spectrum of the city.

Design, Crafts, Fashion and Decorative Arts

Things, those domestic objects with which human beings live so closely, are a testimony to the habits and culture of a people. Spain's is a history of things. And these Catalonian parts of Spain, especially Barcelona, have paid great attention to things, having become a world-class centre of fashion and design.

There is a 5,000 year old tradition behind Barcelona's phenomenal success as a hot-bed of industrial design, fashion, ceramics, jewelry and decorative arts. Hand-made earthenware pots from Neolithic times and the pre-Roman pottery of Ilduro (Mataró) and Cosse (Tarragona) testify to the region's long familiarity with the ceramic arts. And as far as design goes, already back in 1775 the *Escuela Gratuita de Diseño* (Free School of Design) was founded in Barcelona, followed by the FAD or *Fomento de las Artes Decorativas* (Promotion of the Decorative Arts) in 1903. In 1960, the ADI/FAD *Agrupación de Diseño Industrial* (Industrial Design Group) was founded, and today the use of CAD/CAM programs and other electronic aids forms an integral part of a highly developed Catalonian design industry.

Furthermore, Spain has always enjoyed an enviable reputation as a producer of magnificent earthenware glazed tiles or *mosaicos* and other forms of handmade ceramics. Catalonia's vitality and incessant production resulted in a virtual monopoly of the European ceramics trade during the 14-15C, a domination continued up until the arrival of Modernism (19-20C). In other areas, and during the Moorish domination, the kingdom of Al-Andalus ▶ *page* 46 contributed Eastern techniques and sensibilities derived from Arab ceramics. This began in the 10C in Elvira (Granada) and continued during the 11-12C in Málaga. The products included cups, plates, pitchers and flower vases decorated with metallic glazes and relief patterns. The *azulejo*, an ornamental tile that still today reflects a profoundly Spanish style, appeared with the Almojades in Triana, Seville, in the 12C. Under the influence of the Italian Renaissance during the 16C, more floral patterns were added to the geometric motifs of the Almojades design.

Arab craftsmen built the principal ceramic workshops of the Middle Ages: the Levantine **Paterna** during the 13C first produced green and white ware and later blue and white products; **Manises** has been famous since the 14C for its ceramics decorated with reflecting metallic glazes and with botanical motifs and characters. At the height of the splendour of the 15-16C, these lovely wares were keenly sought the world over by the wealthiest and most sophisticated buyers.

The 15C brought the rise of the ceramics centre of Talavera de la Reina (Toledo). This town's pottery replaced the Arabic themes with those of Christianity, bringing a Renaissance spirit to the work and blue and yellow colours to the kiln. The factory of Alcora (Castellón), founded by Philip V in 1727, at first produced Rococo *azulejos* in blue-yellow tones; later, **porcelain** became important there, due mainly to the still internationally famous and sought-after work of Lladró.

As the 18C unfolded, the porcelain plant of the Buen Retiro, founded by Charles III, became the leading manufacturer. In the 19C, Sargadelos ceramics, lovely to look at and resistant to fire, and later, the glazed earthenware and tiles of Pickman (La Cartuja of Seville), decorated with vivid colours and drawings, developed worldwide reputations that have lasted to the present day. At the start of the 20C the tile factories of Triana were working in the Arab-Andalusian tradition as the Catalans to the north experimented with tiling in a more

Modernist style: Butsens y Cía (façade stone of Barcelona), Orsola Solá, and, above all, Escofet.

This long tradition continued into the contemporary period with the ceramic work of Picasso, Miró, the Serró brothers, Sert, Llorens Artigas and Cuixart. It continues still with the work of Durán-Lóriga and many other young artists and craftsmen.

Catalonia has been at the head of **glass** production of jugs, vases and *almorratxas* in Spain since the Early Middle Ages until today, passing through the works of Ponts in the 1940s and the current *Horno del Pueblo Español* in Barcelona.

Spain's **fine metal work** shows its Moslem influence in the copper vases that are popular to this day in Andalusia. The genius of these works of art is found in the clocks, instruments and the Hispano-Arab **automats**, or robots, of the court of Alfonso the Wise. Their zenith came in the **monstrances** of the 16C, enormous and conical towers built replete with columns and statues embossed in silver, in which the host is shown in processions. The Gothic monstrance in Toledo, and the Renaissance monstrances of Santiago and of Seville are the most important in Spain. Iron, just as much as silver, was used with stylized delicacy in the **wrought ironwork** seen in the iron gates of the gardens and courtyards of Seville and the balconies of Ronda (Málaga). These are today's humble inheritors of the **rejería** —grating or grillwork, especially in windows— found in the chapels and choirs of the churches and cathedrals of Toledo, Avila, Jaén and Granada. Fray Francisco de Salamanca, Juan Francés and Francisco Villalpando were some of those whose work was on a massive scale but at the same time extraordinarily delicate.

In Barcelona, the iron-work of Gaudí, the silver-work of Sunyer, Masriera and Mercadé, industrial design objects such as the pressure cooker by Llusca, kettle by Tusquets, Catalonian bench by Tusquets and Clotet, lamp-post by Bernet-Milá, Calder lamp by Franch, fireplaces by Milá, Coderch, Valls and Cornea, and the jewelry of Puig Doria... these are a few examples of Catalan metal craft.

Catalonia also has a long tradition of **furniture-making**. The wooden Romanesque benches of San Clemente de Taüll and the Catalan Gothic furniture of the Middle Ages, the chairs of Gaudí at the turn of the century, and those of Sert and Bonet during the 1930s, as well as the chairs of Galí and the armchairs of Pep Bonet and Tusquets in the 1970s and 1980s all reflect a cultural inheritance of the three great contributions to furniture-making by the Spanish: the **Mudejar hip chair**, decorated with classical Arabic geometric designs; the **friar's armchair**, a harsh and austere piece of Castilian overtones, with leather seat and back fastened with bronze or brass nails; and, above all, the universal contribution of the **bargueño**, the lovely decorated wooden trunks. These portable trunks have sliding drawers and can be opened up into a desk that comes complete with wooden inlays encrusted with insets of ivory and ebony.

The contemporary art of Mediterranean **basket-weaving** is, generally, still more delicate than the stout, angular forms of Galician basketwork and the simpler, linear styles of that of Castile and Extremadura.

Spanish **fashion** is in fashion. It is competing vigorously with the most important fashion centres of Europe: Dusseldorf, Paris and Milan. Clothes have become something of a national obsession in Spain, from prêt-à-porter and sportswear to very expensive and fashionable garments. There is a wide range of accessories: shoe enthusiasts should consider the stylized design of Sara Navarro and Teresa Ramallal, and the product range of Selec Balear, Yanko, Lotusse and Camper; Joaquín Berao and Puig Doria are trend setters in bags, belts, jewelry and costume jewelry Llongueras and Blanco are market leaders in hair creations; Elena Benarroch's fur line is very successful; the Loewe leather goods need no introduction.

The Spanish fashion industry has built on the solid foundations of *haute couture* brand names such as Balenciaga and has found its place in the contemporary designer clothes market. Pedro Morago, Adolfo Domínguez —with shops in Paris, London and Japan—, Elena Benarroch, Sybilla, Jesús del Pozo, Agatha Ruiz de la Prada and Manuel Piña are innovative fashion designers who reflect the present creativity in Spain.

Barcelona has been a major textile centre for over 200 years and is renowned internationally as a dynamic producer of new and innovative fashions. Many of the young creators who have brought Spain to the attention of world markets are Catalan or are working from Barcelona.

The background is a Spanish **textile** tradition that also goes back to prehistory. Among its products stand out the **rugs** of Crevillente which include a tradition of Hispano-Arabic weavings with their geometric decorations, dating from the 10C to the 15C; the technique of the Spanish knot, to which 12C references have been found; the splendour of the richly coloured art produced in Granada for the Holy Week processions in the 14-15C; the workshops at Chinchilla and Cuenca; **tapestry** factories including the Santa Isabel factory in Madrid —dating back to the 17C, and masterfully painted by Velázquez in *Las Hilanderas*— and the Real Fábrica de Santa Bárbara, founded in Madrid by Philip V. In the 18C, Goya painted patterns for tapestries here, and the factory continues as a private enterprise to the present day; and the 9,000 mechanical looms and 3,600 Catalan factories that in the 19C were strongly competitive on an international scale.

It is the same long history of things that underlies Spanish **design**. Since the middle of the last century Spanish designers have shown a flair. Some highlights: Monturiol, the submarine engineer; the Modernism of Gaudí who, in addition to his architectural achievements, created furniture and wonderful iron fittings that continued a tradition established by Herrera, Villanueva and Ventura Rodríguez centuries before; painters like Casas and Rusiñol who designed posters for beverages like *Anís del Mono* and *Codorniú*; graphic artists like Apel.les Mestres, Gual and Opisso; the jewelry of Masriera and, from the 1920s up to the Civil War, the furniture of the architects Luis Feduchi and Sert; the perfume bottles of Myrurgia; the drawings for the magazine *Blanco y Negro* by Rafael de Penagos; the aeronautics of Juan de la Cierva with his autogiro; and the posters of Renau and Miró during the Civil War. More recently, Spain has advanced rapidly toward a post-industrial state, and so the **latest designs** are not only artistic but also functional and industrial. The high-speed train known as the *Talgo*, designed by Goicoechea; the chairs of Oscar Tusquets; the lamps and other objects of André Ricard, Mila, Coderch, Carvajal, Pep Cortés and Cirici; the bookcovers of Daniel Gil; and the general graphic design of Alberto Corazón, Enric Satué and Cruz Novillo; the industrial design of Moneo, Riart and Miralles.

Barcelona is competing with Milan as a world leader in the field of industrial design. A refined, aesthetic taste and 5,000 years of experience and *savoir faire*, together with the latest in high tech, have projected Barcelona's international potential.

History

Spain is an old country, with more than 3,000 years of rich history to boast of; at the same time it is young, modern, forward looking and freedom loving. It is an open country, for millennia a melting pot of peoples —much like the United States— and the cradle of adventurers and emigrants to the five continents of the world. It is linked to the sea, and the sea is one of the reasons why visitors come from all over. Spain is American and Atlantic and it is also European and Mediterranean. Its history is a rich and rare treasure trove.

Catalonia and the County of Barcelona have not only played a vital role in the rich and varied history of Spain but have also been the protagonists of the region's own, distinct history.

Barcelona, tied so closely to the Mediterranean that was the cradle of Western civilization, has historical roots that run deep, even into prehistory. A grave found in present-day c/ Muntaner attests to the Neolithic populations that existed here 5,000 years ago. The Iberians —particularly the Layetanos— followed, meeting colonizing Greeks and Phoenicians some 500 years before Christ. The Carthaginian Amilcar Barca founded the ancient city of Barcino (from Barca, the ruling family of Carthage) in 218 BC.

Conquered by Cornelius Scipios in 133 BC, the city became a Roman colony —Favencia Julia Augusta Pia Barcina. It was made part of the Roman province of Hispania Citerior, subject to the provincial capital of Tarraco (Tarragona). The other two provinces into which the Romans divided Spain were Betica and Lusitania.

The city grew to more than 10,000 inhabitants by the 2C, but was destroyed in the middle of the 3C by a Franco-Germanic invasion. It was later rebuilt and fortified, although that did not stop the Gothic invasion that took place under the command of Ataulfo. They swept S into the Roman province of Tarraco and made Barcino the centre of their court.

In 717-718 the Moslems, marching up from the S of Spain, conquered Barcelona. They installed a tolerant regime: Christianity was not repressed; both the Christian and the Jewish civil authorities were retained, but they had to obey the orders of the *valí*, or Arab governor. A major military operation by Charlemagne in 798 led to a Carolingian occupation across a vast area S of the Pyrenees, from Navarre to Barcelona. As a result, the city now became part of the *Marca Hispánica*, or the frontier of Christian and Moorish Spain. Barcelona was conquered by Louis the Pious in 801. Wilfredo el Velloso (879-897), count of Gothic descent, was an effectively independent lord who established the Catalan dynasty of the *Condado de Barcelona* (countship of Barcelona). There followed a period of real splendour for the city, but it was cut short by the invasion of Almanzor, who sacked the city in 985, taking a great number of captives.

During the ensuing centuries Barcelona grew to 20,000 inhabitants. Its fortifications were rebuilt. Outside the walls, new districts were springing up. The city's shipyards were turning out boats constantly, and merchants used them to plow the Mediterranean on trading missions.

The union of Catalonia and Aragón came about in the 12C through the marriage of Ramón Berenguar IV of Barcelona and Petronila of Aragón. During the reign of James I, king of Aragón (13C), the municipality of Barcelona was established, as well as the first representative institutions: a municipal council (the *Consell de Cent*) that was made up of honourable citizens (merchants), artists (liberal occupations) and craftsmen; and courts that were similarly composed of three classes of citizens. This was the epoch of medieval glory for Barcelona, and it would last to the end of the 14C or the start of the 15C.

New walls came to take the place of old ones, the maritime port was built and, in 1451, the University was founded, bringing Barcelona fully into the modern Age.

The 15C was a period of economic crisis for the region, but in the following century mercantile activity picked up again. Part of the reason for this was that Barcelona, which had received Columbus in 1493 on his return from America, found itself on the route for precious metals (from America to Seville to Genoa). At the beginning of the 16C, the first coins of pure copper were minted and the *Banc de la Ciutat* —whose predecessor had been the *Taula de canvi*— was founded. Charles V arrived in the city in 1519, and made it the capital of the Spanish empire. For more than 100 years, Barcelona prospered under three kings of the house of Austria: Charles V, Philip II and Philip III.

A series of new wars brought ruin to Barcelona and the region. Among them were the wars of Secession, of the Harvesters (who gathered in the city to rise against the viceroy), that of 1640 and of the *Succession*. The war of 1714 ▶ *page* 49 followed, supported by the *Consell de Cent*. Finally, in order to suppress future uprisings, the king ordered the construction of the imposing Ciudadela fortress in the district of La Ribera. Shortly afterwards, the neighbourhood of La Barceloneta rose outside the walls of the city.

The 18C saw an urban expansion —by the end of the century there were some 115,000 inhabitants— and an economic prosperity that was testimony of the Enlightenment of Charles III. Textile production boomed, largely owing to the liberalization of trade with the Americas. The monopoly held by Seville on such trade had been ended and the Americas now provided a rich market for the Catalan textile industry. Despite the bloody toll of the War of Independence —or War of the Spanish Succession, which accounted for some 30,000 dead in Barcelona alone— industrial activity began to expand vigorously in 1826 with the arrival of numerous immigrants looking for work in the factories of Catalonia. A large working class that lived in conditions of poverty grew up. Between 1844 and 1853 the first railways came into existence, joint-stock companies were founded and the first modern banks appeared. The bourgeoisie of the city was rich, flourishing and liberal. The Ensanche ▶ *page* 38 of the old medieval quarter was created.

When the revolution of 1868 dethroned Isabel II, a revolutionary junta took power in Barcelona and decided to demolish the Ciudadela that was built for Philip V and had become a symbol of absolutist oppression. Since then the area of the ancient fortifications has remained a park. In 1888, the Universal Exposition was inaugurated there, and shortly afterwards the first electric tramcars went into service.

At the end of the century, the Barcelonan middle classes had reached a level comparable to that of other European bourgeoisies but virtually unknown in the rest of Spain. The nation, meanwhile, was battered by the loss of its last American colonies. Growing worker protests, anarchist activity and, finally, repression, led to what has come to be known as the Tragic Week, or *Semana Trágica*, during the rule iof Alfonso XII in 1909. A few years later, World War I broke out and commercial and industrial activity in Barcelona expanded briskly.

In 1923, Primo the Ribera inaugurated his dictatorship with the support of the middle classes of Catalonia. There followed a sharp repression of Barcelona's worker organizations and, to a lesser degree, of the most nationalist elements of the Catalan bourgeoisie. The International Exhibition that was held in Montjuïc in 1929 brought with it important urban improvements and the construction of numerous buildings as well as the great Montjuïc fountain ▶ *page* 21.

With the Republican electoral triumph of 1931, Barcelona became once again the capital of an autonomous Catalonia and seat of the regional government, or the *Generalitat.* But with the coming of the Spanish Civil War and the establishment of Franco's dictatorship the autonomy of the region ended: autonomy would only return in September of 1977, ▶ *page* 52, two years after Franco's death.

Between 1950 and 1970 a large number of immigrants, coming to Barcelona from the poor S areas of Spain to participate in the city's industrial and commercial boom, spurred the development of several new neighbourhoods on the city's periphery. A great industrial belt grew around the city at the same time that the first worker dormitory communities were growing nearby. Today, Barcelona is a modern city that remains extremely active economically, a place where artistic and cultural creativity coexist with the development of industrial design and new technology.

Chronological Table

	Origins
-10,000 BC	Middle Paleolithic Period. Remains of cave-dwelling hunters have been found in the provinces of Gerona and Tarragona. Upper Paleolithic Period. Rupestrian paintings in the world-famous caves of Altamira (Santander) and Parpalló (Gandía).
9,000- 4,000 BC	End of the Old Stone Age.
5,000 BC	Neolithic Period. Development of agriculture and domestic livestock.
3,000 BC	Development of the tomb/burial culture; one of their sepulchres was found on c/ Muntaner (Barcelona).
-1,100 BC	Bronze Age. Invasions by Nordic peoples, probably Celts. Colonization by Phoenicians and Greeks, the founding of Ampurias, Tortosa and other coastal trading posts. Coexistence with indigenous Iberian tribes.
900-400 BC	Celtic tribes from northen Europe make their way into the N of the Iberian Peninsula, mixing with the Iberians and giving rise to the Celtiberian race.
400 BC	Iberian culture (the Layetanos) nucleus at Barcino or Barcinona (Barcelona).
	Roman Spain
2C BC	Arrival of the Carthaginians from Africa.
218 BC	The colonization of Spain by the Roman Empire begins with the arrival of Publius Cornelius Scipios' legions at Ampurias.
214 BC	Hannibal attacks Saguntum, a Roman ally. The Second Punic War.
1C BC	Founding of Augusta Barcina (Barcelona) by Romans.
2C BC- 3C AD	A prolonged period of Romanization. The economy flourishes as the subjugated inhabitants adopt Roman engineering, culture, law and architecture, even the Roman currency and language. Iberia —or Hispania—

becomes an important part of the civilized world, making up three provinces of the Roman Empire. It produces philosophers and writers and gives two great emperors to Rome, both of them from the town of Itálica (Seville): Trajan, who rules the Empire from 98-117 AD, and Hadrian, 117-138 AD. Catalonia is incorporated into the Roman province of Hispania Citerior with its capital at Tarragona. Barcelona develops into a prosperous commercial and maritime centre during the 1C and 2C.

2C — Extension of Christianity in Spain.

3C — Crisis of the Roman Empire. Vandals invade the peninsula, destroying Barcelona and Tarragona.

5C — The Visigoths, allies of the Romans, come to defend Spain against invasions of Vandals, Germanic peoples and others. King Teudis makes Barcelona his capital and later integrates it into the Visigoth kingdom based at Toledo.

5-7C — The Visigoths establish a relatively weak kingdom, with its capital in Toledo and its cultural life in the Christian church.

Moorish Spain, Frankish Catalonia, the House of Barcelona and its Independence

711 — The Moors cross the Straits of Gibraltar from N Africa and defeat the Visigoths at Guadalete. In seven years, the invaders conquer the peninsula, and they are not fully driven out again for eight centuries. The emir al-Hurr conquers Catalonia in 717, but Arab domination in Catalonia is never very strong. Christians win the battle of Covadonga. The kingdom of Asturias is founded.

8-11C — Al-Andalus (Andalusia) flourishes culturally and economically. 785-793: Gerona, Urgel and Sardinia surrender to the Franks but Córdoba reacts strongly and by 793 once again occupies N Catalonia. 798: The Frankish emperor Charlemagne gradually conquers and occupies a vast area S of the Pyrenees, stretching from Navarre to Barcelona (taken in 801 by Louis the Pious). This Territory becomes known as the *Marca Hispánica* and is the dividing line between Christian Europe and Moorish Spain. The E section of this *Marca Hispánica* is the nucleus of what will later become Catalonia. Separated into *condados* or counties, the first counts (Besa, 801-820) were vassals of the king of Aquitaine. One of these counts, Wilfredo El Velloso (879-897), unites under his jurisdiction the counties of Urgel, Sardinia, Gerona and Barcelona, and creates a dynasty (the House of Barcelona), which is to rule the new nation for centuries to come. 929: Abd al-Rahman III declares his Western Califate independent and Córdoba becomes the cultural and economical capital of Europe. 985: The Arab Almanzor sacks Barcelona. 987: Count Borrell frees himself from the vassalage imposed by the Frankish King, Hugues Capet.

10C — Modern Spanish develops as a language.

11C — The Caliphate disintegrates into small kingdoms or *taifas*. This weakness gives added impetus to the reconquest and the Catalan counties make spectacular progress.

	Ramón Berenguar I (1045-1076) unites the rest of the Catalonian counties.
1085-1086	The Christians conquer Toledo. Al-Andalus is invaded by the Almoravids.
1090	Ramón Berenguar II, defeated by El Cid, fails in his attempt to dominate the east.
12C	Tension rises between the Christians of the north and the Moors of the south. The Christian Reconquest, or *Reconquista*, is a time of war, but also of peace and mutual influence. Moorish authority is re-established in Al-Andalus by the Almojades. Ramón Berenguar III the Great transforms the County of Barcelona into a western Mediterranean power. Through his marriage to Douce de Provence, he incorporates that part of present-day France into the Catalonian state, which is the name the locals use to describe their territory. His son, the Count of Barcelona Ramón Berenguar IV, marries Petronilla of Aragón thereby uniting the *condado* with the Aragón kingdom and creating the Catalan dynasty of the Crown of Aragón.
	The Height of the 13-14C and the decline of the 15C in Catalonia
13C	By the middle of the 13C, half the peninsula is under Christian domination. The kingdoms of Castile, León, Asturias and Aragón are growing ever more powerful. 1212: The Christians win an important victory at Navas de Tolosa. 1236-1248: Ferdinand III conquers Córdoba and Seville. The Reconquest peters out for the moment. The Moorish kingdom of Granada will enjoy another two centuries of prosperity. Alfonso X presides over a cultural flowering in Christian Spain. In Catalonia, notable economic development gives rise to an enterprising middle class in the cities. 1245: James I of Aragón conquers Majorca, Ibiza and Valencia. 1258: The treaty of Corbeil frees Catalonia from its theoretical status as a Frech vassal state. Spectacular expansion of Catalan commerce. James I founds the *Consejo de Ciento*, a governing body within the city of Barcelona. 1282: Peter the Great defeats Sicily. 1283: Establishment of the Catalan *Cortes*.
14C	With James II (1291-1327) and Alfonso the Benign (1327-1336) Catalonia attains its highest point of prestige and power. Part of Greece is conquered. Catalonia has 500,000 inhabitants. 1356-1375: Wars between Peter the Ceremonious of Aragón and Peter the Cruel of Castile. Economic crises in Catalonia at the end of the 14C with bankruptcy of banks, massacres of Jews, French invasions and wars with Sardinia and Sicily during the reign of Martín the Humane.
15C	The decline of Catalonia. Castile emerges as a dominant power due to its cereals and wool-trade with the Low Countries. After the death of Peter the Ceremonious of Aragón, Aragonese gentry and the Church oppose the Catalan candidate, Jaime de Urgel, and opt for the Castilian Fernando de Trastámara as the royal successor. 1412: The *Compromiso de Caspe* initiates Castilian

hegemony. The termination of the Catalan line within the Crown of Aragón and the beginning of a new dynasty with Ferdinand I. This dynasty enlarges the kingdom still further (in 1442 Alfonso the Magnanimous conquers Naples) and unites it with the Crown of Aragón.

The Catholic Monarchs and the Modern State

1469 — Marriage of Ferdinand V of Aragón —the model for Machiavelli's *The Prince*— and Isabel I of Castile, a match that unites the two greatest kingdoms in Spain. This union does not produce any significant change in Catalonia's international politics. 1486: Ferdinand makes efforts to remedy the economic decadence of Catalonia. His intelligent arbitration over the issue of serfdom, the *Sentencia de Guadalupe*, lays the foundations of Catalonian's later rural prosperity.

1492 — The Conquest of Granada completes the Christian unification of Spain. Columbus discovers America. A Borja from Játiva is elected Pope Alexander VI. The Inquisition is created and the expulsion of 400,000 Jews is ordered.

1493 — Columbus is received by the Catholic Monarchs in Barcelona after his first voyage to the New World.

The Golden Age of the 16C

1500-1512 — Reconquest of the kingdom of Naples by Gonzalo Férnandez de Córdoba who is popularly known as *El Gran Capitán*. Spanish dominion in North Africa: Melilla, Orán, Tripoli, Mazalquivir, and so on. 1503: The *Casa de Contratación* in Seville is awarded the monopoly of Spanish trade with the Americas. 1512: Navarre is annexed. The *Leyes de Burgos* legislation protects Indians in America.

1513 — Núñez de Balboa discovers the Pacific. Two hundred years of glory begin for a completely unified Spain, the first modern and centralized European state and now the pre-eminent power in the world.

1516-1556 — Reign of Charles V. 1519: Cortés conquers Mexico. 1519-1522: Juan Sebastián Elcano becomes the first man to circumnavigate the world. 1532: Pizarro conquers Peru. 1536: Almagro explores in Chile. The Spanish empire stretches from Sicily and Naples in the Mediterranean to the Americas, and includes most of present-day Germany, France, Austria and the Low Countries. Spanish galleons arrive regularly in Seville laden with gold and silver treasures from the New World. Various wars in Europe. The Spanish Church declares itself an enemy of Martin Luther's Protestant Reformation in Germany. Under the Hapsburgs, Catalonia has a population of 400,000 while Castile has 7 million inhabitants. Catalonia becomes a marginal territory in Spain. 1518: The Indias are incorporated into the Crown of Castile; Catalans, however, do not begin to emigrate to the Americas until 200 years later. Charles V is nevertheless fond of Barcelona which he visits in 1519 and, temporarily, makes the capital of his empire. During Spain's Golden Age, under Charles V, Philip II and Philip III, relations between Barcelona and the Crown are excellent and Catalonia's autonomy and institutions are respected.

1556-1598 Philip II rules over the largest empire under one man yet known to history. His domain extends to four continents. 1561: He moves his court to Madrid. 1571: A Spanish fleet defeats the Turks at the Battle of Lepanto. 1580: Unification with Portugal. The Escorial is constructed. It is the start of the *Siglo de Oro*, or Golden Age, in art and literature. But Spain is already squandering her treasures, brought from the New World, in European wars. The Inquisition and the struggles against Protestantism known as the *Counter-reformation* sap the creative energies of the country. 1588: The powerful Spanish Armada is sunk in a disastrous confrontation with Elizabethan England. English naval power is on the upswing. Spain's decline from imperial power has begun.

Decadence

1598-1621 Reign of Philip III, a period that sees the end of Spanish world hegemony and the beginning of its post-imperial decadence. 1605: Cervantes' *Don Quixote* is published and in many ways perfectly reflects the transition from imperial splendour to decline. Spain is momentarily at peace with her neighbours, but an economic crisis has begun.

1609-1648 Expulsion of the converted Moors, or *Moriscos*. 1618-1648: Thirty Years' War. 1640-1653: On Corpus Christi Day, groups of farm workers, gathered in Barcelona, rise against the Viceregent and kill him. It is the *Guerra de los Segadores*. The Count of Olivares orders a punitive expedition against Catalonia to which the Diputation responds with arms. Consequently, the region refuses to acknowledge Philip IV as its king and proclaims France's Louis XIII Count of Barcelona. The war stretches on until 1653, at which time Catalonia, in exchange for general amnesty and internal autonomy, is reintegrated into the kingdom of Philip IV. 1659: Through the Treaty of the Pyrenees, Philip IV cedes the Catalan territory of Roussillon to France, thereby establishing Spain's present border. 1668: The independence of Portugal. Loss of territories marks the decline of Spanish hegemony in Europe.

1700-1715 War of the Spanish Succession between Philip of Anjou (supported by Madrid and France) and the Archduke Charles of Austria (supported by Catalonia, Aragón and England). 1707: Philip V accedes to the throne, the first of the Bourbon dynasty in Spain. On September 11, 1714, Barcelona is defeated by Spanish-French troops. Loss of the Low Countries, Menorca, Gibraltar, Italy, Sicily and Sardinia.

1716 Philip V issues a Decree called the *Nueva Planta* which abolishes local privileges and dissolves the once-great kingdom of Catalonia, turning it into a province subject to the laws and dictates of Castile. It is a decisive moment in the creation of a central Spanish state. The Bourbon regime is stabilizing rapidly and Catalonia begins to overcome its economic crises.

1759-1788 Reign of Charles III. Aided by competent ministers (Floridablanca, Aranda), Charles III enacts sweeping reforms under the banner of the *Enlightenment*. Aid to the U.S.A. during their struggle for independence (Florida, 1783). Wide economic expansion and respect for the monarchy. New trade laws end the monopoly of Seville and benefit the port of Barcelona and the entire region. The textile industry expands in response to American markets. 1763: The founding of the Chamber of Commerce. 1771: The protectionist decree. 1780: Introduction of English looms. 1783: One of the first textile printing factories is established in Barcelona. Within 60 years, Catalonia's population doubles to a total of 870,000 inhabitants and the cotton industry employs over 80,000 workers. Massive agricultural investment, especialy in vineyards. Catalonia prospers.

Romantic Spain: The Turbulent 19C

1789-1805 The French Revolution. 1793: Charles IV goes to war with revolutionary France after Louis XVI is guillotined. 1804: Napoleon becomes Emperor. 1805: Spain collaborates with Napoleon in the war against England. Disaster strikes at *Trafalgar* with Admiral Nelson's victory. Spain, no longer a maritime power, suffers economic depression. Catalonia becomes more influential in the affairs of the nation.

1808 Popular pressure against the powerful minister Godoy and Charles IV forces the abdication of the monarch and his heir, the future Ferdinand VII. Napoleon foists his brother, Joseph Bonaparte, as king on Spain. On May 2, citizens rise up against the French in Madrid, and the *War of Independence*, or Peninsular War, against the French occupiers is underway.

1812-1813 The parliament at Cádiz proclaims a liberal Constitution. 1813: Several American colonies declare their independence from Spain: Colombia, Chile, Paraguay, Uruguay and Buenos Aires (La Plata).

1814-1877 With the aid of the British and after a pitched guerrilla war, the Spanish forces finally succeed in expelling Napoleon following the Batlle of Vitoria, Ferdinand VII regains the throne and promptly repeals the Constitution of 1812, an act that serves to mark the start of the Romantic period, a turbulent era of struggle between the *absolutism* of the ancien régime and the new *liberalism*. 1820: Riego, a charismatic young officer stages a liberal insurrection. 1821: Mexico wins its independence. 1821-1824: Venezuela and Peru gain their independence. Spain is administratively organized into its present-day provinces. 1830: Isabel II is crowned. 1833-1839: The First Carlist War breaks out between supporters of Don Carlos and Isabel II. French, English and German Romantic writers discover Spain. 1835: Suppression and expropriation of the religious orders. 1840: A keynote military rebellion, led by Espartero, supported by progressive Catalonia. 1843: Revolution and rising of Narváez. 1847-1849: Second Carlist War. 1848: Construction of the Barcelona-Mataró railway.

1850: End of the economic crisis and beginning of prosperity under Queen Isabel II. The Catalan middle classes thrive spectacularly. Since the beginning of the century, Catalonia's poulation has doubled to a total of 1.6 million inhabitants. Catalonia's Pi i Margall proposes political federalism. 1868: Prim's insurrection forces the abdication of Isabel II. 1869: Progressive Constitution adopted. 1870: Amadeus of Savoy is elected constitutional king. 1872-1876: Third Carlist War. 1873: Amadeus of Savoy abdicates. The First Republic and a Catalan State within this new Republic are proclaimed. 1874: Pavía dissolves the *Cortes*, Spain's parliament. Peasant and worker rebellions break out and the middle classes pin their hopes on a restoration of the monarchy. A military coup brings back Alfonso XII, Isabel II's son, as king. The Catalan bourgeoisie enjoy a living standard practically unknown in the rest of the country. The anarchist violence rocks Barcelona (bombing of the Liceo, 1893, and others). Catalan nationalism headed by Prat de la Riba.

1898 Spain loses colonies of Cuba, Puerto Rico and the Philippines in the Spanish-American War. An intellectual resurgence gets underway ▶ *page* 55.

The 20C

1902-1921 The reign of Alfonso XIII coincides with the growth of socialist and republican movements, as well as of trade union organizations like the socialist UGT and the anarchist CNT. 1901: Electoral victory for Catalans as represented by the *Lliga Regionalista* (Regional League). From the *Diputación de Barcelona*, Prat de la Riba modernizes public services, schools and culture (foundation of the Instituto d'Estudis Catalans in 1907). 1909: Demonstrations and anarchy (*Semana Trágica* in Barcelona). 1914-1918: Spain remains neutral throughout World War I and prospers economically as a result. Catalonia regains some of its lost autonomy through the *Mancomunidad* (concessions by federal to regional governments), led by Prat de Riba. 1917-1921: A nationwide general strike, peasant strikes and conflicts between tenant farmers and their landlords follow. Rebellion by Catalan ministers headed by Cambó, leader of the Lliga, and the bourgeoisie. Disorder and shootings (almost 400 victims in Catalonia in 1920 alone). Military disaster in Annual, Morocco.

1923-1930 The Catalan Captain General, Primo de Rivera, installs a *military dictatorship*. The *Mancomunidad* is abolished. Spain enjoys seven years of prosperity due to peace in Morocco and a huge public works plan. But the international financial crisis of 1929 and the restiveness of the opposition brings Primo de Rivera's resignation. There is a renewed surge of cultural activities ▶ *page* 56. 1929: The International Exhibition is held in Montjuïc, Barcelona.

1931-1935 Republican supporters of democracy in Spain win municipal elections. Alfonso XIII abdicates. On April 14, 1931, the Second Republic is declared; but revolutionary pressure exercised by peasants and workers shakes the new regime. An abortive right-wing coup is followed by a centre-right victory in the 1934 elections and worker insurrections in Asturias and Catalonia. 1931: Catalonia recovers its autonomy with its new regional government, the Generalitat, led by Francesc Macià. 1932: The Autonomy is approved by the Spanish *Cortes*.

1936-1939 The Spanish left, running as a united front, wins the elections; Manuel Azaña is Prime Minister. On July 18, 1936, Generals Franco and Mola lead a right-wing military insurrection, sparking the three-year *Spanish Civil War*. The conflict involves untold cruelty and destroys the nation. In Catalonia, the anarchist groups foment a social revolution by collectivizing the industries. Franco enters Catalonia in April 1938 and abolishes its statute of Autonomy. Barcelona is taken on January 26, 1936. Exile of Spanish Republicans.

1939-1975 Franco's dictatorship. The early years are especially hard, with strong repression of the Catalan language and culture. Spain remains neutral in World War II, but sends a volunteer division to help Hitler on the Russian front. 1953-1955: American bases are set up in the country and Spain is admitted to the United Nations. 1959: An economic stabilization plan opens Spain's closed economy to the world. The tourist boom begins, accompanied by a decade of growth and modernization.

1975 Franco dies. Juan Carlos I is proclaimed king. The transition to democracy begins in 1977 under centre-right prime minister Adolfo Suárez. Victory for the leftist parties in Catalonia. Re-establishment of the *Generalitat* on September 29, with Tarradellas as President. Political parties are legalized.

Modern Spain: The Democracy

1978-1981 The modern Spanish Constitution is adopted, a liberal document that allows for political power at the regional level. 1980: Statutes of autonomy for Catalonia and the Basque country are approved. General elections in Catalonia. The *Convergencia i Unió* party voted to power with Jordi Pujol at the head of the Generalitat. 1981: On February 23, a military coup attempt is aborted by the king's intervention.

1982 Socialist Prime Minister Felipe González takes office.

1986 Spain enters the Common Market on January 1. The Socialists win again in general elections. Forty-six million tourists a year are visiting Spain.

1992 Seville hosts the Universal Exhibition and Barcelona hosts the Summer Olympics. It is the 500th anniversary of Columbus' discovery of America.

Literature

Like a multi-coloured fabric, Spain's pre-Golden Age literature is woven with threads of at least three colours: the Latin, the Moslem and the Hebrew. The towering Christian intellects, King Alfonso the Wise and the anonymous author of the *Cantar del Mío Cid* take their place in the rich pantheon of Spanish literature alongside captivating Arab poets, sagacious Moslem scholars and the great Jewish writer and royal physician, Moses Ben Maimon, better known to the world as Maimónides. Spain's 20C intellectual giants include Federico García Lorca, José Ortega y Gasset, Miguel de Unamuno and Antonio Machado.

Barcelona is an important focal point of Spanish literature and it is also the heart of *Catalonia's own literature*, a literature whose sentiments, values and language reflect the identity of the Catalan people and nation.

A quick checklist of contemporary Spanish letters includes mature writers such as Cela, Delibes, Mercé Rodoreda, Juan Goytisolo, Martín Gaite and Marsé, poets, among them Gimferrer, José María Alvarez, Martínez Sarrión and Leopoldo María Panero, and novelists such as Guelbenzu, Eduardo Mendoza and Jesús Ferrero. Political themes are no longer predominant as was the case during the Franco years. In fact, the political decentralization that has accompanied the restoration of democracy in Spain has meant a new literary vigour in Spain's several, distinct regions. A case in point is the manner in which the language and literature of Catalonia, long repressed by the Franco regime, have gained new energy.

But to start at the beginning.... Seneca the Elder, known as the Rhetorician, and his son, Seneca the Stoic, were revered for the purity and grace of their Latin. Christian literature, coming with the Roman adoption of Christianity, was less creative in Spain, for the Moorish invasion in 711 severed it from western European currents.

The Moorish kingdoms on the Iberian peninsula were, however, rich in literature and scholarship. They produced a wealth of classical Arab poetry, Moslem religious tracts and finally, Maimónides (1135-1204), who has been compared to St. Thomas Aquinas for his attempts to reconcile reason and faith. The Castilian language began to achieve predominance with epic poetry in the 12C. The *Cantar del Mío Cid* (*Song of My Cid*), which recounts the heroic deeds of Rodrigo Díaz de Vivar, the great hero of the Christian Reconquest, is the greatest work to survive. In the 13C, Alfonso X the Wise made Castilian the language of the court and of scholarship, replacing Latin. He was very well-regarded as a writer, of both prose and verse, and a nephew, Juan Manuel, followed with a wonderful collection of tales in the 14C, while the Archpriest of Hita wrote a brilliant satirical work, *El libro del buen amor*, in verse.

The dominance of the Castilian language in literature on the Iberian peninsula was stalwartly resisted by the Catalan tongue, which developed beside but separately from the speech of Castile. During the 12-13C, a pleiad of Catalan poets formed part of the popular troubador literature of the time. But the true beginnings of Catalan literature took place in the 13C with the prose chronicles of James I, Desclot, Muntaner and Peter the Ceremonious, with the treaties of Arnau de Vilanova, doctor of popes and kings and, above all, with the works of Ramón Llull, one of the most important figures in 13C Europe —a mystic, philosopher, theologian, scientific encyclopedist, poet and novelist— the first realistic novelist to create bourgeois and city characters. He also contributed many new words of his own invention to the Catalan language.

The Golden Age of Catalan literature can be situated between the end of the 14C and the beginning of the 15C. The survival of Medievalism can be seen in the writings of Eiximenis and the sermons of St Vincent Ferrer and Catalan humanism can be traced to the rationalism of Turmeda and Bernat Metge. Poetry was italianized in the work of Febrer and Jordi de Sant Jordi while the verses of Ausias March, a poet free from provincialism, were harsh, profound and heartrending; Roís de Corella was the last great classical poet, and Jaume Roig was one of the first poets to celebrate the daily life of Valencia. During the mid-15C, two great chivalric novels appeared: *Curial e Güelfa*, anonymous, and *Tirant lo Blanch*, by Joanot Martorell, praised and immortalized by Cervantes, which has recently been translated into English. Finally, the religious presentations titled *Cant de la Sibil.la*, concerning the three mysteries associated with the Virgin, constitute an interesting precursor to the theatrical genre.

Returning to Castilian literature, since Catalan literature entered a crisis at the beginning of the 16C which would last all through the Renaissance and Neoclassicism and up to the first part of the 19C, we find that theatre reached a peak with the *Tragicomedia de Calixto y Melibea*, better known as *La Celestina* after its bawdy central character, by Fernando de Rojas (about 1500).

At the dawn of Imperial Spain's Golden Age, a period which was to be exceptional in the history of world literature, we find Bartolomé de las Casas, a Sevillian member of the Dominican order and later a bishop, who was a tireless literary champion of the Indians in the New World and a critic of the often brutal excesses of the *conquistadores*. The Golden Age, which extended through the 16C and part of the 17C, coincided with the reigns of Charles V, Philip II and Philip III and was both Spain's and the world's literary heyday. After a period of Italian influence, the Salamanca school —Friar Luis de León (1527-1591)— and the Seville school —Fernando de Herrera (1534-1597)— began to make their mark in the theatre. Renaissance drama, however, reached its peak with Lope de Vega (1562-1635), one of the world's most prolific playwrights and a poet who excelled in beautiful imagery and musical cadence. Tirso de Molina (1584-1648), who created Don Juan, the mythical lover, and Pedro Calderón de la Barca (1600-1681) were well-known colleagues and fellow dramatists. Francisco de Quevedo y Villegas (1580-1645) was famed for his all-round literary personality and for his virulent temper.

With Miguel Cervantes (1547-1616) Spanish writing reaches its pinnacle in the Golden Age. *La vida del Ingenioso Hidalgo Don Quixote de la Mancha* is undoubtedly Spain's greatest contribution to world literature. Cervantes led a life of incredible adventure: he lost his left hand at the Battle of Lepanto, was captured by Barbary pirates and sold into slavery for five years before being ransomed and becoming Deputy-Purveyor to the Invincible Spanish Armada. He was imprisoned twice over financial matters and died disillusioned a few days after becoming a Franciscan friar. Somehow during this frenetic life, Cervantes wrote what has been hailed as the world's first modern novel. He anticipated literary forms by several centuries and succeeded in influencing writers from Shakespeare to Fyodor Dostoyevsky, James Joyce and Vladimir Nabokov.

Decadence and a loss of energy in the arts marked the end of the Golden Age at the close of the 17C, and was accompanied by the nation's preoccupation with a growing French influence that made itself felt in the Spanish arts. This uninspired era lasted from the death of Calderón until the advent of Romanticism at the start of the 19C. The memorable lyric poetry of Gustavo Adolfo Becquer (1836-1870) was post-Romantic rather than Romantic. Several outstanding writers rose to prominence in the first half of the 19C: Pedro de Alarcón

(1833-1891), author of *The Three-Cornered Hat*, the revolutionary José de Espronceda (1810-1842), who fought at the barricades in Paris in 1830, and the deeply sceptical journalist Mariano José de Larra (1809-1837) were foremost among them.

Toward the end of the 19C, the realistic novel, acidly critical and chronological in its storytelling, made its appearance in Spain. The leading novelist of the time, Benito Pérez Galdós (1843-1920), rejected the social injustice he saw around him, as did his contemporaries, Countess Emilia Pardo-Bazán (1852-1921) and Leopoldo Alas, better known as Clarín.

In Catalonia, along with industrialization and a thriving, flourishing middle class, the 19C also witnessed the *Renaixença* (renaissance). Aribau's poem *La patrià* was the first milestone of the *Renaixença*, and also of the other movement that dominated the age, Romanticism. *Jocs Florals* (poetry competitions) helped to promote popular poetry as of 1859. At the turn of the century, Jacint Verdaguer rose to prominence in the circle of Catalan poetry; his Catalan romanticism and deep mysticism were expressed in such epics as *L'Atlantida* and *Canigó*. Milá i Fontanals established high standards of erudition while in the theatre, Catalonia's great dramatist and poet, Angel Guimerà, triumphed with his realistic play *Terra Baixa*. Novels of the time include the naturalist narrations of Narcís Oller and *Victor Catala*, a pseudonym for Caterina Albert, and the modernist work of Santiago Rusiñol. The turn of the century also ushered in the poetry of Margall, Costa i Llobera and Alcover. During this period, as Catalonia flourished, the rest of Spain sank into the crisis of '98.

The *Generation of '98* was the name given to a group of writers who faced the moral crisis and general break-down of the Spanish spirit in the aftermath of Spain's humiliating defeat in the Spanish-American war of 1898 and loss of her last colonies (Cuba, the Philippines and Puerto Rico). The group was deeply critical of Spanish decadence and sought the regeneration of the nation. The most famous member of this group, which was very diverse but was bound together by a common commitment to a reborn Spain, was the Basque Miguel de Unamuno (1864-1936). His copious output included philosophical works, essays, novels and volumes of poetry. An austere intellectual, Unamuno had a profound impact on his own and on succeeding generations of Spaniards.

Other members of the Generation of '98 included Ramón María del Valle Inclán (1869-1936), who became famous for his four *Sonatas*; José Martínez Ruiz, a critic and essayist who wrote under the pen name Azorín, the novelist Pío Baroja and the historian Menéndez Pidal. The philosopher José Ortega y Gasset (1883-1955) was a key intellectual whose *Invertebrate Spain* and *The Revolt of the Masses* achieved lasting notoriety in Europe. Spanish poetry achieved outstanding lyricism with the work of Antonio Machado (1875-1939), who though a Sevillian born was principally inspired by the landscapes of Castile, and Juan Ramón Jiménez (1881-1958), who is best known for his book of lyric prose *Platero and I*, and who won the Nobel Prize for Literature in 1956.

At the beginning of the 20C, the Catalan bourgeoisie stimulated and promoted many ambitious cultural projects. Their taste in literature was cosmopolitan and exceedingly preoccupied with style and form. Eugeni d'Ors set the standards for this so-called *noucentisme* movement. Poets of the time were Carner —*Nabí*—, Carles Riba —*Elegies de Bierville*—, the *avant garde* poet Salvat-Papasseit, and J. V. Foix. From the 1920s onward, Catalan novelists have broadly concentrated on the psychological novel, in contrast to the rest of Spain where language has been the principal concern.

Federico García Lorca (1898-1936) deserves special mention. A member of the so-called *Poetic Generation of '27*, Lorca developed his own form of lyric poetry, based on the folk poetry of his native Andalusia and the songs of the Gypsy flamenco singers so prominent in his home town of Granada. His chief poetical works are *Gypsy Ballads* and *The Poet in New York, and Blood Wedding* and *The House of Bernarda Alba* are his major plays. His genius was cut short soon after the outbreak of the Spanish Civil War when he was executed in Granada by rebel Francoists. Other members of the Generation of '27 were Vicente Aleixandre (Nobel Prize for Literature in 1977), Dámaso Alonso and Jorge Guillén. Outside this group, but in the same period, the poet Miguel Hernández gained prominence for his haunting verses of great beauty. He was strongly identified with the Republic and did not survive the prison term that the ensuing Franco regime imposed on him. Manuel Andújar, Ramón J. Sender, Rosa Chacel, Corpus Barga, Rafael Cansinos-Asséns and León Felipe were other writers of the period. The majority of them fled Spain after the war ended in 1939. Sender, who wrote *La Tesis de Nancy*, the tale of an American student in Spain, spent most of his life living in exile in the United States. Ramón Pérez de Ayala, Republican ambassador in London until 1936, and Ramón Gómez de la Serna went to Argentina.

A generation of new novelists appeared after the war. Many of them, and the many poets belonging to the *Poetic Generation of '36* who began writing then as well, attacked the Franco regime or dwelled on themes of human rights and oppression. Among the more important novelists were Miguel Delibes, Camilo José Cela (who founded the school of *Tremendismo*), José María Gironella and Ana María Matute. Martín Santos and Benet are contemporary authors who were already well known in the fifties. Juan Goytisolo was one of those who followed the forms of the *nouveau roman* and North American writing. Cela, and Sánchez Ferlosio are leading novelists of the time. Torrente Ballester and Alvaro Cunqueiro were leaders of a trend of magic realism.

Catalan literature began to break away from the *noucentisme* trend in the 1930s, but this transition lasted well into the 1960s. Lorenç Villalonga wrote a novel about a crepuscular mythological world that passes away, *Bearn*, while Mercé Rodoreda manifested her lyricism in *La Plaça del Diamant*, Manuel de Pedrolo constructed historical allegories, Porcel reflected on everyday reality, and Terenci Moix created a personal world brimming with fantasy. Mixing journalism with prose, Josep Plá lucidly described life in modern Catalonia in his popular *Els Payesos*. Catalan poetry has also been enriched by Pere Quart, Joan Brossa, Gabriel Ferrer, Pere Gimferrer and Salvador Espríu with his *La Pell de Brau*. Espríu was also a dramatist, as was Josep Sagarra, a key figure in the Modernist movement of Catalan theatre.

In theatre, the century produced the high comedy of Benavente, winner of the 1922 Nobel Prize, and the comic sketches of Arniches. They were succeeded by Casona and the outstanding figure of Buero Vallejo. Alfonso Sastre brought ideological tension to the stage, whereas Miguel Mihura, Tono and Alfonso Paso worked on uniquely humorous comedies. Luca de Tena entertained audiences with his literature of manners, and Pemán with his originality. Modern theatre passed its infancy among the shifting sands of these diverse playwrights. Today, the theatre features the plays of Antonio Gala,

Fermín Cabal, as well as García Lorca, who is currently being successfully revived. *Avant garde* theatre techniques have led to a new and daring approach to stagecraft, as can be seen in the work of companies such as *La Fura dels Baus* and *Els Joglars*.

One should finally mention the influence of essayists such as José Luis Aranguren, Pedro Laín Entralgo and María Zambrano who have become national institutions. And a younger group of philosophers, spearheaded by Fernando Savater and Javier Sádaba, has started to emerge over the last few years.

Music

Spain is a musical country, a place where the people both sing and dance, and where an array of styles and types of music coexist. It is a music above all marked by a joy of living.

Lyrical Music

Montserrat Caballé, Plácido Domingo, Alfredo Kraus and José Carreras are opera names that have gained international fame and prestige. Nevertheless, the great popular tradition of Spanish music owes more to the ***zarzuela***, a form of operetta that is genuinely Spanish and has its roots in the 18C, than it does to opera properly speaking. The Spanish court in those days was much taken with hunting. After the hunts, it was normal to sleep out in a tent surrounded by brambles, somewhere in the countryside around Madrid. There, the evening's entertainment was enlivened with theatrical presentations accompanied by music and song. This was the birth of the *zarzuela*. The form was much influenced by Italian opera until the 19C. Subsequently the ***género chico*** —the genre comprising *zarzuelas* and one-act comedies— lost ground to the great German operas. Spanish work returned to prominence, however, with Tomás Bretón's *La Verbena de la Paloma* in 1894 which was purely Spanish and Goyaesque in its aesthetics. Torroba, Sorozabal and Guerrero are also in the front line of major *zarzuela* librettists.

Classical Music

The *Cantigas*, written by Alfonso the Wise, is an impressive legacy of the Middle Ages. During the Golden Age, when the guitar became a highly popular instrument displacing, in the process, the more courtly vihuela (an ancient type of guitar), Tomás Luis de Victoria won international renown for his beautiful religious choral music.

As Romanticism laid down roots in Spain so did that most Spanish of all instruments, the **guitar**, spread its influence. Modern guitar-playing is largely based on the work of a native of the Valencia area, Tárrega (1852-1909). The aficionado will recognize one of his most beautiful pieces, *Recuerdos de la Alhambra*, played with Indochinese instruments for the soundtrack of the movie *The Killing Fields*.

Romanticism developed into what critics term musical nationalism through the work of Turina (1882-1949), Albéniz (1860-1909) and Manuel de Falla (1876-1946). Turina's compositions reveal solid technique and descriptive rigour. In *La Procesión del Rocio, Mujeres Españolas* and *Danzas Gitanas*, perceptible French influences are balanced by Turina's pronounced Spanishness.

In Albéniz's suite *Iberia*, a collection of 12 highly original piano pieces, Spain's musical nationalism reached its zenith. The influence of Albéniz, together with that of French impressionism, can be traced in the refined and colourful work of the Andalusian Falla, who wrote *El Amor Brujo*, the *Concerto for Harpsichord and Five Instruments* and *Atlantida*, which was completed by his disciple, Ernesto Halffter.

The musical renewal of the 20C was a mixture of classicism and newer movements. The synthesis was apparent in the work of Frederic Mompou, a fine pianist and composer of works for a range of instruments —*Suburbios* (piano), *Becquerianas* (voice) and *Suite Compostelana* (guitar). Joaquín Rodrigo, author of the world-famous *Aranjuez Concerto*, and Xavier Montsalvage are the best-known postwar composers.

Contemporary Spanish composers no longer cultivate nationalism. Instead, they have immersed themselves in the more advanced Western tendencies, such as **electroacoustics**. Luis de Pablo, C. Halffter, Bernaola, Guinjoan and Tomás Marco are among the prominent musicians of this genre.

Spain's major musical interpreters are the guitarists Andrés Segovia (1894-) and Narciso Yepes (1927-). The most revered was the late Pau Casals who in the course of a career that spanned the first half of this century became an international musical institution. Casals composed the *Hymn to the United Nations*. Teresa Berganza and Victoria de los Angeles are firmly established sopranos, and López-Cobos is unquestionably Spain's leading conductor.

Flamenco

The origins of flamenco music are little known and much debated —in Roman times writers such as Martial discussed the dancers of Cádiz. Truly flamenco **folk songs** and **dances** have blended with Andalusian popular singing to the point where it is difficult to mark the precise boundaries of this exotic and picturesque art form.

Whatever flamenco's origins, there is no doubt that the genre constitutes *an entire people's form of expression*. The universality of the forlorn, heartrending laments sung by such legendary figures as Antonio Chacón, Antonio Mairena or *la Niña de los Peines* not only express the sorrows, tribulations and hopes of a *pueblo*, but they are an intrinsic part of the day-to-day life of the people. Today, Chiquetete and other young singers carry on this timeless tradition. The fiery aesthetics of flamenco dancing can be enjoyed and appreciated in the graceful movements of Barcelona's Carmen Amaya or in the fascinating steps of Spain's most famous dancer, Antonio Gades, who has brought the joy, spontaneity and exhilaration of flamenco to all parts of the world. Barcelona's well established gipsy community has a long-standing flamenco tradition.

To see and hear flamenco is not difficult. But keep in mind that there is an abundance of highly commercial shows of more than doubtful quality and authenticity. The best advice: go informed.

Spanish Popular Music, Rock and Pop

Apart from traditional and classical music, Spain produces some of the most wild, aggressive and sometimes even sinister rock and roll in Europe. A multitude of young groups are constantly being born, breaking up, reforming.... In melodic composition, there is a series of soloists and well-known groups whose recordings include the more or less involved ballads of Joan Manuel Serrat, Mocedades, Ana Belén and Victor Manuel; the songs of urbane sentiment and indifference of Luis Eduardo Aute and Joaquín Sabina; the beautiful tones of María del Mar Bonet which recall musical forms with deep roots in Majorcan and Mediterranean tradition; and the voice that is known on five continents, that of Julio Iglesias. All styles coexist in what is broadly known as the

Spanish song. This is not to be confused with flamenco, although there are sometimes common melodic and rhythmic roots as well as common themes of love, passion, sorrow and hope.

The Music of Barcelona

It may be that Barcelona's international renown stems from its unique painters and artists such as Dalí, Picasso, Miró, Tapiès and the rest. But if there is one cultural element, apart from language, that is intimately connected with the Catalans, it is music. Music is everywhere: on every corner and at every hour of the day. As far back as the Middle Ages, musicians were permanently employed by Barcelona's nobility. The year 1599 saw the founding of the *Cofradía de Músicos de Barcelona*, a local musicians' association, whose purpose was to unite all those who earned their living through musical activities.

The traditional temple of classical music in Barcelona is the **Liceo** (the full name of which is the *Gran Teatro de Liceo*), one of the major European houses since the 19C. Regular concerts have been held here since the foundation of the Barcelona Philharmonic Society in 1844. Lizst was invited to conduct the orchestra the following year. The **Palau**, or *Palau de la Música Catalana*, Barcelona's second musical centre, was inaugurated by Richard Strauss and the Berlin Philharmonic in 1908. The *Banda Municipal* (Municipal Band) and the *Escuela de Música* (School of Music) were created in the city in 1886. Names such as *Agrupació Polifónica de Vilafranca del Penedés, Orquesta de Cambra del Conservatorio de Terrassa, Orquesta de Cambra Solistas de Sabadell, Orquesta de Cambra de L'Hospitalet*, among many others, illustrate how the love of music is shared throughout Catalonia.

Catalonia is a land of internationally renowned musical artists: interpreters of the category of Montserrat Caballé, Pablo (Pau) Casals, Victoria de los Angeles and José Carreras; flamenco dancers like Carmen Amaya; composers such as Casals, Albéniz, Enric Granados, Amadeu Vives, Frederic Mompou and Xavier Montsalvaje; music-hall singers like Raquel Meller, who began her career in the Arnau theatre and now has a monument erected in her honour on Av Paralelo; jazzmen such as Tete Montoliú, who began here, and *cantautores* (literally singer-composers) like Joan Manuel Serrat...

If the Liceo and Palau appeal to the well-to-do strata of society, then the *coros* belong to the common people. In the mid-19C Josep Anselm Clavé founded the *Coros Clavé* with the idea of organizing the groups who strolled through the streets and taverns singing. This very Catalan and highly popular tradition is still alive and well in Catalonia. Preeminent among these choral groups are *Orfeó Catalá*, founded by Millet and Vives in 1891, the *Coral de Sant Jordi*, and the very old *Escolanía de Montserrat*. Choral societies of this kind proliferate all over Catalonia: *Coral Joventut Sardanista de Puig-Roig. Orfeó Vicentí, Orfeó Parroquial El Delme, Orfeó Manresà, Grupo de Canto de Artés* and *Orfeó Nova Salsona* are some of the names that spring to mind.

Another Catalan musical tradition are the *coblas* or brass bands that play on the street to provide the accompaniment for the ***sardanas***, Catalonia's national dance. The *sardanas* are danced everywhere and by everyone; from the small villages to the large cities, by young and old alike. Although its origin is not documented, legend has it that the dance came from Crete or Greece. Others claim that it originated in Sardinia (*Cerdeña*, in Spanish), since old Catalan and Castilian texts refer to it as a *cerdana*. The *sardana* owes its present form to the modifications introduced in the mid-19C by Pep Ventura, a native of the Ampurdán.

The *sardana* is a group dance in which participants form a ring —as large as necessary to accommodate all dancers— with arms raised and hands joined, dancing in complete silence to the repetitive rhythms provided by the *cobla* (derived from the Latin word meaning cupola, couple, union). For some the *sardana* is a symbol of solidarity employed by the community in times of adversity, a rallying point for the expression of national identity and peaceful resistance to oppression. Today there are several plazas in Barcelona where the *sardanas* are still danced, especially on Sunday mornings. Try Pl Sant Jaume and Pl del Rey among others.

The Musical Season of Barcelona

This is a musical city *par excellence*. All year long there are classical and modern music festivals, concert cycles, performances by groups, ensembles and singers. The calendar that follows lists only the major musical events that have a fixed date. To find out more about local musical events, consult the periodicals *Vivir en Barcelona* or *Guía del Ocio*, as well as other local publications ▶ *page* 96.

Jazz

Besides the many shows that take place during the year in clubs and other places in Barcelona dedicated to Jazz ▶ *page* 71, the city celebrates its Jazz Festival in September.

Opera

January

Festival of Romantic Music

March

Music Week in Barcelona. Palau de la Música, c/ Amadeo Vives, 1 ☎ 301 11 04.

April

Cycle of Polyphonic Music

May

Festival of Ancient Music. Tinell Room and Palau de la Música.

July and *August*

Summer Serenades (*Serenatas d'Estiu*). A variety of concerts under the aegis of the summer *Grec* festival ▶ *page* 84.

September

International Music Festival of Barcelona.

Painting and Sculpture

From the cave paintings of Cogul (Lérida) to the world famous canvasses of Picasso, Dalí, Miró and the murals of J.M. Sert, Catalonia has had a truly rich and millenarian tradition in the field of the plastic arts. If one had to choose one field in which Spain has contributed more than any other to the world, it would be in this. And Barcelona today is the focal point of the plastic arts for the whole of Spain.

Prehistoric Legacies

The bisons, deer and wild boars of the Altamira caves (Santander) are Spain's most important Paleolithic cave paintings. Executed with great naturalness and force in several colours —they have been called the *Sistine Chapel* of rupestrian, or cave, art— they are believed to be over 10,000 years old. The Levantine paintings and engravings of the cave of Parpalló and Cogul (Lérida) are also Paleolithic.

Roman, Visigoth and Romanesque Influences

Included in this period are the Paleo-Christian paintings at Centcelles Constantí (Tarragona). Statues and sarcophagi are examples of Roman and Visigoth sculptures whose themes extended into the art of the

Christian kingdoms of Asturias and Catalonia. Only when Moslem culture began to mix with pure Catalan Romanesque after the Moorish invasion in 711 —as at Taüll (Lérida), in the paintings of Vic and Ripoll, and the virgins and dressed crucifixes of the 12C— did strong new influences on Spanish art come into play.

Gothic Art, 13-15C

Gothic painting in Spain is derived from three major sources: France during the 13C; Siena and Florence, especially in Catalonia (Ferrer Bassa) during the 14C; and the Flemish school, which made itself felt in the courts of Aragón and Castile during the 15C. Nonetheless, the naturalism and picturesque details of these works was entirely Spanish. In sculpture, this was the time of the great retables. Sculpture grew more delicate and its relief more accentuated than in the Romanesque era. This was a period of fine work in the porticos and sepulchres of many cathedrals. A good example is the *Doncel* in Sigüenza.

From the master Bartomeu in the 13C to the great Pere Johan in the 15C, Catalan Gothic sculpture has given rise to many illustrious names. These men produced works of art such as the sepulchres of Queen Elísenda de Montcada (Monastery of Pedralbes, Barcelona) and of Peter the Great and James II (Monastery of Santes Creus). The Santa Tecla retable (Cathedral of Tarragona) is the work of Pere Johan.

Renaissance Art, 16C

Several Spanish sculptors studied in Italy, including Diego de Siloé —cathedrals of Burgos and Granada— and Alonso Berruguete, —works in Toledo and Valladolid— whose lyricism and tormented human forms approached in power those of Michelangelo. Juan de Juni —works in Valladolid— used a more theatrical style. It was during this period that the famous Milanese bronzesmiths Leone and Pompeo Leoni were at work on the monastery of El Escorial for Philip II.

By the time of the Renaissance, Catalonia had fallen into decadence and consequently no remarkable artistic monuments were created during this period. The Padelles mansion (Barcelona), the main altar retable in the monastery of Poblet and the fountain in Prades' main square are notable exceptions.

The Renaissance deeply influenced the study of perspective, the glorification of the human body and clarity in composition. Juan de Juanes, known as *the Spanish Raphael*, was one of the great Levantine painters of the period. In Castile, the great master of the late 15C was Pedro Berruguete, although the work of Sánchez Coello and Pantoja de la Cruz is also admirable.

Towering above the rest, however, was El Greco, the Greek immigrant whose real name was Domenico Teotocopuli and whose unique style defies easy characterization. El Greco settled in Toledo in 1577, and it was there he developed his elongated, mystical and strangely dark works. Some of them, such as *The Burial of the Count of Orgaz*, are in Toledo still. His lengthening of human figures and vibrant colours helped give his paintings their feeling of religious intensity.

Baroque Art, 17-18C

The Baroque era, a period that unfolded during the *Siglo de Oro*, or Golden Age, produced an extraordinary wealth of painters in what was truly one of the high moments in European art. The sculptors of the time were also a rich and diverse group: Gregorio Fernández, of Valladolid; Martínez Montañés and his excellent disciple Juan de Mesa of Seville; Alonso Cano of Granada, known for the unusual grace and delicacy of his *inmaculadas*, while his disciple Pedro de Mena was known for his realism. In Murcia, Salcillo was already extremely famous.

The most representative examples of the Baroque style in Catalonia can be seen in the altars and retables of the churches of Roser and Santa María (Arenys de Mar), the Basilica of Santa María (Mataró), the Chapel of Santa Tecla (cathedral of Tarragona), the parish church of Sitges, and the Sanctuary of Sant Pau (Sant Pere de Ribes), as well as in the organ of the Church of San Salvador (El Vendrell).

The exceptional Spanish painting of the 17C began with the penetration of an Italian influence, which is obvious in the assimilation of Caravaggio by Francisco Ribalta. José de Ribera stands at the head of the schools of painters established in both Valencia and Naples. He was the painter of martyrs, saints and ascetics.

The Sevillian school also produced several masters of painting. Zurbarán painted cycles of religious exaltation (monastery of Guadalupe) and still life. Murillo was a painter of intense realism who was famous for his *inmaculadas*. Valdés Leal painted macabre profiles —*Las Postrimerías de la Vida*— and sacred compositions. The painter, sculptor and architect Alonso Cano worked in Granada. In Castile, Claudio Coello, Carreño and Carducho painted, like Murillo, in a carefully realistic style.

The greatest painter of the epoch was doubtless the Sevillian Diego Velázquez, court painter to Philip IV. His work included portraits —*Felipe IV, Conde Duque de Olivares, Inocencio X*—, history —*Rendición de Breda*—, mythology —*Fragua de Vulcano, Los Borrachos, Las Hilanderas*—, and landscapes —*Villa Medicis*. *Las Meninas* is painted with a stroke so skilful that it puts Velázquez alongside the twin giants of Spanish painting, Goya and Picasso.

Neoclassical Art, 18C

During the 18C, there was a resurgence of Catalan painting. Artists from the period that spring to mind are the Tramulles (*El Vigatà*) brothers and A. Vildomat (Basilica of Santa María, Mataró). The Lonja School of Art (Barcelona) also opened its doors at this time.

The Bourbon monarchs in this period founded the San Fernando Academy and brought foreign painters, such as Mengs and Tiepolo, to teach there. But head and shoulders above these and others was a man of complete genius who was to lead the way into the Romanticism of the 19C. Francisco de Goya, a multi-faceted, dynamic and sarcastic man, broke with all the academic principles of painting and anticipated in his work artistic trends characteristic of 20C contemporary art. His two paintings of the rebellion in Madrid against the French —*The Charge of the Mamelukes and the Imperial Guard in the Puerta del Sol* and the chilling *Executions of the Second of May*— haunt the imagination. No less interesting are the series of engravings *The Disasters of War*, the suggestive and erotic pair of paintings *The Maja, Clothed* and *The Maja, Unclothed*, the terrifying lines of *The Insane Asylum* and the bright tenderness of *Children Playing*, one of a series of joyful and colourful paintings of daily life. His so called black period works must be seen as well. Goya was a painter of extraordinary depth and irony. A *Goyesca* school followed him; Eugenio Lucas was the best of his followers.

The 19C

The shadow of the great 18C painters reached into the 19C, affecting profoundly the character and attitudes of its painters and sculptors. Some developed a dark cast to their work, such as Rosales; others were airy, cosmopolitan and almost frivolous, like Fortuny; there were portraitists, like Vicente López, and those who revelled in depicting the bourgeoisie, like the Madrazo family.

Detail, *Complainte du lezard amoureux*, Joan Miró

In Catalonia, the work of such artists as Casas, Nonell, Rusiñol and Mir was clearly related to the currents of European art, while the Valencian Sorolla brought a Mediterranean brightness to French impressionism in his paintings of beaches bathed in light. In sculpture, naturalism and an impressionist cast also feature in the work of Mariano Benlliure, especially in his bullfight scenes.

The 20C

Pablo Picasso, who was born in Málaga and raised in Barcelona, was, in a sense, the embodiment of the history of Spanish painting and sculpture. Living in exile in France since the Spanish Civil War, his prolific work ranged over a wide variety of themes but was executed with the same consummate skill everywhere. Along with Picasso, the 20C also produced the great Spanish Surrealist painters Salvador Dalí and Joan Miró, who was also a skilled muralist (Cincinatti, Harvard and Barcelona), ceramicist and sculptor. Their works made Surrealism known around the world. Juan Gris was an analytical Cubist, while Solana and Zuloaga painted everyday life with careful realism. J.M. Sert was known for his large frescoes.

Blay, Llimona, Clará and Casanovas, Catalonian sculptors, acquired international renown at the beginning of the 20C.

After the Civil War, several schools of painting and sculpture developed. They included the Catalan group Dau al Set formed by Ponç, Tapiès, Cuixart and Tharrats; the neo-figurative group which brought together Clavé, Pancho Cossío and Vázquez Díaz; the informal work of Feito; the Madrid group called El Paso which included Millares, Saura, Canogar and Viola; the Levantine movement incorporating Sempere, Genovés and Mompo. Highlights in Catalonia are Ràfols Casamda's post-cubist experiments together with those of Guinovart, Viola and Viladecans. The period's better-known sculptors included Chillida, Hugué, Mallol, Gargallo, Picasso, Ferrant and Subirachs.

Antonio López, a hyperrealist, has become internationally famous. Now, new values are making their appearance in present-day Spain. Artists such as Barceló and Pérez Villalta already have solid reputations despite their youth.

The Museums and Art Showrooms of Barcelona

Important works of the artists mentioned above can be viewed in the numerous museums of Barcelona which are reviewed in the 'Places of Interest' section ▶ *page* 99 of this guide. But Barcelona also has other institutions dedicated to the arts. They include showrooms and cultural centres with constantly changing programmes of great interest. And one should not forget the art galleries ▶ *page* 65.

Caja Postal, Av Infanta Carlota, 66.

Casa Elizalde, c/ Valencia, 302 ☎ 318 06 81. Dedicated to showing works of Barcelonan artists who dwell on themes related to the city.

Fundación Caja de Pensiones, La Caixa, Paseo de Gracia, 2; c/ Jaume I, 2; c/ Arcs, 5; c/ Montcada, 14; Paseo de San Juan, 108; and Vía Layetana, 56. The various showrooms run by this institution have exhibits of the highest interest.

Palace of the Vicereine, Rambla, 99 ☎ 301 77 75 and 318 23 83. A changing series of shows. Closed Monday mornings.

Palacio Meca, c/ Montcada, 19. Interesting art exhibits from all periods.

ENTERTAINMENT

It is hard to speak of a *single Barcelona* when it comes to entertainment. There are worlds and sub-worlds here, many of them fast asleep during the daytime, emerging at night time. Jazz, rock of all kinds, flamenco *tablaos*, traditional music halls, discotheques, bars, pubs are just the beginning of what's happening here. The night has its rhythms, its different and changing environments; it is a time of a thousand sensations. Take advantage of this city's nocturnal offerings. It's *your* night.

Beyond the *Barrio chino*, with its port atmosphere of cheap sex and labyrinthine streets, the rest of Barcelona is a whole universe, impossible for a one-time visitor to take in completely. There is always another intriguing bar, a café known for its cocktails, some interesting-looking new place with a rose-coloured neon sign blinking insistently overhead, some attractive person to meet... And there is also the quiet corner bar, a place to get a quiet *copa* and reflect for a moment on this absolutely polymorphic city.

Amusement Parks

on the highway to Mataró, near Exit 6, Vilassar de Dalt ☎ 751 45 53 and 751 52 60.

Parque de Atracciones, Ctra Montjuic, s/n ☎ 241 70 24 and 242 31 75.

Tibidabo, Pl Tibidabo, s/n ☎ 417 03 38 and 211 79 90.

Bars, Cafeterias, Terraces, Pubs and Similar Establishments

There are thousands of these in Barcelona and they come in all shapes and sizes to suit every taste. New establishments appear every day, as styles and tastes change, and others stay as they have been for ages.

Alt Heidelberg, c/ Ronda Universidad, 5. German beer and sausages.

Amarcord, c/ Provenza and Paseo de Gracia. An ideal terrace for a mid-afternoon drink. Open all day, in the marvellous Pedrera building by Gaudí.

Antiquari de la Plaça del Rei, c/ Veguer, 13 (Gothic quarter). Extremely animated. Music and cocktails last until 5 in the morning.

Azulete, Vía Augusta, 281. Cocktails in the very agreeable garden terrace of a Barcelonan house. Sophisticated environment.

Balmoral, Av Diagonal, 500. Teas and pastries.

Barcelona-Jabugo, c/ París, 175. Excellent Jabugo ham, stuffed pork loin and other pork sausages.

Bar dels Encants, Pl dels Encants, 10. Unusual.

Bar-Librería Cristal-City, c/ Balmes, 294. Very peculiar establishment where one can drink and eat unusual appetizers like Canary Islands ham and fish pastries... and where you can also buy books.

Batucada, c/ Bailén, 7. Offers a Brazilian drink known as a caipiriña.

Belvedere, Pasaje Mercader, 3 (between c/ Balmes and Rambla de Cataluña). A romantic scene for an afternoon or evening drink. Garden and outdoor terrace with tables.

Berimbau, Paseo del Born, 17. The pioneer and still the best of the garden terraces, with good Rio de Janeiro cocktails, Brazilian rums, whisky and music.

Bijou, Vía Augusta, corner of c/ Luis Antúnez. A somewhat difficult place to find, but worth the trouble.

Illuminated fountains at Montjuïc

Boadas, c/ Tallers, 1, nearly on the corner of the Ramblas. The palace of cocktails, more than half a century old and with a reputation for quality and service.

Brut, c/ Trompetas, 3. Typical place for drinking the local sparkling cava wines after taking in a show. Reasonable prices.

Café de la Opera, Ramblas-Liceo. Cosmopolitan and unusual with a terrace that is also an observatory.

Cairo, c/ Aviació, 5. Fashionable with trendy young people, the *movida*. Music.

Casablanca, c/ Buenavista, 6. This is also a very typical establishment for a drink after shows. Canapés and a wide selection of cavas.

Cava de Olimpia, c/ Loreto, 10. Cavas, *tapas* (hors d'oeuvres) and small, open meat sandwiches known as *bocaditos*.

Chicago Pizza Pie Factory, c/ Provenza, 300. Pure United States in Barcelona. There's American pizza, Yankee decoration, music, even videos of American football.

City Arms, Pl Narcís Oller, 9. An English tavern with Victorian decor. Irish coffee, cocktails and canapés.

Compañía General de Sandwiches, c/ Santaló, 155 and c/ Moya, 14. A wide variety of sandwiches of all kinds.

Crêperie Bretonne, c/ Balmes, 274. Exquisite crepes in a small place with a young atmosphere and long tradition.

Croissant, c/ Ganduxer, 28. Very good croissants of all types. Always very busy.

Distrito Blanco, Av Meridiana, 140. Pub with a nice atmosphere.

Dos Torres, Vía Augusta, 300. Good place for an afternoon aperitif. A select atmosphere. Garden terrace.

Dry Martini Bar, c/ Aribau, 162. Pioneer of the *martini* in Barcelona. Wide selection of gins. High quality drinks and service.

El Born, Paseo del Born, 26. Cocktails in a pleasant ambience. There is also a buffet.

El Particular, Av del Tibidabo, 61. Musical bar with good views and a welcoming terrace. Its locale is one of the most beautiful in the city.

Gimlet, c/ Rech, 24, in the Born, and c/ Santaló, 46 in Sant Gervasi. Both locations are splendid, but the second is more chic. One of the best places in Barcelona.

Gold Lions, c/ Aribau, 163. Two large rooms, a heterogeneous public, cocktails of every type. Play backgammon and drink Irish coffee or cocoloco.

Ideal Cocktail's Bar, c/ Aribau, 89. Good selection of whiskies in an elegant, classic and welcoming place decorated in the English style. This establishment is a real cathedral of cocktails, with one of the most professional bar staffs in Spain.

Jamón Jamón, c/ Maestro Nicolau, 4. Exquisite and authentic Jabugo hams. Modern decoration, restaurant, bar and delicatessen.

K.G.B., c/ Alegre de Dalt, 55 (Gracia). This is the height of fashion in Barcelona. It seems that *practically everyone* visits this place. Bar with music that is sometimes live.

La Cava del Palau, c/ Verdaguer i Callís, 10. A traditional place facing the Palau de la Musica. Cavas, cocktails, cheeses and anchovies.

La Folie, c/ Bailén, 169. Well decorated. A good champagne bar for a cava or cocktail after midnight.

La Jijonenca, Rambla de Cataluña, 35. Perhaps the best terrace in Barcelona. Excellent ice creams.

La Xampanyería, c/ Provenza, 236. An excellent cava and champagne list. Good prices, too.

Maison Dorée, Rambla de Cataluña, 104. Inside, a single bar. Outside, during the summertime, a welcoming terrace. Some of the best croissants, brioches and so on, in Barcelona, both to eat there and to take away.

Merbeyé, Pl del Funicular, s/n. At the foot of Tibidabo mountain with a very special view. Very fashionable. Aperitifs in the mornings and cocktails in the afternoons and evenings.

Mundial, Pl San Agustín el Viejo, 1. Fish, shellfish and barbecue appetizers.

Nick Havanna, c/ Rosellón, 208. The latest in the city: a kind of haven for post-industrial design and aesthetics.

Paraigua, c/ Pas de l'Ensenyança, 2 (near the City Hall). A good place for a Bloody Mary in a modern atmosphere. Classical music.

Pastis, c/ Santa Mónica, 4 (Atarazanas). Traditional ambience, of special interest to nostalgics.

Pinte, c/ París, 18. German beer and other specialities in an informal environment that is, however, not very comfortable.

Piscolabis, Rambla de Cataluña, 49-51. Varied menu of sandwiches, patés, pastries and so on, in one of the most prestigious spots in the city.

Ricos y Bellas, c/ Aribau, 242. Elegant and sophisticated ambience, with very comfortable sofas.

Samba Brasil, c/ Lepanto, 297. Good cocktails and tropical drinks.

Sandor, Pl Francesc Macià, 5. A terrace in the area of the city that is always in fashion. A nice spot to meet for a coffee or a drink.

Santos Lugares, c/ Eures, 4. In a basement. A dark place, lit only by circles of light beamed from the candles illuminating images of saints that are affixed to the walls. There are no tables or seats or bar stools —instead there are wooden church pews. The smell is of incense. Informal and fashionable among the trendy.

Snooker, c/ Roger de Lluria, 42. A fashionable spot with young people and for social events. Cocktails, canapés and good beer, as well as facilities for the English billiard game that gives the place its name.

Soviet's, Av Paralelo 169. Well known for its large screen video and its vodka-based drinks.

Taita 1 and 2, c/ Mestre Nicolau, 10 and 11. *Tapas*, Artistic and intellectual atmosphere.

Tandem, c/ Aribau, 86. A perfect dry martini. Authentic daiquiris.

Torquemada, Av Diagonal, 676. Luxurious and relaxed, in accordance with the area in which it is located, Pedralbes. Comfortable and welcoming, this is a good place to have a relaxing drink.

Torre de los Leones, Pl Doña Carolina, 1-3 (Ciudad Diagonal), next to Pedralbes. A very pleasant place.

Tres Tres, c/ Amigó, 33. Well decorated, fashionable establishment. A good place to drink cava or cocktails.

Tropeziens, Paseo de Gracia, 83. Sandwiches, milk shakes and pizzas that are among the best in the city.

Turo, c/ Tenor Viñas, 1. A fun terrace with lots of atmosphere.

Universal, c/ Mariano Cubí, 184 (Sant Gervasi). One of those places known for chance encounters. A heterogeneous atmosphere.

Velódromo, c/ Muntaner, 213. A place with much tradition. Well decorated with antique mirrors and serving excellent *tapas*, sandwiches and potato chips. You can play dominoes, billiards, Parcheesi and other games here. Very popular; jampacked at night.

Victory's, Pasaje Concepción, 16. A small, English style spot of very high quality. Excellent whiskies and cocktails.

Xampú Xampany, c/ Gran Vía, 702. Very much in vogue among the trendy.
Zig-Zag, c/ Platón, 13. Pleasant environment. Good music.
Zurich, Pl Catalunya, 35. A spectacular terrace. Good coffee.

Casinos

Gran Casino de Barcelona ☎ 893 36 36, in Sant Pere de Ribes, very close to Sitges and some 40km from Barcelona. There, in between winning or losing at roulette, blackjack, *boule, chemin de fer* or the slot machines, you can do a number of things. On Fridays and Saturdays the casino restaurant offers a *buffet*, an orchestra plays at the dance hall Friday nights; and some of the best international shows come to perform at the casino during the summer months.

Cultural and Sporting Events

While the sun shines and in the early evening hours, Barcelona offers visitors and its own natives a wide gamut of amusements, especially in the areas of culture and sports. There are all kinds of movies, theatres, art exhibitions, concerts, opera and more; check the local publications, ▶ *page* 96, to find out what's showing. Football (soccer) is played almost right through the year. And there are competitions in a whole range of sports —motor racing, equestrian events, bicycling, swimming, basketball and athletics are the most common among them. Consult the sports periodicals ▶ *page* 96, as well as the newspapers and magazines mentioned which cover cultural events. Further sporting possibilities include:

El Karting, Autovía de Castelldefels, km12.500 ☎ 662 36 52. Go-karts circuit, bumper cars, mini-golf and trampolines. Open daily from 11.00 a.m. to midnight.

Sport Center, Ctra N150, km14.700 (exit at Sabadell N by the A18 highway) ☎ 726 66 44. Tracks for mini-motorcycles, go-karts, electrical cars, bicycles, roller-skating, ping-pong and other games. Open daily from 8.00 a.m. until midnight.

Dance Halls

For those interested in dancing late into the night to the music of an orchestra, there are a number of choices.

Bolero, Av Diagonal, 405, has its own orchestra, and you can dance until 4.00 in the morning. There are modern decorations, comfortable sofas and occasional dance contests here.

Cibeles, c/ Córcega, 363, is for many the best dance hall with its own orchestra in the city. It combines a middle-aged public with a younger set interested in older social customs.

Imperator, c/ Córcega, 325, is the easiest to find at the intersection of Av Diagonal and the Paseo de Gracia. It caters to a middle-aged clientele who are impeccably and conservatively dressed.

La Paloma, c/ Tigre, 27, is a true jewel from the past, with mouldings and angels made of gilded plaster and great red drapes. It is a place where all epochs are celebrated —the fox trot, mambo, bolero, tango, cha cha and also a bit of rock. On Tuesdays, there are boxing bouts in a ring erected on the dance floor. The discreet charm of the *turn of century* is very evident in this old hall.

Sutton, c/ Tusset, 13, is probably the most successful hall in recent times. It is elegant, with doormen to park your car, its own orchestra and a clientele that includes the rich and famous in pursuit of 19C delights.

Discotheques and Live Music

The most **elegant** places in Barcelona, with a select clientele that includes members of the European *jet set*, are *Up and Down* and *Regine's*. Both are for card-carrying members, at least in theory. But the doormen will admit those they like the looks of without asking for membership cards. Members of both these clubs tend to be middle-aged. In Regine's the crowd gets younger as the night advances into the early morning hours; at Up and Down the older crowd eats and dances on the upper level while younger people use the space below.

Chic Privee, Gran Vía de Carlos III, 97. A discotheque for members only.

Quartier, c/ Santa Catalina de Siena, 28 (Pedralbes). It specializes in staging parties, contests and similar events which are well-attended by the personalities featured in the *revistas del corazón* —Spain's lively gossip magazines. This place is also a club with membership cards.

Regine's, Pl de Pio XII, next to the Princesa Sofía hotel, is something out of a summer in Marbella —there is a discotheque, a bar and a restaurant, as well as a separate discotheque for private parties.

Up and Down, c/ Numancia, 179, has a similar tone. It is known as a meeting spot for *the best* in Barcelona. It has two floors; on the second is a restaurant and a more formal atmosphere (suit and tie are required); on the first the music is loud and the clientele young.

Spain's so-called ***movida*** —a kind of hip, underground night life scene that is also known as the *marcha moderna*— lives in every district of Barcelona, in all kinds of places. You will find it in simulated garages, old theatres and restored movie houses transformed into discotheques and done up in pink and grey. The members of this cultural movement wear clothes that seem to be somewhere between ballroom wear and designer fashion and the decor of their venues is probably best described as postmodern.

666, c/ Llull, 145. In 666 the tone is set with leather, plastic and an aesthetic of dark tones. There are three levels, each with different music. Occasionally, one can see live groups or cultural performances at this place. It is an original establishment, with tables made of coffins, walls with recesses and a black altar.

BCN, c/ Mariano Cubí, 183. Bar, performance hall and discotheque. Various levels and a distinct clientele. Modern, in a good area.

Bikini, Av Diagonal, 571. Bikini is done up in the styles of the 1950s and has two sections: downstairs there is African music, while above they play hard and funky music.

Café de las Artes, c/ Valencia, 234 (corner of Balmes). From 9.00 a.m. to 6.00 p.m., breakfasts, appetizers and quick meals. From 6.00 p.m. until after midnight, modern, African and funky music, as well as fashionable Spanish groups.

Distrito Distinto, Av Meridiana, 140. This is one of the most modern discos, very informal and a centre for young people. A favourite spot is the terrace.

Duetto, c/ Consejo de Ciento, 294. This disco offers video upstairs and dancing below.

Ebano, c/ Roger de Flor, 114. It sounds an exotic note in Barcelona's night life. Customers dance to African and tropical salsa rhythms; this is a place much frequented by Africans resident in the city. Very cheap prices.

Els Quatre Gats, c/ Montsió, 5. Jazz shows. Bar, social area.

Falstaff, c/ Sant Pere Mitjá, 9-11. Classical music and whisky.

Heavy Metal, c/ Sants, 387. A place that is frequented by young people from the suburbs.

Karma, Pl Real, 10. Live shows at weekends. Usually crowded.

K.G.B. c/ Alegre de Dalt, 55. At KGB the decoration and the public are the show, although there are also live shows by Spanish and foreign bands.

Necronemicón, c/ Riereta, 20-22. This disco has an area for watching videos and the theatre here offers good modern music well past midnight.

Otto Zutz, c/ Lincoln, 13. Otto draws trendy people in expensive clothes. There are sizeable queues and the doormen exercise strict control on who gets in —often in a less than friendly way. This is one of the *most* selective places in the city.

SiSiSi, Av Diagonal, 442. This is another place to find *movida* life.

Studio 54, Av Paralelo, 54. A more disco-type, electronic place; you can dance bathed in the flashing lights of lasers, or take a dip (during the summer) in the swimming pool.

Zeleste, c/ Platería, 65. It is the vanguard spot as regards new musical groups in Barcelona. It is famous for the very modern live pop and rock shows it puts on, as well as a delightful freebie —the view, as you leave the place sometime after midnight, of the beautiful Gothic church of Santa María del Mar. The most interesting time to go to Zeleste is after midnight.

Flamenco and Jazz

Flamenco every day becomes more a part of Barcelona's life. The professional dancing is increasingly better, and recently it has become a real fashion for amateur extroverts to dance *sevillanas* as well.

El Patio Andaluz, c/ Aribau, 242, has white walls, forged iron window gratings, large carnations, guitars, singing, dancing and dinner-shows until 3 in the morning.

La Venta Andaluza, c/ Obradors, 11, has professional and improvised shows.

Los Tarantos, Pl Real, 17 ☎ 317 80 98, also has a good flamenco show, a classic in Barcelona.

Jazz has both its *aficionados* and its *temples* in this city.

Abraxas, c/ Gelabert, 26, is a much frequented jazz spot.

Els Quatre Gats, c/ Montsió, 5, has first-rate performances.

L'Auditori, c/ Balmes, 245, offers orthodox jazz in a relaxed atmosphere.

La Cova del Drac, c/ Tuset, 30, rivals the preceding club with its shows.

Music Halls and Night Clubs

The tradition of ports everywhere impregnates the area of *Av Paralelo,* running from Paseo de Colón by the wharf to the Pl de España —that is to say, a novelish atmosphere of murky eroticism. This is the area of liaisons on the streets and in dark doorways, of foggy lights and equivocal gestures from ladies of the night. But it is also the place where Barcelona has its *music halls,* places that are real relics of another era with their bawdy shows and dancing.

Arnau, Av Paralelo, 60. The shows at Arnau, with its house ballet, have always attracted customers.

Bagdad, c/ Conde del Asalto, 103. This establishment has a porno show.

Barcelona de Noche, c/ Tapias, 5. A cabaret with a transvestite flavour.

Belle Epoque, c/ Muntaner, 246. This music hall has modern decorations and sophisticated technical facilities.

Bodega Apolo, Av Paralelo, 59. Offers very Spanish shows reminiscent of the 1950s.

Bodega Bohemia, c/ Lancaster, s/n. This is a nostalgic spot, with professional and amateur imitations of old artistes who sang here in times long past.

El Molino, c/ Vila Vila, 99. The house shows have not stopped drawing customers.

No, c/ Aribau, 242. This is a discotheque for young and fashionable people in the afternoons, and an entertainment hall at night.

Scala, Paseo de San Juan, 47-49. This is the most important entertainment hall in Barcelona, with huge props, spectacular sets and international artistes. There is usually a dinner show and a second show afterwards.

Zoos

Zoo de Barcelona, Parque de la Ciutadella, s/n ☎ 309 25 00. Every kind of animal. Ecology shows on Saturdays. Open daily from 9.30 a.m. until 7.30 p.m.

EXCURSIONS

The region around Barcelona is varied, beautiful and interesting; there is, as a result, a wealth of places and sites to visit. Here is a sample of short distance excursions around Barcelona.

Costa Dorada

The Costa Dorada, literally the Golden Coast, is a 250km band of the Spanish Mediterranean coastline that stretches NE from Sitges to Calella and SW from Tarragona as far as the Ebro delta. It is a splendid coastline with golden sandy beaches scattered along its impressive length. The Costa Dorada's warm, stable climate has made it a favourite place for swimmers and sunbathers.

For our purpose, it is best to divide the Costa Dorada into two distinct zones. One is centred on the **Maresme** coast, which runs NE from Barcelona to Calella and the Tordera River which marks the boundary with the province of Gerona and the Costa Brava. The other is the **Tarragona** area that extends SE as far as Sant Carles de la Rápita at the mouth of the Ebro River, marking the beginning of the Valencian *Comunitat* or autonomous region.

Leaving Barcelona and heading in a NE direction along the N-II coastal road, the visitor will arrive at the most northerly part of the Costa Dorada, the **Maresme**, which stretches 64km through the province of Barcelona to the Tordera River. Because of its rich agricultural production, this fertile corridor, irrigated by a number of small rivers, is known as the *jardín y mercado de Barcelona*, that is to say, Barcelona's garden and market. Ever since the Middle Ages this coast has been dotted with fishing villages, but with the coming of the Industrial Revolution in the 19C, many were converted into chemical industry and textile centres.

Beyond Badalona (the old Roman *Baetulo*, now an industrial centre) and Santa Coloma de Gramanet (formerly an Iberian village but now a dormitory town) there are a number of interesting coastal towns. **Masnou**, with its 3km beach, active marina, and rural Catalan architecture in the old town, is a favourite with Barcelonans. For dining here try *Les Caves*, c/ San Cristobal, 4. After **Premiá del Mar** the visitor arrives at Vilassar de Mar, an 18C village which is now devoted to tourism and the growing of carnations. There is an excellent spot to do a little food shopping called *Gran Chef* on c/ J. Marsal, 19. Finally you arrive at **Mataró**, the capital of Maresme (formerly the Iberian village of *Ilduro* and the Roman city of *Iluro*), which received its present name towards the end of the 13C. Today it is a thriving industrial and commercial centre dedicated to textiles and the cultivation of fruit and flowers. Curiously, Mataró was the first town in Spain to have a railway (1848) and a paved highway, which connected it with Barcelona. Places to visit here include the Renaissance basilica of Santa María (16C) with its Baroque Roser altar (18C), the Antoni Viladomat paintings (18C) in the Dolores chapel, the Town Hall, the Hospital church (13C) and the two 10C Romanesque hermitages on the outskirts of the town. Mataró also has an extensive beach and an excellent restaurant, *Can Dimas*, on Paseo Callao, s/n, which serves typical Maresme dishes.

About 12km beyond Mataró and just a little more than 34km from Barcelona (heading NE on Ctra N-II) is **Arenys de Mar**. This town was once populated by the Iberians and, later on, the Romans settled here.

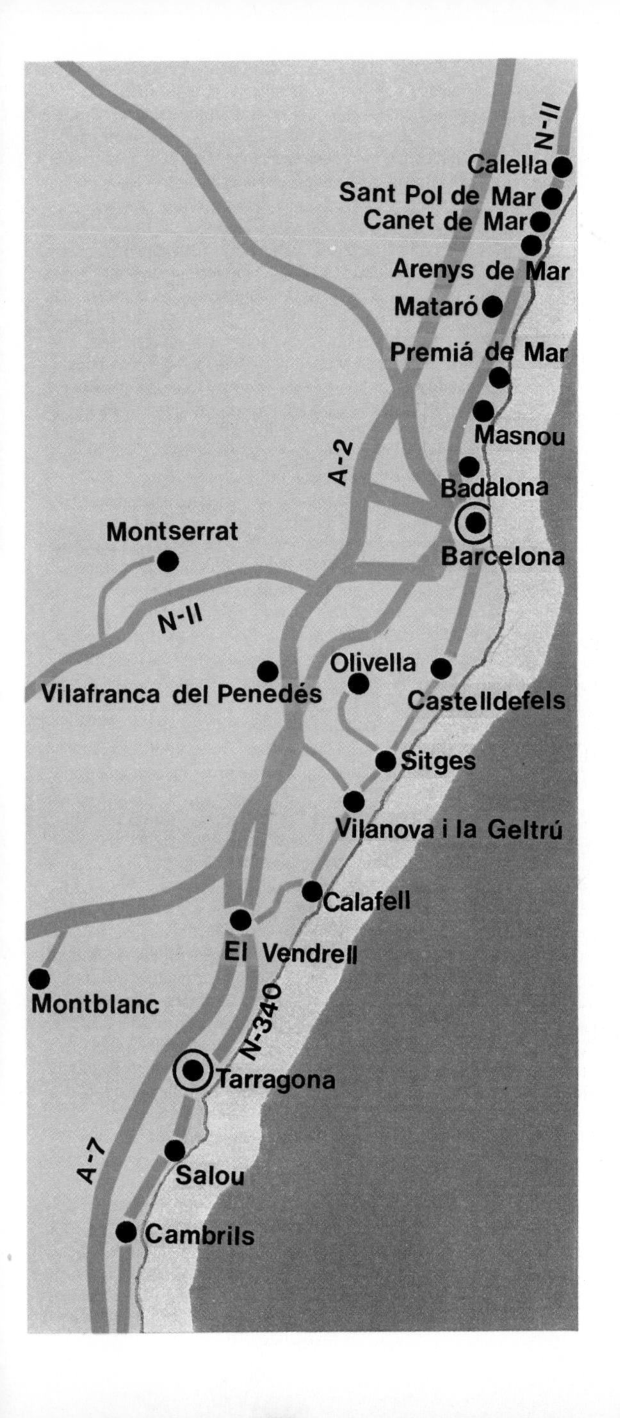
N-II
Calella
Sant Pol de Mar
Canet de Mar
Arenys de Mar
Mataró
Premiá de Mar
Masnou
A-2
Badalona
Montserrat
Barcelona
N-II
Olivella
Vilafranca del Penedés
Castelldefels
Sitges
Vilanova i la Geltrú
Calafell
El Vendrell
Montblanc
N-340
Tarragona
A-7
Salou
Cambrils

During the 18C it conducted a significant trade with the Americas and in the 19C it boasted a shipyard and nautical college. Today it is a major sports and tourist town as well as a base for the local coastal fishing industry. But above all Arenys is a **water sports centre** and international regattas are held here every year. Typical snacks here are *almendras garrapiñadas* (sweet almonds) and if you feel like a drink try one of the local liqueurs that are made in the town's distilleries. Traditional cooking can be enjoyed at the *Hispania*, c/ Real, 54 ☎ 791 04 57, which offers excellent dishes not usually found in most restaurants. Another distinguished Catalonian restaurant is the *Portinyol*, situated in the port area ☎ 972 13 31, where you can enjoy fish and sea food dishes. Interesting places to visit in the town are the Fidel Fita Museum, c/ Riera del Bisbe Pol, 10, which displays Catalonia's seafaring history; the **Marés Museum**, c/ Iglesia, 43, which houses one of the most important fine-lace collections in Europe; the Church of Santa María (18C) with its baroque reredos designed by Pau Costa, and the romantic Sirena cemetery, located at the top of a small hill that offers a view of the sea. This cemetery was immortalized by the great Catalan poet Salvador Espriú ▶ *page* 56.

From Arenys to Pineda de Mar the coast is dotted with enchanting villages. **Canet de Mar** is very much a tourist town. The Castle of Santa Florentina, a 10C battlement for defence against pirate raids, is located here. It was renovated in the 19C and today contains an interesting art collection. Further on lies **Sant Pol de Mar**, a pleasant, relaxing village with narrow, winding streets in its old town. The Martina Tower, a Roman construction, stands just outside the town and the hermitage of Sant Pau stands on the ruins of the monastery that was widely influential during the Middle Ages. The town also has a small Museum with Catalan paintings from the 19-20C. Finally, a few minutes from Sant Pol de Mar is the popular tourist village of **Calella**. There is a long beach here dominated by a lighthouse that rises from the rocky shoreline at the end of the beach. It has the usual marketplace and is very lively during the summer.

The second stretch of the Costa Dorada reaches from Barcelona toward the SW as far as the Ebro delta. Taking Ctra C246, you will pass the industrial areas on the S side of Barcelona and the region of *Bajo*, or lower, Llobregat. The main population centres before you reach Castelldefels are Espluges, Sant Joan Despí, Sant Boi de Llobregat and Gavá. **Castelldefels** has a large beach that is highly popular among the visiting Barcelonans. The 12-15C watchtowers on the outskirts of the town are the only ruins that remain of the old fortifications that once stood there. For dining in the area, try *La Bonne Table*, Av Constitución, 390 ☎ 665 37 55; *Las Botas*, Av Constitución, 326 ☎ 665 18 24; or *El Elefante*, Paseo Can Viñas, 10 ☎ 665 21 32.

Some 15km beyond Castelldefels, the visitor will pass through the picturesque **Garraf Coast**. These cliffs overlooking the sea are part of the mountain range and county that bear the same name.

The next place to visit along the coast is **Sitges**, a tourist town of great attraction (see the *Sitges* title published in this *Everything Under the Sun* travel guide series).

Sitges dates back more than 2,000 years, to a time before the arrival of the Romans. This medieval fishing and agricultural village is the home of many emigrants to America who returned to invest their fortunes here. It was also an early spot for tourism in the 19C, and later became a place that captivated many intellectuals —painters like Santiago Rusiñol and architects like Utrillo— along with many wealthy families from Barcelona. The flavour of the village, maritime and cosmopolitan at the same time, turned Sitges into a privileged sanctuary only half an hour from Barcelona, the great city of the Mediterranean.

The enchantment of Sitges derives not only from its picturesque and beautiful urban centre, but also from its traditional, stately Catalan character that combines surprisingly well with the eccentric and cosmopolitan artistic life of the town. Its fine city beaches and its excellent range of water and other sports make it even more special.

A part of Sitges' special charm comes in the form of its attractive *modernist houses*, many of them built by emigrants who made their fortunes abroad during the late 19C. Some of the best examples of this type of house are seen in the San Bartolomé, Isla de Cuba, San Gaudencio and Jesús streets. Of special note are the *Hotel Romántico* and the *Casa Rosa*. The Cau Ferrat Museum is inside an old fisherman's house and contains an interesting exhibition of ironwork and a gallery that features works by El Greco and Rusiñol, who was responsible for opening the museum. The Maricel Museum and the Romantic Museum complete the interesting cultural offering in this town, dominated by a beautiful parish church with a rose-coloured façade. But Sitges is known for more than its museums. It is famous, among other things, for its **Corpus Christi** festivities, featuring streets strewn with flowers, its **carnivals**, its night-time **entertainment**, its **International Film Festival**, the summertime **Menéndez Pelayo University**, and its **Vintage Car Rally**. The town is the equivalent of London's Brighton or Paris' Deauville.

Sitges, whose culinary specialities include fish and shellfish, has a number of good restaurants. Try *Fragata*, Paseo Ribera, 1 ☎ 894 10 86; *Mare Nostrum*, Paseo Ribera, 60 ☎ 894 33 93: *La Masía*, Paseo Vilanova, 164 ☎ 894 10 76 or *El Velero*, Paseo Ribera, 38 ☎ 894 20 51.

Only 6km down the road from Sitges are Vilanova i la Geltrú, Cunit and Calafell. Vilanova i la Geltrú, capital of Garraf county, is a seafaring city with a population of 45,000 inhabitants. Since the beginning of the century it has been an active industrial centre. Of interest to the visitor are the Balaguer Library-Museum, Av Victor Balaguer, s/n, with its collection of notable paintings that includes an El Greco; the *Museo de Curiosidades Marineras de Roig Toques*, or **Museum of Rare Nautical Objects of Roig Toques**, c/ Almirall Cervera, 2, which displays models of boats and nautical instruments and the Romantic Museum, in the Papiol House, c/ Mayor, 32. This building was erected between 1790 and 1801 by the wealthy landowner Francisco Papiol. It contains furniture and all kinds of objects used in daily life with exquisite details that show the refined luxury of the age. Everything is so naturally placed that it seems as if the people who lived in it at the time could casually walk in at any moment. Vilanova is also known for its traditional cuisine. For excellent sea food try *Peixerot*, Paseo Marítimo, 56 and *Chez Bernard y Marguerite*, c/ Ramón Llull, s/n.

El Penedés

Penedés is the land of wine, an immense wine growing district that extendes across a wide plain that slopes gently toward the Costa Dorada between Barcelona and Tarragona. A wine producing district since the Middle Ages, this gigantic vineyard has indelibly marked the character of the entire county. The landscape, the rhythm of life, the architecture in the villages and towns and even the popular celebrations and festivals have been fashioned and influenced by this ancient Mediterran product.

To get to **Vilafranca del Penedés** take Ctra A7 going toward Vilanova i La Geltrú. In Sant Miguel d'Olérdola, travelling by Ctra C244, you will find the historic **ruins** of the same name.

Vilafranca is also the capital of the Penedés wine-growing region. If you are a wine aficionado, do not miss the impressive *Museo del Vino* or **Wine Museum**, with its beautiful Gothic patio. Furthermore, many of the *bodegas* welcome group and private visits. Try the famous *Miguel Torres*, c/ Comercio, s/n and *René Barbier-Segura Viudas*, near Sant Sadurní. If you wish to visit a particular wine cellar, information is available at the Municipal Tourism Council in the town hall, or at the *Consejo Regulador de la Denominación de Origen Penedés* (the Institute of Officially Regulated Wine Regions), c/ Amalia Soler, 27 ☎ 890 48 11. Generally, the *bodegueros* in Vilafranca and the surrounding area are friendly and will allow visits to their wine cellars. Here are a couple of addresses that may be of interest to wine lovers: *Estación de Viticultura y Enología* (Viticulture and Oenology Board), INCAVI, c/ Amalia Soler, 27 ☎ 890 02 11 and *Consejo Regulador de los Vinos Espumosos* (Institute of Officially Regulated Sparkling Wines), Av Tarragona, 24 ☎ 890 31 04.

If you eat in Vilafranca try *Casa Juan* or *Can Toni*.

Some 8km from Vilafranca along Ctra C243 is **Sant Sadurní d'Anoia**. This town is the centre of the *País del Cava* (the land of sparkling wine), the renowned sparkling wines of Catalonia ▶ *page* 156 that are today successfully penetrating the international wine markets. If you are in the Pl del Ayuntamiento ask someone to direct you to the house of Antonio Mestres. This friendly and talkative *cavista* (sparkling wine specialist) will be glad to give you all the information you need.

Beneath your feet, in Vilafranca, there are endless tunnels which provide storage space for millions of bottles of *bubbly*. They rest quietly and undisturbed in these enormous cellars until they are ready for the table. This small town produces more than 100 million bottles of sparkling wine every year. The two largest *bodegas* are *Codorníu* and *Freixenet*. Freixenet is the leading sparkling wine brand in the USA, ahead of French champagne, and also sells to such unlikely customers as the People's Republic of China. These two companies produce almost 80% of the town's output. The other producers, such as *Marqués de Monistrol, Juve Camps, Segura Viudas* and *Conde de Caralt* make up most of the rest. However, there are about four dozen small scale producers who carry on Sant Sadurní's traditional methods and only supply some few hundred thousand bottles per year. Most of them are situated in town and their names are known among connoisseurs: *Mestres, Recaredo, Gramona, Llopart* and *Nadal*, among others. If you knock on their doors at a reasonable hour they will almost always show you through the cellar and perhaps offer you a taste of their carefully nurtured cava.

The visitor should be aware that in Sant Sadurní large-scale production does not mean lower quality. On the contrary, the big manufacturers are just as proud of their product as the small producers. There is nothing easier than arranging **visits to the cellars** of *Codorníu* ☎ 891 01 25 and *Freixenet* ☎ 891 07 00. *Can Codorníu* —with its splendid **Modernist buildings** which have been declared a National Monument— is the largest sparkling wine producer (using the

French champagne method) in the world. The tours are very interesting and if the visitor wishes he can also visit the *Segura Viudas* cellars —☏ 899 51 11— just outside town. But there is more to Sant Sadurní than bubbly wines. There is the **Espiells chapel**, a noteworthy 11C Romanesque building, and the **Roman bridge**, also just beyond the town limits. *El Mirador dels Cavas*, on Ctra C246 on the way to Ordal ☏ 899 31 78, is an excellent local restaurant.

Further along the same road lies **Cunit**. There is a first class and luxurious restaurant here that serves sea food and original dishes made from the vegetables grown in the area; the *L'Avi Pau* ☏ (977) 67 48 61.

Inland Routes: Attractive Villages and Monasteries

Some 27km NW of El Vendrell, and some 95km from Barcelona by way of Ctra A7 to this town and then along Ctra A2, stands another of Spain's architectural jewels, the **Monastery of Santes Creus**, Poblet's twin. This monastery, like Poblet, was protected by the Catalan nobility and the monarchs of Aragón during the Middle Ages. Built between the 12-14C, it has an outstanding Gothic **cloister** —which is reached through the *Puerta Real* or Royal Portal on the right side of the church—, a **capitular room**, and an austere Cistercian style **church** that was begun in the 12C and houses the royal tombs of Peter the Great and his son James II the Just. There is a beautiful **rose window** in the apse. The **infirmary cloister** with its modest design, fountain and cypresses is a peaceful and relaxing haven within the confines of the monastery walls. The **patio** is pleasingly proportioned and contains a beautiful stairway. From Barcelona, El Vendrell can be reached by taking Ctra N340 or Ctra A7 in a SW direction.

Montblanc is reached by heading N from Vendrell as far as the A7 and A2 road intersection and then taking Ctra A2 in the direction of Lérida. This small village, which exudes a strong medieval flavour, is one of the most beautiful in Catalonia. Montblanc was once the seat of the Catalonian Monarchs Peter III, Alfonso III and James II. The town saw its greatest splendour during the 13-14C. The 14C **walls** and the no less imposing **church of Santa María** stand out against what Spanish writer Gabriel Miró called 'the rich, exuberant fields steeped in blue', and contrast sharply with the rocky contours of the Sierra de Cabra mountain range. The attractive 14C single-naved church merits a visit, as do the narrow winding streets like c/ Plebanya which descends from the church to the old Jewish quarter. Also of interest are the arcaded **Plaza Mayor**, a small **museum** with prehistoric pieces and local handicrafts, and the Gothic **Hospital of Santa Magdalena** with its refreshing Gothic patio and 14C bridge over the Francolí river. For dining try *Fonda Colón*, Ctra de Civadeira, 5 or *Les Fonts de Lilla*, at km30 of Ctra N240.

Situated some 8km from Montblanc stands one of Catalonia's four great monastaries, the **Monastery of Poblet**. Ripoll was the crucible of the first reconquest of Catalonia ▶ *page* 47 and the sepulchre of its ancient nobility, and Poblet was to become the centre of the Catalan-Aragón kingdom and the mausoleum of its monarchs. The monastery was founded in 1149 by Ramón Berenguer IV, Count of Barcelona, in thanksgiving for the recovery of the Prades and Siurana mountain ranges from the Arabs. Poblet was, much like nearby Santa Creus (see above), a favourite retreat of the Aragón royalty, who would come here to hunt and relax in the monastery's natural surroundings.

Although its political importance declined in the 16C, Poblet continued to thrive and remained a monastic community without interruption for almost 700 years. Poblet was sacked during the War of Independence, abandoned and then laicisized following the suppression of church orders and expropriation of church property in 1835 ▶ *page* 50. The monastery suffered over a hundred years of solitary desolation before it was restored in 1940.

An avenue beyond the first wall leads to the 15C *Puerta Dorada* or **Golden Gate**. From here the monastery is entered through the **Royal Gate**, a 14C example of military architecture. Sobriety, purity of line, and the large dimensions (40 x 35m) typical of Cistercian construction, characterize the magnificient **cloister**. The slow march towards the Gothic style can be perceived in the worked stone and the floral decorations of the **capitals**. The **kitchen** and the **refectory** date from the 12C, while the **library** was completed in the 13C. The **chapter room** is noted for its delicate columns and stylized capitals. The spacious Cistercian **church**, with its barrel-vaulted naves, was built by Alfonso II in the 12C.

The **Royal Pantheon**, built by Peter IV in 1350 for the Crown of Aragón (the Aragón monarchs were buried here from 1196 to 1497), is the most beautiful and ornamental element in the church. In 1835, the two enormous Gothic sarcophagi were restored by the sculptor Frederic Marés. The 16C Renaissance **retable of the high altar** is a monumental work by the artist Damiá Forment. Also noteworthy are the **Palace of King Martin the Humane** with its sumptuous chambers and huge windows, commissioned by the king in 1400, and the **museum**, formerly a dormitory for elderly monks and later the main dormitory in the monastery, with an impressive 87 x 10m nave.

If you want to delve deeper into the 12C world of the Catalan-Aragonese kingdom, take the local road W from Poblet for 20km. Here you will find, nestling on the top of a mountain almost 1,000m above sea level, the stunning medieval village of **Prades**. The town is commonly known as *villa roja*, literally red town, because of the dark red colour of the stone used in the construction of the town buildings. Places of interest here include the 13C exterior walls, the arcaded plaza, the Sant Roc gate with its spacious Gothic transept, the Gothic apse in the town church, and the picturesque street that connects the Sant Roc gate with the attractively arcaded Plaza Mayor and its Renaissance fountain. Prades' two typical main streets, Major and Sant Llorenç, and the steeply inclined Carrer Nou del Pont, with its attractive porches, are also agreeable spots to enjoy an afternoon's walk.

For almost one thousand years **Montserrat** has been Catalonia's holy mountain. This ancient centre of Marian pilgrimages is only 73km from Barcelona by Ctra A17 travelling toward Tarragona until the detour at Olesa, where you should leave the motorway to pick up the highway that goes to Munistrol, a village that sits at the foot of the incredible mountains in which the famous monastery is perched. The way up with the best **views** is from the W. The monastery can also be reached by a cable car or *teleférico* from the foot of the mountain.

The **site** alone is highly impressive, consisting of gigantic blocks of granite sculptured by wind and water into fantastic forms and crowned by the ragged, saw-toothed summits of the *sierra*. Montserrat has always induced spiritual contemplation and mysticism and it has been inhabited since the times of the first Evangelists. By the 9C there were already five hermitages on its slopes. The Montserrat we know today

Montserrat

dates to the powerful Abbot Oliba, great-grandson of Wilfredo El Velloso ▶ *page* 43. Abbot of Ripoll and Sant Martí del Canigó, Bishop of Vic and Elna, Oliba was a dynamic and inexhaustable builder of Romanesque Catalonia. He founded the **Monastery of Our Lady of Montserrat** in 1205.

Montserrat's power increased continuously as growing numbers of pilgrims came to worship before the **Virgin of Montserrat**, a polychromatic 12C statue of a black virgin popularly known as *la Moreneta*. The monks of Montserrat soon acquired a reputation for erudition and the monastery became wealthy for its patrons included James I the Conqueror, the Emperor Charles V who visited the monastery at least nine times, and Pope Julius II, patron of the Renaissance, who was a former abbot of Montserrat. Although assailed by the troops of Napoleon in 1812 ▶ *page* 50, the symbolic power of the Monastery as the nucleus of Catalonian identity and the Marian devotion of the people remained intact. The actual monastery buildings visited today were rebuilt in the 19C.

Montserrat is also renowned for its ***Escolanía***, one of the oldest traditional boy's choirs in the world dating back to the 13C. Nobody, whether Catalan, Christian or not, who hears the choir sing the *Salve* at noon, vespers in the evening, and mass on Sundays and feast days, can fail to be moved by the sheer beauty of these young voices joined in harmony. While here, the visitor should not miss the opportunity of exploring the **mountain paths** that lead to the five old **hermitages**: *Sant Jeroni*, which from its height of 1,238m offers **panoramic views** that take in the Pyrenees Mountains and the Balearic Islands; *Santa Cecilia*, with its 9C Romanesque church; *Santa Cova*, where, according to the legend, the sculpture of the virgin was found; *Sant Miguel*, which offers an excellent view of the Montserrat complex, and *Sant Joan*, which also offers **scenic views** of the surrounding area.

Romanesque Catalonia

This is an excursion to the region of **Ripolles**, where the finest Romanesque monuments in Catalonia are to be found. The route of the excursion includes intermediate stops in Vic and its environs, an area rich in medieval architecture. Going N from Barcelona, the traveller should take Ctra N152. The route crosses the Vallés Oriental or Eastern Vallés region, leaving behind its capital, **Granollers**, today an important nucleus that is known for its traditional *market*. The market has been celebrated since the 16C in the famous *Porxada*, a hall covered by a roof supported on columns.

Some 22km from Barcelona is **La Garriga**, a town set on the SW slopes of the Sierra de Montseny mountain range. It is a spa and resort centre whose hot baths made it well known as far back as Roman times. The town has a number of interesting buildings such as the modern villas of *Manzana Raspall* and the ancient parish church of Sant Esteve, located in the outskirts of the town and better known as *la Doma*. La Garriga is the home of perhaps the very best *butifarra* ▶ *page* 27, a famous type of Catalan sausage. The sulfhydric waters for which it is known are also to be found in Tona, 21km from La Garriga and a very busy summer resort and spa. Some 3km from Tona is the village of **Malla**, where the Romanesque church of Sant Vincent dates to the 11-12C.

Vic, situated 10km from Tona and 68km from Barcelona, is an important commercial centre with an intense artistic and cultural life. Capital of the region of Osona, Vic is graced with lovely old homes and with murals by Sert —the Catalan painter buried in the Cathedral cloister— in its cathedral. Several small Romanesque churches are found outside Vic, such as the **Santa Eugenia de Berga** church, 7km SE on a local highway, and the church of **Sant Pere de Casserres**, 4km from the Parador of Sau. To eat in Vic, try *La Taula*, Pl Miguel de Clariana, 4 ☎ 889 32 29.

Following the same highway, Ctra N152, some 38km from Vic, you will find Ripoll, the true **seat of Romanesque Catalonia**. The Santa María Monastery in Ripoll was a centre of arts and letters during medieval times. Unfortunately, all that remains of its original structure is the extraordinary portal with a central arch and, on the sides, horizontal reliefs depicting Biblical scenes, and the cloister with its double arch built between the 13C and the 14C. Seeing this building is itself worth the trip to Ripoll. Reconstruction of the façade as we see it now was completed toward the end of last century. Another church in Ripoll, the **Sant Pere**, still retains portions of the old pre-Romanesque structure.

Finally, 10km NE of Ctra C151, there is a small but historically interesting village called Sant Joan de les Abadesses. Its monastery, the seat of an order of Benedictine women who were expelled in the year 1017, is one of the Romanesque monuments of Catalonia that shows the greatest French influence. It contains several artistic jewels, including the retable and Gothic figure of **Santa María la Blanca**, the 13C sculpted group of the **Holy Mystery**, and several other works of Gothic art.

Among the many other places worth exploring, consider the National Park of Aigües Tortes, the Costa Brava, Tarragona, Gerona and Seo de Urgel.

FIESTAS AND FESTIVALS

All Spain loves a *fiesta*. This is a land replete with festivities that run throughout the year, and the Spanish people are true lovers of these celebrations. They are held for countless reasons, in every region and town, but most of them have their roots in the cycles of nature (*fiestas* of spring, of San Juan, of the summer solstice and so on), in religious holidays (many of them superimposed on pre-Christian, pagan precedents) and in historical events. Every region's celebrations have their peculiarities, and Catalonia's in particular has some with very special features. The Catalans celebrate Holy Week and Corpus Christi, among other events, with due solemnity, and special features of Catalonia's *fiestas* include the *sardana* dance, the *gigantes y cabezudos*, or carnival figures with large heads, and the human towers formed by the *xiquets* of Valls and elsewhere. Whatever its size or rank, every town and village holds a festival for its patron saint. Several of these local celebrations date back to the Middle Ages. All Catalonia celebrates the *Diada*, the national day of the Catalan people. It may appear to the casual visitor that the Catalans are a serious people, and, indeed, they are very industrious. But in their *fiestas* Catalans show their other face. They are equally passionate about merry-making.

Barcelona is a city famous for the way in which it enjoys its *fiestas*. In addition to the citywide celebrations, there are those of each neighbourhood, or *barrio*, so much so that the calendar of festivals is practically uninterrupted throughout the year.

The celebration of Christmas and New Year is traditional and very popular here, and fills the city with light, trees and mangers. The annual Santa Lucía Fair, which takes place during this season, fills the area around the cathedral with nativity scenes and handmade figures of Bethlehem. The procession of the Three Wise Men that takes place on January 5 in the centre of the city ends this cycle of holidaymaking and opens the way for the carnivals that follow. The carnivals, picturesque and theatrical occasions marked by costumes and disguises, are timed to brighten the gloomy days of winter. The city of Barcelona has its own carnival, but the visitor should also know of two Shrovetide celebrations that take place outside the city, just 30 to 40 minutes away by car. They are in Sitges and Vilanova i la Geltrú (see the *Sitges* title in this *Everything Under the Sun* travel guide series).

During Holy Week (*Semana Santa*) in Barcelona, a series of religious festivals begins with a Palm Sunday procession through the Rambla de Cataluña and continues with a number of processions through the city. But the festival with the longest tradition is without doubt that of the representation of *La Passió* (the Passion) in Olesa de Montserrat, some 40km from Barcelona. It has been celebrated since 1642, almost 350 years. Hundreds of people participate in this sacred drama on the Sundays and holidays of Lent (*Cuaresma*) and Holy Week.

The festival of Sant Jordi (Saint George), patron saint of Catalonia, is on April 23 and coincides with the Book Fair that is celebrated throughout Spain. All Barcelona is full of book stalls and flowers which are traditionally exchanged by couples. Four days later, on April 27, comes the *fiesta* of the Virgin of Montserrat, a deeply religious festival. For more information, see 'Excursions' ▶ *page* 78.

On May 11, the *fiesta* of San Ponç —a traditional market of aromatic and medicinal herbs, honey and other natural products— is held on Hospital street, near the Ramblas.

The festival of Corpus Christi is celebrated on a Thursday in May, a date that varies according to the liturgical calendar. It is a particularly well-known festival in two towns of the province of Barcelona. In Berga, some 120km NW of Barcelona, the **Patum** features hand-crafted giants and the large-headed figures known as *cabezudos*, the traditional Catalan *sardana* dances and, above all, representations of the struggles between Christians and Moors that include monsters, angels and animals. In Sitges, a bare 40km from Barcelona on the Costa Dorada, the *fiesta* is celebrated with flowers. The visitor will see the famous **carpets of flowers** that cover the streets, as well as a carnation show and a competition for the best flower decoration of a building façade. Among all these flowers the procession of Corpus Christi, one of the finest in Spain, takes place (see *Sitges*, a sister guide in the *Everything Under the Sun* series of which this book forms a part).

The month of June brings the **International Film Festival of Barcelona**, before Cinema Week, expanded in 1987 to become a major event with several categories and a number of retrospective and other special film cycles.

On the evening of June 24, the summer solstice and the *fiesta* of **San Juan**, all Barcelona becomes a scene of light, fireworks and fire. Apart from the central bonfire that is built in Montjuïc, every neighbourhood, street and plaza has its own bonfire and dance that lasts into the early morning hours.

From the end of June until July the **Grec** festival is held, a series of shows in several areas —theatre, classical music and pop and rock. See one of the information guides listed in 'Local Publications' ▶ *page* 96 for details of this year's celebrations.

The *verbenas*, or dances generally held on the eve of a saint's day, take place in the various neighbourhoods of Barcelona throughout the summer, coinciding with the day of the patron saint of each district. Among the many such *fiestas*, that of the Barrio de Gracia, which climaxes on August 15, is probably the best known.

The most important *fiesta* in all Catalonia, the **Diada**, takes place on September 11, and has a political character. It celebrates the values of autonomy (from the rest of Spain), consists of demonstrations and other gatherings and is marked by the profuse waving of the *senyera*, the flag of Catalonia.

The celebration of the patron saint of Barcelona, the *Virgin of Merced*, takes place on September 24. This *fiesta* lasts an entire week —**Setmana Gran**— and features *verbenas* and *sardana* dancing, contests, parades, concerts, musical and theatrical shows, sports competitions and more. One of the most popular traditions during this period is that of the gathering of mock *giants* from all over Catalonia in the Pl Sant Jaume facing the City Hall, and the later procession of these same oversized representations through the streets of the central city. Bullfights are also a part of this *fiesta*.

Bullfights and Football

As a general rule, Catalans are not over fond of the bullfight. Nevertheless, Barcelona has its aficionados who show up at the *corridas* every Sunday from April until October, the normal bullfighting season. **Football**, on the other hand, has a large and enthusiastic following here. *Barça*, or the Football Club of Barcelona, is the eternal rival of *R.C.D. Español*. Both teams play in the first division and take part in European competitions and friendly games virtually throughout the year.

Calendar of Festivities

February

In all Catalonia: **Carnivals**, on variable dates.

In Barcelona: **Festivity of Santa Eulalia**, the co-patron saint of the city, with a range of events with a medieval flavour, a parade of giant figures, theatre depicting witches and the Spanish Inquisition, and medieval dances.

March

In Sitges: **International Barcelona-Sitges Vintage Car Rally**, on variable dates.

Human towers

April

In all Catalonia: **Holy Week**, or *Semana Santa*, changes dates according to the religious calendar but is in March or April. It features popular processions such as that of *Gran Poder* and the *Macarena* in Barcelona, a replica of the original Sevillian processions. On **Palm Sunday** palm fronds are used in decorations that range from the very simple to the elaborate. Traditionally, godfathers buy them for their godchildren. In Barcelona craftsmen sell these decorative items in the plazas of Sants, Sagrada Familia and on the Rambla de Cataluña (between c/ Diputación and c/ Aragón). Also in all Catalonia: **Easter Monday** (*Lunes de Pascua*) is a festival on which the godmother gives her godchild the traditional *monas*, chocolate sweets filled with caramel.

In all Catalonia, April 23: Day of the province's patron saint, **Sant Jordi** (Saint George). In Vilanova i la Geltrú there are incredible **human towers** that reach as high as nine men. In general, but especially in Barcelona: on the **Day of the Book and the Rose** (*Día del Libro y la Rosa*), with the Ramblas and the Pl Sant Jaume full of roses, the Palau de la Generalitat opens its doors to the public (the only such time during the year) and there is, in the Salon Sant Jordi, an exhibition of roses that have won a local competition. Booksellers set up stalls in public places.

In the Abbey of Montserrat, April 27: The festival of the **Virgin of Montserrat**, includes liturgical acts, chanting of the Salve by the choirboys and a performance of traditional *sardana* dances.

May

In Barcelona, May 11: ***Fira de Sant Ponç***, in c/ Hospital, Pl Padró and in Sants, there is an exhibition of natural products, herbs, honey, candied fruits, among others.

June

In Sitges: *Fiestas* take place sometime between April and June to mark **Corpus Christi**, including the procession of Corpus, the **National Exhibition of Carnations, Floral Contest of Building Façades**, and the **Flower Carpet Contest**.

In Barcelona and on the coast, June 23-24: **San Juan** bonfires and fireworks, celebrations of the summer solstice. In Sant Pere de Ribes: *verbena* dancing and bonfires.

July

In Barcelona, at the end of June and during the month of July: ***Grec***, with numerous acts and shows, including theatre, dance, flamenco dancing, classical and contemporary music concerts, movies (International Film Festival of Barcelona), jazz, pop music and more.

September

In all Catalonia, September 11: ***Diada***, national day of Catalonia. Commemorative festival that is particularly interesting in Barcelona.

In Sitges: **Menéndez Pelayo International University**, with courses, conferences, seminars and round table discussions, is attended by foreign and Spanish intellectuals over the course of the month. On the second fortnight of the month: the ***Fiesta de la Vendimia*** is especially interesting in Sitges.

In Barcelona, September 24: ***Fiesta de la Verge Mercé*** honouring Our Lady of Mercy (*Nuestra Señora de la Merced*), patron saint of the city.

October

In Sitges, variable date: **International Fantastic Film Festival of Sitges**.

LODGING

Barcelona boasts a total of more than 14,000 hotel beds. There are six five-star hotels with a capacity of 3,000; 22 four-star hotels with space for 4,500; 30 three-star hotels able to accommodate more than 4,000 people; 12 two-star hotels with a combined capacity of 1,400 and finally 14 one-star hotels with space for 1,400 people.

The *Barcelona Hotel Association*, on Vía Layetana, 47 ☎ 301 62 40, offers information on the facilities offered by specific hotels.

Aside from hotels, there is accommodation of other kinds for more than 5,000 visitors, everything from luxury to third class apartments or rooms with a variety of services. Reservations can be made directly, or through travel agencies in your native country. It is also possible to go through one of Barcelona's many real estate agencies.

In addition, the newspaper *La Vanguardia* and the weekly *Segond ma* publish notices of apartments, houses, and so on for rent as well as for sale.

For those interested in camping, the province and city of Barcelona offer a combined total of 38,000 camping site spaces. Practically all coastal towns and villages offer camping spaces and many in the interior do so as well. The *Asociación de Campings de Barcelona*, c/ Diputación, 279 ☎ 317 44 16, offers detailed information on camping sites.

All this availability of space does not guarantee, however, that the visitor will easily find a place to stay. Barcelona is a major commercial and industrial centre, and the hotels are often full of people attending conventions, exhibitions, congresses or meetings. The number of such visitors has been climbing in recent years. **Making reservations** in advance is the best way to avoid problems.

Apartments

There are a great many apartments available in Barcelona that rent by the day, the week or the month. The majority are in modern buildings located in central areas of the city. There is a lot of variety as far as size and category are concerned, and the prices vary accordingly. Rates may drop to some degree for those who rent for longer periods. As a general rule, apartment prices include water, electricity, bed and table linen, rubbish collection and use of common facilities. You will have no problem finding a place like this at any time of the year. It is a matter of minutes to take care of the preliminary legal work. The contract a tenant signs is standard, and it is usually accompanied by an inventory of furniture, household appliances and linen. Check it over to make sure everything listed is there. You will be asked for a deposit, generally known as a *fianza*, that should not exceed 25% of the total rental fee. You are advised, however, to rent through real estate agencies, property administrators or other professionals or professional firms. Avoid any potential problems in this way.

Like hotels and restaurants, tourist apartments are rated on a scale ranging from one to four keys. Minimum requirements for the different ratings are as follows:

Luxury (Four keys). This indicates a high-quality building, well situated. Air conditioning. Lifts in buildings higher than two floors. Service lift. Private parking. Reception and advice desk. Lobby. Telephone. Rubbish tip with collectors on every floor. Bar service. Restaurant cafeteria. 24-hour hot water.

First class (Three keys). You can expect, as a minimum, a well-built structure of first class materials. Lifts in buildings of more than three floors. Heating. Hot water. Reception and advice desk. Small lobby. Telephone communication to reception from every room.
Second class (Two keys). This indicates a well-built structure. Lifts in buildings of more than three floors. Heating. Hot water. House telephone at the reception and on every floor.
Third class (One key). This guarantees a lift in buildings of more than four floors. Hot water and at least a shower.

Real Estate Agencies in Barcelona

Abarca Leandro, c/ Mallorca, 221 ☎ 253 36 07.
Alustrey García, Vía Layetana, 57 ☎ 317 26 00.
Andreu Alcacer, c/ Espronceda, 304 ☎ 340 93 12.
Bassegoda Hombravella, c/ Angel Guimerá, 12 ☎ 201 95 61.
Bel Martí, c/ Provenza, 471 ☎ 235 47 42.
Bertran Torné, Gran Vía de les Cortes Catalans, 464 ☎ 224 39 00.
Bou Vidal, c/ Balmes, 44 ☎ 318 76 28.
Eurofincas, Vía Layetana, 57 ☎ 317 26 00.
Fincas Fradera-Api, Paseo Gracia, 90 ☎ 215 14 12.
Fincas Inter, c/ Capitán Arenas, 22 ☎ 203 13 04.
Fincas Sacristán, c/ Balmes, 23 ☎ 302 72 53.
Fontanet Mola, c/ Mallorca, 75 ☎ 321 10 53.
Fornieles Raya, c/ Nicaragua, 100 ☎ 321 70 34.
García Sánchez, c/ Villarroel, 233 ☎ 230 83 08.
Gálvez Sesé, c/ Canuda, 11 ☎ 318 78 48.
González Ferrero, c/ Comte d'Urgell, 55 ☎ 253 42 01.
González Martínez, c/ Trafalgar, 14 ☎ 317 00 97.
Marcos Buerg, Av Diagonal, 477 ☎ 230 85 02.
Múgica Goicoechea, c/ Aragó, 210 ☎ 253 18 69.
Plans Gelabert, Ronda Universidad, 20 ☎ 302 50 90.
Pointres-api, c/ Aragón, 259 ☎ 215 10 77.
Porta Bachs, c/ Comte Borrell, 179 ☎ 323 57 62.
Riera Solá, c/ General Mitre, 181 ☎ 212 57 00.
Roca Torrás, Pl de Urquinaona, 6 ☎ 318 27 28.
Sánchez García, c/ Roselló 55 ☎ 321 69 14.
Segui Vandellos, c/ San Antonio, 54 ☎ 301 51 42.
Serrano Muller, c/ Comte Salvatierra, 5 ☎ 237 85 10.
Vallbona Gaurdia, c/ Mallorca, 192 ☎ 254 70 01.

Camping sites

There are more than 38,000 available spaces on sites located in Barcelona. It is best to reserve a space ahead of time in the high season because the sites can become crowded. The National Tourist Office publishes a useful and cheap little guide, *Guía Oficial de Campings*, that contains all the information you need on existing camping sites and provides you with the details you need for making your reservation. Under Spanish law, no type of discrimination is permitted on camping sites. And you should not be charged for drinking water, showers or washing facilities, garbage collection, postal service or security. Camping is generally freely permitted except on mountains, on beaches, on river shores, or within 1km of a town, 50m of a highway or 150m of a drinking water supply. Camping on private property requires prior permission from the owner. It is extremely important to be careful with fire and matches as Spain is prone to forest fires, especially this region.

THOMSON

Hotels and Hostels

Hotels are officially classified on a scale ranging from ★ to ★★★★★. You will see the rating on a blue sign, under the letter H. Other possibilities are the signs HR, HA and RA which stand for Hotel Residence, Hotel Apartment and Residence Apartment respectively. The rating classifies the hotel's installations and services. Prices are regulated by the tourist authorities in Spain. If you have any questions about this, ask at the reception desk. There is a mandatory rates card in the lobby, and individual sheets showing the rate for each room usually hang on the inside of the entrance door in each room. Hotels are legally required to mantain these prices, but there are some variations, such as when the national sales tax VAT, known as *IVA*, is added. The tax is included in some hotel prices, not in others. If a single room is not available, you should not be charged more than 80% of the price of a double. For a room with an extra bed, you should not be charged more than 60% the price of a single or 35% the price of a double. There are usually discounts for children, according to their age. Finally, you should not be surprised at any differences between these official prices and those paid by organized groups or package tours that include hotels and other services; tour prices can be much lower or about the same.

★ Central heating. Lift when there are more than four floors. Lobby. Shower, washbasin and toilet in 25% of the rooms; washbasin in 50% of them; common bath available for every seven rooms. Laundry service available. Telephone on every floor.

★★ Central heating. Lift when there are more than three floors. Lobby. Bar. Complete bath in 15% of the rooms; shower, washbasin and toilet in 45% of them; washbasin in 40% of the rooms; common bath every six rooms. Laundry service available. Telephone in all rooms.

★★★ Central heating. Lift. Lobby. Bar. Complete bath in 50% of rooms; shower, washbasin and toilet in 50% of them. Laundry service available. Telephone in every room.

★★★★ Air conditioning in all common rooms and bedrooms, unless the local climate demands central heating instead. Lift. At least two lobbies. Bar. Garage (in cities). Complete bath in 75% of rooms; shower, washbasin and toilet in 25% of rooms. Laundry service available. Telephone in every room.

★★★★★ Air conditioning in all common rooms and bedrooms. Central heating. Two or more lifts. Several lobbies. Bar. Garage (in cities). Hairdressers. Complete bath in all rooms. Several suites including reception rooms. Laundry service available. Telephone in all rooms.

Avenida Palace

★★★★★ H (Open 1/1-31/12) Gran Vía, 605. Telex 54734 08007 ☎ 301 96 00 211 ✕ 🍸 El Candelabro and La Pinacoteca ✂ TV parabolic antenna AE, DC, EC, MC, V, CB $$$$$.

Splendidly situated in the nerve centre of the city, this stately and comfortable hotel is lavish with 1950s decorations. The service is cordial and attentive, if not always brilliantly efficient. The hotel restaurant, *El Candelabro*, is English in style and sober in atmosphere. The main lobby is in the Windsor style. Frequented by business men and women, this hotel has three meeting rooms for its clients.

Diplomatic

★★★★★ H (Open 1/1-31/12) c/ Pau Claris, 122. Telex 54701 08009 317 31 00 213 AE, DC, EC, MC, V, CB $$$$$.

Magnificent location, next to the Paseo de Gracia. The rooms are comfortable, but they do not have interesting views. The hotel functions well and efficiently. It has five pleasant bars, one of them an English-style establishment. Shops, swimming pool and an agreeable solarium. All bedrooms are soundproof, which can be a boon to visitors unaccustomed to keeping late Spanish hours, or who like to lie in late in the mornings.

Gran Hotel Sarriá Sol

★★★★★ H (Open 1/1-31/12) Av Sarriá, 50. Telex 51638 ghsbe 08029 239 11 09 314 AE, DC, EC, MC, V, CB $$$$$.

This hotel is located in the residential area of Sarriá, near the upper part of Av Diagonal. It is much used by conventioners and those attending congresses of various kinds, and has several meeting rooms, one of them with a capacity for 600 people. Gallery of shops, gymnasium and sauna.

Presidente

★★★★★ H (Open 1/1-31/12) Av Diagonal, 570. Telex 52180 08021 200 21 11 161 AE, DC, EC, MC, V, CB $$$$$.

Centrally located and consequently a bit noisy at certain times of the day. Comfortable, with large meeting rooms well suited to conferences and interviews. Well-served bar. Generally, however, the service at this hotel is somewhat old-fashioned and less than efficient. Rooms are comfortable, with telephones in bathrooms. On the ground floor there is a shopping gallery or mall.

Princesa Sofía

★★★★★ H (Open 1/1-31/12) Pl Papa Pio XII, 4. Telex 51032 sofie 08028 330 71 11 505 AE, DC, EC, MC, V, CB $$$$$.

Although a bit distant from the city's centre, the *Princesa Sofía* remains the city's finest hotel. It is a favourite among international travellers who value modern comfort and luxury. It has a number of restaurants, two bars that offer music and dancing at night, a covered swimming pool, gymnasium and sauna. There are also a number of salons and meeting rooms for conventions and other gatherings, one of them with a capacity for over 1,000 people. Under the hotel, reached by a separate entrance, is *Regine's* discotheque.

Ritz

★★★★★ H (Open 1/1-31/12) Gran Vía, 668. Telex 52739 08010 318 52 00 186 AE, DC, EC, MC, V, CB $$$$$.

Founded in 1919, the *Ritz* remains today a symbol of prestige hostelry. With high ceilings, marble friezes, brocade cloths and huge crystal chandeliers, it recreates the atmosphere of the *belle époque*. Some of its well-appointed rooms come equipped with Roman baths and mosaics from Seville. Among its famous clients are Xavier Cugat and Salvador Dalí, who on one occasion left the hotel straddling a beautiful white colt. The imperial lobby is magnificent, and its restaurant is numbered among Barcelona's best. The service is impeccable.

Arenas
★★★★ HR (Open 1/1-31/12) c/ Capitan Arenas, 20. Telex 54990 hare 08034 204 03 00 59 AE, DC, EC, MC, V, CB $$$$$.
Located in the upper residential zone of Barcelona, this hotel is not centrally located, but it is peaceful and has good communications. Service is efficient and rooms are pleasant.

Balmoral
★★★★ HR (Open 1/1-31/12) Vía Augusta, 5. Telex 54087 hoba 08006 217 87 00 94 AE, DC, EC, MC, V, CB $$$$$.
Centrally located, this functional hotel is equipped with a staff that gives good service. The restaurant offers particularly quick service and there are various cafeterias. The meeting rooms are large and comfortable.

Barcelona
★★★★ HR (Open 1/1-31/12) c/ Caspe, 1 to 13. Telex 54990 hare 08010 302 58 58 64 $$$$$.
Located in the nerve centre of Barcelona, next to the Pl de Cataluña, this totally renovated and modern hotel has functional decoration and reasonably adequate service.

Calderón
★★★★ HR (Open 1/1-31/12) Rambla de Cataluña, 26. Telex 51549 hoca e 08007 301 00 00 244 AE, DC, EC, MC, V, CB $$$$$.
Very close to the Pl de Cataluña. Modern, comfortable and functional ambience. A good-quality restaurant and a bar recommended by many. Good service.

Colón
★★★★ H (Open 1/1-31/12) Av Catedral, 7. Telex 52654 colon 08002 301 14 04 161 AE, DC, EC, MC, V, CB $$$$$.
For some people, this hotel is in the best spot in Barcelona, right in the middle of the Gothic Quarter. From several of the bedrooms the Cathedral can be seen lit up at night. The rooms are comfortable and the salons well furnished. The hospitable bar, decorated in a sober but pleasant style, has excellent *Bloody Marys* among its specialities. Good service, if sometimes slow.

Condes de Barcelona
★★★★ H (Open 1/1-31/12) Paseo de Gracia, 75. Telex 51531 ecbre 08008 215 06 16 100 AE, DC, EC, MC, V, CB $$$$$.
This is the newest of the four-star hotels. Situated inside the Old Batlló House, it is a splendid building in the Modernist style. Elegant lobbies, bar and restaurant, the *Brasserie Condal*, that is not top-notch quality. There are three large halls for conventions and banquets, the Picasso, the Gaudí and the Miró salons, with capacities ranging from 40 to 100 people. There are 100 rooms, including some suites. This hotel is always full; reserve in advance.

Cóndor
★★★★ HR (Open 1/1-31/12) Vía Augusta, 127. Telex 52925 hocon 08006 209 45 11 78 AE, DC, EC, MC, V, CB $$$$.
Centrally located and well-served by public transport. Functional and practical service. Many of the rooms have nice balconies. Several meeting rooms and a good number of shops.

Cristal

★★★★ HR (Open 1/1-31/12) c/ Diputación, 257. Telex 54560 ☎ 301 66 00 148 $$$$$.

Dante

★★★★ HR (Open 1/1-31/12) c/ Mallorca, 181. Telex 52588 ☎ 323 22 54 81 $$$$$.

Derby

★★★★ HR (Open 1/1-31/12) c/ Loreto, 21. Telex 97429 08029 ☎ 322 32 15 116 AE, DC, EC, MC, V, CB $$$$$.

Centrally located but tranquil and pleasant. Rooms with every type of furnishing. The special Derby breakfast is much prized by regular clients. Its scotch bar won the Spanish National Cocktail Award in 1976. Live music shows at night. The *Dickens Pub* in this hotel is authentically British.

Europark

★★★★ HR (Open 1/1-31/12) c/ Aragón, 325 ☎ 257 92 05 66 $$$$.

Gran Derby

★★★★ HA (Open 1/1-31/12) c/ Loreto, 28. Telex 97429 08029 ☎ 322 32 15 39 AE, DC, EC, MC, V, CB $$$$$.

This Apart-hotel is new and the only one of its kind in Barcelona. All the rooms are suites or duplexes, and most of them have a small balcony overlooking the hotel's interior garden. Situated facing the *Derby*, this hotel apartment shares its sister hotel's restaurant, bar and pub.

Gran Hotel Cristina

★★★★ HR (Open 1/1-31/12) Av Diagonal, 458. Telex 54328 ☎ 217 68 00 123 $$$$.

Hesperia

★★★★ HR (Open 1/1-31/12) c/ Los Vergos, 20. Telex 98403 pviae ☎ 204 55 51 144 $$$$$.

Majestic

★★★★ H (Open 1/1-31/12) Paseo de Gracia, 70. Telex 52211 08008 ☎ 215 45 12 344 AE, DC, EC, MC, V, CB $$$$$.

A functional and modern hotel. All the rooms face the street and are sunny as well as comfortable. The hotel is well placed on the stately Paseo de Gracia. Its convention hall seats 1,000 people. It also has an attractive terrace, swimming pool, gymnasium and sauna. In the hotel's busy bars you can order a very good *dry martini* or *pisco-sour.*

Manila

★★★★ HR (Open 1/1-31/12) Ramblas, 111. Telex 54634 ☎ 318 62 00 210 $$$$$.

Núñez-Urgel

★★★★ HR (Open 1/1-31/12) c/ Urgel, 232 ☎ 322 41 53 121 $$$$$.

Putxet

★★★★ HA (Open 1/1-31/12) c/ Putxet, 68. Telex 98718 aphoe 08023 ☎ 212 51 58 125 AE, V $$$$ to $$$$$.

This hotel is in a quiet area in the upper part of town, some distance from the old centre, but it has good communications. It offers apartments with cooking facilities. Service is good and hygiene optimal. From the hotel's fine balcony you can see all of Barcelona to the sea. Gymnasium.

Regente

★★★★ H (Open 1/1-31/12) Rambla de Cataluña, 76. Telex 51939 ☎ 215 25 70 78 $$$$$.

Royal

★★★★ HR (Open 1/1-31/12) Ramblas, 117. Telex 97565 ☎ 301 94 00 108 $$$$$.

Victoria Hotel Apartamentos

★★★★ RA (Open 1/1-31/12) Av Pedralbes, 16. Telex 98302 lihve ☎ 204 27 54 79 $$$$$.

Located near the entrance to the A2 motorway (Zaragoza-Lérida) in a quiet area some distance from the centre of town but with good comunication system. Apartments with living rooms and cooking facilities. The hotel has car rental facilities at daily, monthly or seasonal rates.

Aragón

★★★ HR (Open 1/1-31/12) c/ Aragón, 569 bis 571. Telex 98718 apho 08026 ☎ 245 89 05 72 AE, V $$$$ to $$$$$.

Located near the entrance to the motorway from the north, on the way to the fairgrounds. Some of the rooms have cooking facilities and can lodge up to 3 or 4 persons. Good communications.

Astoria

★★★ HR (Open 1/1-31/12) c/ Paris, 203. Telex 97429 dehoe 08036 ☎ 209 83 11 114 « AE, DC, EC, MC, V, CB $$$$.

Centrally located but quiet, set at the intersection of two little-travelled streets. The upper storeys house duplexes that are modern and comfortable and have balconies with magnificent views of the city.

Atenas

★★★ H (Open 1/1-31/12) Av Meridiana, 151 (corner with c/ Mallorca). Telex 98718 aphoe 08026 ☎ 232 20 11 166 (22 suites, 66 VIP rooms, 78 doubles) AE, DC, EC, MC, V, CB $$$.

Located at the entrance to Barcelona from the French border, this hotel is very close to the Metro and several bus lines. Comfortable rooms, all of them facing outwards. Swimming pool, solarium, and a pleasant terrace for dining during the summer.

Augusta

★★★ RA (Open 1/1-31/12) c/ Lincon, 32 ☎ 218 33 55 30 $$$$$.

A new hotel situated between the residential zone and the old city centre. Better facilities than average for its class. Large terrace with fine views of the city.

Condado

★★★ H (Open 1/1-31/12) c/ Aribau, 201. Telex 54546 hcoe ☎ 200 23 11 89 $$$$.

Corts

★★★ HR (Open 1/1-31/12) Travesera de las Corts, 292 ☎ 322 08 11 80 $$$.

Covadonga

★★★ HR (Open 1/1-31/12) Av Diagonal, 596. Telex 93394 cvhte ☎ 209 55 11 76 $$$.

Expo Hotel
★★★ HR (Open 1/1-31/12) c/ Mallorca, 1 to 23. Telex 54147 325 12 12 432 $$$$.

Ficus
★★★ HR (Open 1/1-31/12) c/ Mallorca, 163. Telex 98203 253 35 00 78 $$$.

Fornos
★★★ HR (Open 1/1-31/12) Ramblas, 44 318 20 24 30 $$$.

Gala Placidia
★★★ HA (Open 1/1-31/12) Vía Augusta, 112 217 82 00 31 $$$$$.

Gaudí
★★★ H (Open 1/1-31/12) Carrer Nou la Rambla 12. Telex 98974 hogae 317 90 32 71 $$$.

Gran Vía
★★★ H (Open 1/1-31/12) Gran Vía Corts Catalanes, 642 08007 318 19 00 48 AE, DC, EC, MC, V, CB $$$.
In a stately palace dating from the mid-19C, this hotel retains an authentic air of Old World ostentation. It has a magnificent *Art Nouveau* staircase, enchanting telephone booths and wardrobes. Breakfast is served in a mirrored salon arranged in the French style. The old chapel of the palace is still intact. Comfortable rooms and good service.

Gótico
★★★ HR (Open 1/1-31/12) c/ Jaime I, 14. Telex 97206 315 22 11 72 $$$$.

Habana
★★★ HR (Open 1/1-31/12) Gran Vía, 647 301 07 50 65 $$$.

Mikado
★★★ HA (Open 1/1-31/12) Pl de la Bonanova, 58. Telex 98718 aphoe 08017 211 41 66 46 doubles, 5 suites, 15 VIP rooms AE, DC, EC, MC, V, CB $$$$$.
Located in a residential area, this hotel has large rooms and a very fine solarium from which you get a really good view of the city, the sea, and the Tibidabo. Snack bar and good service in the dining room.

Mitre
★★★ HR (Open 1/1-31/12) c/ Bertran, 9 and 13. Telex 51531 ecbre 08023 212 11 04 57 AE, DC, EC, MC, V, CB $$$$.
Located in the residential area of the upper part of town, this is a quiet hotel with easy access to public transport. Comfortable rooms and modern facilities.

Montecarlo
★★★ HR (Open 1/1-31/12) Rambla de los Estudios, 124. Telex 93345 srmse 317 58 00 73 $$$.

Numancia
★★★ HR (Open 1/1-31/12) c/ Numancia, 74 322 44 51 140 $$$$.

Oriente
★★★ H (Open 1/1-31/12) Ramblas, 45 and 47. Telex 54134 302 25 58 142 $$$.

Pedralbes

★★★ H (Open 1/1-31/12) c/ Fontcoberta, 4 203 71 12 28 $$$$.

Rallye

★★★ HR (Open 1/1-31/12) Travesera de las Corts, 150 339 90 50 73 $$$$.

Regencia Colón

★★★ HR (Open 1/1-31/12) c/ Sagristans, 13 to 17. Telex 98175 318 98 58 55 $$$.

Regina

★★★ H (Open 1/1-31/12) c/ Vergara, 2 08002 301 32 32 102 AE, V $$$.

Very close to the Ramblas, on a quiet street. Family atmosphere, comfortable rooms and fine service.

Rubens

★★★ HA (Open 1/1-31/12) Paseo Nuestra Señora del Coll, 10. Telex 98718 aphoe 08023 219 12 04 136 AE, DC, EC, MC, V, CB $$$$ to $$$$$.

This hotel in the residential part of Barcelona is comfortable and accessible; it has the added attraction of being near the Güell Park. Some rooms have cooking facilities. Solarium with excellent views, meeting room and board room.

Suizo

★★★ H (Open 1/1-31/12) Pl del Angel, 12. Telex 97206 315 41 11 50 $$$$.

Terminal

★★★ HR (Open 1/1-31/12) c/ Provenza, 1. Telex 98213 321 53 50 75 $$$$.

Tres Torres

★★★ HR (Open 1/1-31/12) c/ Calatrava, 32 and 34. Telex 54990 hare 417 73 00 56 $$$$.

Villa de Madrid

★★★ HR (Open 1/1-31/12) Pl Villa de Madrid, 3 317 49 16 28 $$.

Wilson

★★★ HR (Open 1/1-31/12) Av Diagonal, 568 08006 209 25 11 52 AE, V $$$$.

A peaceful and well located hotel with comfortable and quiet rooms. The service is cordial, but somehow unevenly efficient.

Zenit

★★★ HR (Open 1/1-31/12) c/ Santalo, 8. Telex 54990 209 89 11 61 $$$$.

Antibes

★★ HR (Open 1/1-31/12) c/ Diputación, 394 232 62 11 65 $$.

Augusta

★★ HR (Open 1/1-31/12) Vía Augusta, 63 08006 217 92 50 44 AE, V $$$.

A new hotel set between Barcelona's residential area and the city centre. The facilities are above average for its category, and it has a fine terrace with lovely views.

Auto Hogar

★★ HR (Open 1/1-31/12) c/ Paralell, 64 241 84 00 156 $$.

Hostels and Boarding Houses

Like the hotels, hostels are officially classified on a scale from ★ to ★★★. This rating will appear on a blue sign under the letters Hs. Another possibility is the sign HsR, which stands for hostel residence. The minimum requirements of hostels, or *hostales*, are:

★ Washbasin in all rooms, with cold water; common bath every 12 rooms. A public telephone.

★★ Central heating. Lift for buildings of more than four floors. Vestibule or small lobby. Washbasin in all rooms; common bath every 10 rooms. Public telephone.

★★★ Central heating. Lift for buildings of more than three floors. Vestibule. Complete bath in 5% of rooms; shower, washbasin and toilet in 10%; shower and washbasin in 85% of them; common bath every eight rooms. Washing and ironing service available. Telephone in all rooms.

Boarding houses and pensions —indicated on a sign under the letter P— are a very cheap way to stay in Spain; they generally include a meal taken with the family that runs the establishment and laundry service.

Casal
★★★ HsR (Open 1/1-31/12) c/ Tapinería, 10 ☎ 319 78 00 36 $$$.

Continental
★★★ HsR (Open 1/1-31/12) Rambla de Canaletas, 138 ☎ 301 25 08 32 $$$.

Cuatro Naciones
★★★ Hs (Open 1/1-31/12) Ramblas, 40 ☎ 317 36 24 34 TV P $$$.

Monegal
★★★ HsR (Open 1/1-31/12) c/ Pelayo, 62 ☎ 302 65 66 12 $$.

Paseo de Gracia
★★★ HsR (Open 1/1-31/12) Paseo de Gracia, 102 ☎ 215 58 24 34 $$.

Rubí
★★★ HsR (Open 1/1-31/12) Vía Layetana, 42 ☎ 319 95 00 15 TV $$.

Taber
★★★ HsR (Open 1/1-31/12) c/ Aragón, 256. Telex 93452 htbre ☎ 318 70 50 65 TV $$$.

Urbis
★★★ HsR (Open 1/1-31/12) Paseo de Gracia, 23 08007 ☎ 317 27 66 61 43 with baths and 17 with showers in some rooms AE, DC, EC, MC, V, CB $$$.
A fine choice as an inn or pension, a jewel among family-run pensions. A stately 19C house, it is beautifully decorated and has a very colourful lobby. It is centrally located and provides good service.

Neutral
★★ HsR (Open 1/1-31/12) Rambla de Cataluña, 42 ☎ 318 73 70 28 $$.

Nuestra Señora de Nuria
★★ Hs (Open 1/1-31/12) c/ Lauría, 147 ☎ 217 13 22 14 TV $$.

Orléans
★★ HsR (Open 1/1-31/12) c/ M. de Argentera, 13 ☎ 319 65 09 10 $$.

MAIL

Post offices are open from 9.00 a.m. to 1.00 p.m. and from 5.00 to 7.00 p.m. Facilities include a *poste restante*, in Spanish *lista de correos*, for mail sent care of the post office in question. You need to present an identity document or passport to pick up your *poste restante* mail. Private agencies like Thomas Cook and American Express have similar services, though the latter company only serves cardholders or purchasers of its traveller's cheques.

Normal letter boxes are painted yellow, with two red, horizontal stripes. The letter boxes for express mail are red. Stamps can be bought in the *estancos*, or tobacconists, as well as at the lobby counters of most hotels, where you can also generally leave mail for posting.

To send *telegrams*, you can go to the post office in person —easiest if you don't speak the language— or dial a special telephone number and send the message by phone. Telegrams may also be handed in at most hotel lobbies.

To send a *telex* you must go to the post office or to the lobby of a hotel with telex facilities.

The main *Post Office* in Barcelona is in Pl Antonio López, s/n, at the end of Vía Layetana, facing Paseo Colón. It offers a Postal Express service for sending urgent mail. The main post office is open all day; the branch office at c/ Aragón, 282 ☎ 216 04 53, is open during office hours, while all other branch offices close at 1.00 p.m.

MASS MEDIA

Newspapers and Magazines

The best-known and oldest representative of the Barcelona press is the daily newspaper *La Vanguardia*, published now for more than 100 years. With the return of democracy more than a decade ago, *El Periódico* appeared, a newspaper with a somewhat more progressive orientation. *Avui*, a newspaper published in the Catalan language is considered centre-right politically. *Diario de Barcelona*, called *El Brusi* by its readers, is also written in Catalan. It has recently begun appearing again after several years. The biggest and most influential daily newspaper in Spain, *El País*, considered centre-left politically, puts out a special edition for the region that is published in Barcelona.

The *Guía de Ocio* (literally, Leisure Guide) is a weekly, small-format publication that lists all kinds of entertainment, from cultural events to shows of various kinds and other forms of entertainment. It is cheap and very informative.

Vivir en Barcelona (literally, Living in Barcelona) is a similar publication that has come out monthly in a large, all colour format since May, 1985. It has a full listing of cultural, social and gastronomic details for the city, including an extensive listing of theatre, cinema, concerts, books, exhibitions, restaurants and afternoon and evening entertainment spots.

There are two daily local sports papers; —*El Mundo Deportivo* and *Sport*— both of them tabloids.

British and American newspapers and magazines are readily available in the kiosks and newsagents in the city centre, generally within a day of publication.

Radio and Television

There are a great many FM radio stations of all types in Barcelona and its environs. On television, in addition to the two national channels, there is a regional channel, TV3, that broadcasts in Catalan. Its programming is informative and narrowly focused on Barcelona and Catalonia.

ORGANIZED TOURS

The majority of travel agencies offer a full programme of tours, most of them quite similar. The tour operators generally pick up participants at their own hotels or at a central point. Since these tours are programmed for large groups, the prices are reasonable. Comfort and price compensate for a very strict schedule; individual adventures are sacrificed to the economy of the group as a whole.

Andorra

Trips to this small, mountainous country sandwiched between Spain and France last a day or a weekend. Day trippers leave Barcelona early in the morning to allow as much shopping time as possible in Andorra. Weekend trips usually leave on Saturday morning, returning to Barcelona Sunday evening, and their prices —between 5,500 and 6,500 pesetas— include all meals and lodging. The day trips cost about 3,400 pesetas.

Barcelona City Tours

There are several types of tours of the city: half-day trips (morning or afternoon) that take visitors to sites such as the Gothic Quarter, the Ramblas, Montjuïc, or to the Church of the Holy Family, Tibidabo, the Picasso Museum, the University campus and Güell Park, and night tours that generally include a trip through the city's main streets, a flamenco show (*tablao*) and a visit to a nightclub. The night tours cost something like 6,000 pesetas, while the half-day tours run to an average of about 2,300 pesetas.

Costa Brava

Tours to this beautiful part of the Spanish coast, just off the city of Gerona, take the visitor to the principal points of interest between Arenys de Mar and Tossa. Some agencies include a short boat trip as well. These tours, including lunch, cost approximately 5,000 pesetas. Weekend trips are also offered.

Montserrat

This is normally an excursion lasting a day, and includes visits to several spots around the mountain of Montserrat, as well as a trip to the monastery itself, a world-famous symbol of Catalan tradition ▶ *page* 78. The tours to Montserrat usually also take the tourist to *miniature Catalonia*, an exhibition of scale models of the principal monuments of the region. The price of a full day's excursion, including lunch, ranges from 4,500 to 5,600 pesetas. There are also afternoon-only trips priced at around 2,700 pesetas.

Ski Resorts

During the ski season there are many organized trips to the ski resorts ▶ *page* 149 of the Catalan Pyrenees. In general, they leave Barcelona on a Friday afternoon to allow a full day's skiing on Saturday and most of the day Sunday. The return trip to Barcelona leaves on Sunday evening. A wide range of prices is offered, depending on the type of lodging the visitor is seeking. As a rough guide, there are weekend offers that include lodging for as little as 5,000 pesetas.

PHOTOGRAPHY

Spain is a beautiful country, and Barcelona is one of Spain's most beautiful cities, providing the photographer with plenty of occasions to take outstanding shots of its monuments, beaches and open areas. The strong light, however, calls for certain precautions.

Care of Camera and Film

Barcelona can be a very sunny place. The heat can damage film and is also capable of seriously damaging your camera. Do not leave cameras in the open sun: not in a car, or near a window or out in the open while at the beach. The beach poses another danger: hot sand can jam certain mechanisms in the camera, as well as scratching the lens. Always carry a lens-cleaning brush with your camera to remove sand from the lens without damage. Stains left by sun tan lotion or other oils can be removed with alcohol; on the lens, however, use a special liquid that can be purchased in photography stores or clean in carefully as best you can. It is wise keep photographic equipment always inside a sealed plastic bag when near the sea or on a beach.

Repairs and Film Developing

If your loaded film is stuck —that is, if you can't rewind or advance it— do not force the camera's rewind or advance levers. Before you try anything else, check to see if the film is used up. Are you sure, for instance, you put in a roll of 36 frames, rather than one of 24? Don't open the camera in the light; you will expose the film and ruin it. If you must open it, do so in a completely dark room; or better yet, take it to a photo store. As far as serious camera repairs are concerned, remember that in Spain, as anywhere else, this type of repair takes a good deal of time.

There are plenty of places in Barcelona for developing films. Some photography stores will take several days; but the vast majority give a 24-hour service, and photo shops that will develop films in an hour become more common every day. Give any special instructions you have to the shop assistants. Quality is uniformly good in most Spanish photo shops.

Taking Good Photos

Especially in summer, the bright light can affect your pictures, making them harsh and overly contrasted. You may also get glare, whited-out areas and other problems. You can get advice at a local photo store as to the most suitable film types and filters. As a general rule remember that you are likely to get better pictures in the early morning or late afternoon, when the light is weaker but still adequate. An ultraviolet filter will protect your lens from environmental damage. A polaroid filter will help get rid of glare: the pictures are clearer and the colours more true, especially when you are photographing the sea and sky —the blues, as well as bronze skin tones, will stand out nicely. The chances are you will normally be using 100 ASA film. When the light begins to fade or early in the day, 200 ASA film will probably be the most useful. Generally speaking, to use 400 ASA you will almost certainly have to have a reflex camera that allows you to close down the F-stop to 16 or 22.

PLACES OF INTEREST

Cathedral

The old cathedral of Barcelona was erected in 1046 under the auspices of the Counts of Barcelona and the Bishop Guisalberto. It was constructed on the site of an ancient basilica razed in 968 by Almanzor. From what we know now, this was a Romanesque church built in the Lombardine style. Part of it was on the site of the present cathedral, and it extended onto the plaza that faces the cathedral today.

In 1298 workmen laid the first stone of the modern cathedral, incorporating elements of the old structure into the new building. The first outstanding feature in the centre of the principal nave is the **crypt**. It was constructed in honour of Santa Eulalia and the Virgin from plans by Jaume Fabre. The crypt features an arch of triumph and a ribbed vault supported by smaller, hanging vaults creating the effect of a fan. On the keystone, which dates from 1337, there is a depiction of the coronation of Santa Eulalia, presided over by the baby Jesus, who sits in the lap of the Virgin. The remains of Santa Eulalia are in the crypt, inside a sarcophagus whose reliefs have been attributed to Nicola Pisano. At the base of the eight marble columns that support the coffin there are carvings of Hercules, draped with the pelt of a lion, between images of the Evangelists. Scenes of the life of Santa Eulalia and of the transfer of her remains from the ancient church of Our Lady of the Sands to the original cathedral are also depicted. Apart from the coffin, the crypt also contains the Saint's original 9C sepulchre and an inscription that recalls the discovery of the saint's remains in 887.

In the presbytery there is an altar supported by two Visigothic capitals, doubtless taken from the original cathedral. The main altar, completed in 1357, was inexplicably moved to the Church of San Jaime in 1970, and a bronze scene of the crucifixion was put in its place. The Pontifical seat, crafted in the second quarter of the 14C, is set with alabaster plaques. On both sides of the presbytery, next to the transept pillars, there are two great Baroque candelabra. Decorated with the city's coat-of-arms, they were installed in 1674. The organ is located over the door of San Ivo. Underneath, you can see a Moorish head that has been used for ages to dispense sweets to children on certain *fiesta* days.

The Chapel of San Antonio Abad, the Virgin of Carmen and San Francisco de Asís (St. Francis of Asisi) was built in 1319. It houses a 17C Baroque retable, or altarpiece, which substituted the original retable decorated with paintings of the saints by Luis de Borrasà. The chapel is closed off from the rest of the church by a 1746 iron grille.

The Chapel of the Visitation, formerly that of San Miguel, belonged to the brotherhood of the *Vidrieros de la Luz* (Glassmakers of the Light) until the 15C. It had a retable by Jaume Huguet, the remains of which may be seen today in the *Sala Capitular*, or Chapter House, of the Cathedral Museum. An 1880 tryptich there was made from the remains of a 15C retable. It was painted by order of the canon Nadal Garcés and dedicated to the Visitation.

In the Chapel of the Transfiguration of the Lord and of San Benito there is a lovely Gothic retable dedicated to San Salvador, executed by Bernat Martorell in 1447.

The Chapel of the Heart of Mary, San Sebastián and Santa Tecla has a magnificent Gothic altarpiece dedicated to San Sebastián and Santa Tecla. It is by Vergós y Alemany.

The Chapel of Our Lady of the Rosary (*Nuestra Señora del Rosario*) contains a Renaissance reredos by Pujol. It was completed in 1617.

The great historian Cirici called the cloister of the cathedral *the most beautiful spot in the city.* Vaulted galleries surround a delightful garden of palm trees, magnolias and medlars. The galleries are enriched by the exquisitely forged iron grillework.

Next to the Door of Piedad you will find a small temple with a Gothic fountain and water jet. Every year, on the eighth day of Corpus, it is adorned with broom plants and cherries. An eggshell is balanced atop the spout of water, where it dances as if it were accompanied by music; and from this it gets its popular name, *ou com balla*. Next to this little temple there is an ornamental lake where geese swim and children gather to play.

Passing through the cloister, the visitor arrives at the Chapter Museum and the **Sacristy**. The sacristy, or vestry, has three sections. The oldest, under a groin vault, is rectangular; while the treasure chamber of 1408 and the canonical sacristy of 1502 are both irregular in shape. You can see the processional monstrance, dating of the 14C, over a seat of silver. The figure of Santa Eulalia, the mitre of San Olegario and a 16C retable are other attractions here.

The *Sala Capitular*, or **Chapter House**, of the museum contains a wide range of valuable pieces. Among the most interesting are the **Calvary** scene which belonged to the San Benardino retable; the **Guardian Angel** by Jaime Huguet; the **Pietà** ordered by the archdeacon Desplá and executed by Bartolomé Bermejo; and the gilded silver throne of Martin I in which the Ostensory (a monstrance containing the bones of saints) is placed during the Corpus Christi procession.

Chapels, Churches and Monasteries

Belén, Church of (*Iglesia de Belén*)

This church was founded by the Jesuits in 1533, burnt down in 1671, rebuilt and then destroyed again by fire in 1936 at the start of the Spanish Civil War. The original church was located where the present apse is. The church has only one nave, with chapels on both sides separated by arches. The arches support the galleries, and the dome rises above them. The ground plan of the apse is semicircular. The façade of the church facing the c/ Carmen is in two sections: a lower part with stone coussinets and an upper section with a crown of hewn stone. The main door is inscribed with architectural insignia depicting San Ignacio de Loyola and San Francisco de Borja, flanked by wreathed columns; above them is a relief of the Nativity.

Holy Family, Church of the (*Sagrada Familia*)

(Pl de la Sagrada Familia). The incredible Church of the Holy Family is set at the back of an enormous plaza of the same name, whose gardens are now adorned with Falques stone and iron lamp posts, previously located at the intersection of the Paseo de Gracia and Av Diagonal.

In 1891, Gaudí was assigned to continue the work begun on the church dedicated to the Holy Family. Gaudí changed the plan for the building, but kept in mind the four basic theses of Martinell —utility, iconography, art and construction. From the symbolic point of view, the four towers that flank the dome refer to the four Evangelists: the 12 towers grouped by fours on the façade symbolize the 12 apostles; and the four angular bodies recall the four cardinal virtues.

The church is arranged in the shape of the Latin cross, with five naves, a retrochoir and an extremely imaginative system of arranging space. Gaudí began the front part of the construction early, and toward 1910 the beginnings of the façade of the Nativity were erected. Juan Rubió, Francisco Berenguer, Domingo Sugranyes and Francisco Quintana all collaborated with Gaudí in this stage of the construction.

If the building appears from the interior an adventurous and playful combination of intersecting planes, the exterior shows a profusion of naturalistic decorations. Four towers with parabolic profiles, each of them 107m high and topped with polychromatic mosaics, crown the three doors of the façade. These three entrances are dedicated to Faith, Hope and Charity. On the right is the door of Faith, with the anagram of San José and sculptures alluding to the Visitation and the infancy of the Baby Jesus. The pinnacle is constructed in the forms of the grapes and cereal grains symbolising the Eucharist and of the Virgin over a simple heart, image of the Trinity.

The Door of Hope is on the left, crowned by the anagram of Mary and with scenes of the Holy Family. In the upper part of this door there is a rock from the mountain of Montserrat, site of the famous monastery.

The door of Charity is in the centre. In the mullion over the door there is a genealogical tree of Jesus, the Annunciation of the Virgin, the Nativity and the Coronation of the Virgin. At the top is the anagram of Jesus.

Gaudí considered the Church of the Holy Family to be the ultimate goal of his career. He always took his work terribly seriously, using earlier constructions as experimental tests for later projects —and the cathedral was the last of Gaudí's buildings. When, at the age of 58, he completed the Milá House ▶ *page* 111, he decided to accept no more projects and to dedicate the rest of his life to his masterwork, the cathedral. He did not abandon work he had already undertaken, Güell Park and the cathedral of Majorca, but he took on no new projects.

When you visit this impressive and unfinished work, you will probably spot Josep María Subirach, the renowned Catalan sculptor who has undertaken the tremendous responsibility of finishing Gaudí's work. Subirach expects to spend the next 15 years completing the master's last work.

Marcús, Chapel of (*Capilla de Marcús*)

(Pl de Marcús, s/n). This 12C Romanesque chapel is the only remaining part of the old hospital for the poor. It is located on one of the main roads out of the city. The local association of postal workers —a great many of whom lived in this district— consecrated the chapel to the workers' protector, the Virgin de la Guía.

Merced, Church of (*Iglesia de la Merced*)

The foundations of this church were built in the second quarter of the 13C when the Mercedarians (an order of Our Lady of Mercy) established themselves in Barcelona in the Santa Eulalia Hospital. The hospital was the work of Ramón Plegamans and was on the site occupied by the Merced church today. The original church was completed in 1267, but underwent substantial modifications in 1336 and 1408. The present church was begun in 1765 and finished in 1775. It has a large central nave with a transept, dome and cupola, and two smaller attached naves with four chapels on each side.

The **choir** is set in a projecting section of the façade, while the galleries stand over the vaults of the two smaller naves.

The **main altar** dates from 1794 but has undergone several modifications. It is dominated by the seated image of Our Lady of Mercy, which was created in the middle of the 14C. The monastery building, much changed, is now on the spot where the old orchard of the Mercedarians was located. The main body of the building, the cloister and the refectory, date from the middle of the 17C, the work of the Santacana architects.

The **cloister**, built in a square, is enclosed by two floors of galleries supported by stone columns. The lower galleries have four arches on each wing; while the upper galleries have eight smaller arches each, resting on the balustrade. The façade is one of the very few examples of Baroque architecture in Barcelona.

San Agustín, Church of (*Iglesia de San Agustín*)

(Pl de San Agustín). Wrought by Alexandre de Rez in the 18C, this church has three naves with a vast transept which has a cupola in the centre of its ceiling. It is a sober work in the academic Baroque style.

San Justo, Church of (*Iglesia de San Justo*)

Legend says that this church, which is very close to the *Casa de la Ciudad*, is the oldest in Barcelona. In any case, up to the 15C it was the parish church of the local kings. It is important also because it carries the privilege, unique in Spain, of judging the validity of sacramental testaments.

San Justo and San Pastor, Church of (*Iglesia de San Justo y San Pastor*)

The original church was erected in the 10C with a cemetery and a chapel dedicated to San Celedonio. Construction of the present building began in the 14C and work continued into the 16C. The church has one nave in five sections, with a polygonal apse and rectangular chapels set between the buttresses.

San Pablo del Campo, Church of (*Iglesia de San Pablo del Campo*)

(c/ Huerto de San Pablo). An ancient Roman church, rebuilt three times, which contains the gravestone of Count Wilfredo II, who died in 911. The main façade includes Merovingian capitals from the 7C to the 8C, and parts of the wall date back further still. In the lintel over the door there is a commemorative inscription; in the tympanum, *Christ between the Apostles Peter and Paul*. The ornamental aspects of the building are completed with 13C representations of the hand of God and of the Evangelists.

The interior is in the shape of a Greek cross, and there is a cupola over the intersection of the cross. There are carvings on the walls and in the three parallel apses, window lintels. The **cloister** is 12C, square in layout, and has a number of arches that are supported by matching columns. The capitals of the columns are decorated with scenes of men fighting wild animals and with plant motifs. There are 13C to 15C stone tablets and sepulchres. The **chapter house**, which has been converted into a chapel, has a front façade made in 1300. The 14C abbot's residence is the present-day *Casa Rectoral*.

San Pedro de las Puellas, Church of (*Iglesia de San Pedro de las Puellas*)

(Pl de San Pedro). This is also said to be the oldest church in Barcelona. It is said that Louis the Pious ordered it built while laying siege to Barcelona in 801, on a hillock known as the *Cogoll* N of the city walls. The church, which was on the route across the Pyrenees, was dedicated to San Saturnino de Tolosa. It is mentioned again in 945, in a document consecrating the Church of San Pedro, built just across from what was called in Latin the *Atrium Saturnini Domini Testis*. Count Sunyer established a community of Benedictine monks in

San Pedro at that time. In the year 986, both churches were razed by Almanzor. By the 12C, after a number of successive restorations, there is no mention of San Saturnino. In 1147, in a document consecrating a new reconstruction, San Pedro is the only name mentioned. There were more modifications and renovations during the Gothic and Renaissance periods. After a fire in 1909, there was little of the original Romanesque structure left beyond some capitals and funeral tablets dating to the 9C, some of the vaulted ceilings and the cupola.

Santa Agueda, Palatine Chapel of (*Capilla Palatina de Santa Agueda*)

(Pl del Rey, s/n). A 14C Gothic chapel that is a part of the Main Royal Palace (*Palacio Real Mayor*). There is an important work in the chapel, the 15C retable of Condestable, by Jaime Huguet.

Santa Ana, Church of (*Iglesia de Santa Ana*)

(c/ Santa Ana). This church and monastery were founded in the 12C, after the Order of the Sacred Sepulchre established itself in Barcelona in 1141. The construction of the church is attributed to a member of the order known as Carfilius. The first architectural changes came in the 13C, when the nave was extended.

In the second quarter of the 15C, the regular clergymen of San Agustín, dedicated to Santa Eulàlia de Nierida and coming from the Montesion monastery (which was ceded to the Dominicans), were united with the canons of Santa Ana. The result was a number of new works, including the construction of the cloister, the *sala capitular*, or chapter house, and several chapels.

The 12C church was in the shape of a cross. It had thick walls with narrow, trumpet-shaped windows. The nave was built in the 14C with two spans of ribs, or ogives, reaching higher than the transept. The exterior walls are supported by thick buttresses, which mark out the outside ornamental covering into sections. The 15C **cloister** is rectangular in shape, with four gallery sections. The galleries are two tiers high, and the lower set features pointed arches. They are supported by square columns made of Gerona stone, with typically Catalan capitals. Overhead, a ceiling of wooden rafters is held up by consoles with stone arches in the corners. The arches in the galleries are very low. The chapter house is square in plan, and covered by an octagonal, cupola-shaped vaulted ceiling.

Santa María de los Reyes, or Pino Church (*Iglesia de Santa María de los Reyes*)

Construction of this church began in 1320. The side door retains Romanesque capitals and a polygonal tower rises behind the apse. The magnificent, huge windows of the upper part of the tower, dating from the 15C, are attention-grabbing. Inside, the church has one nave under seven sections of ogive ribs; and the polygonal apse, with five closed sides and two square side chapels, has a similar ceiling. There are other chapels in the nave, wedged in between the buttresses. The chapter house (*sala capitular*), in the form of a chapel with a polygonal apse, is covered with ogives and is on the south side of the church.

Between 1572 and 1573 the crypt was built under the main altar, under a low vaulted ceiling marked with ogives. The crypt was later to hold a relic of the crown of thorns. The glass windows, executed in the 18C, include some designed by the painter Antonio Viladomat. Other notable features of the church are the 18C **retable of San Miguel** and an interesting collection of gold and silver pieces from the period between the 15C and the 18C.

Santa María del Mar, Church of (*Iglesia de Santa María del Mar*)

A symbol of the power of Barcelona in the 13C, this church was the

Church of Santa María del Mar

owner of extensive Mediterranean properties and the protagonist of commercial development centred in its riverside neighbourhood. Construction began in 1329 to plans by Berenguar de Montagut. From the façade facing the Pl Santa María, one can admire the pure lines that characterize the Catalan Gothic style; take note, especially, of the octagonal towers and their terraces. On both sides of the door are images of Saints Pedro and Pablo (Peter and Paul).

The flamboyant **rose window** dates to the middle of the 14C and is a replacement for the original, destroyed in a fire. The stained glass windows date from various periods. Those depicting the *Ascension* (Chapel of Santa María) and the *Lavatorio*, or Maundy (Chapel of San Rafael), date from the 14C, and the window showing the *Last Supper* from the 17C, and those in the apse are 18C. The simple naturalness of the octagonal pillars is notable. They are placed 13m apart, an unusual distance for the architecture of the period, and represent an advanced concept in the use of space. In the presbytery, there is an interesting recumbent sculpture topping the tomb of Peter IV of Portugal, chosen king of the Catalans in 1464. The church treasury contains many valuable pieces of goldsmithery of the 16C and 18C.

The concerts that are given in this church, especially performances of Baroque music, are a real pleasure and highly recommended.

Santa María de Pedralbes, Monastery of (*Monasterio de Santa María de Pedralbes*)

(At the end of the Av de Pedralbes). This convent of Clarist nuns is an outstanding example of isolated religious life. It was walled from the start, and the complex included the main structure, its outbuildings, a street with residences for the beneficiaries of the secular clergy and a small convent known as the *Convetet*, which was assigned to the Franciscans and dedicated to the service of the feminine community. The N and S gates in the walls have been preserved, each of them protected by 14C and 15C **towers**.

The convent was founded in 1326 by King James II and his fourth wife, Elisenda de Montcada. The following year the church was consecrated and the convent given to the community. The Gothic **church** has one nave with an apse of seven panels, under an pointed vaulted arch. Chapels are ensconced between the buttresses. The nave is divided by an iron grille into two parts, one public and the other reserved for the monastic community. That second has a lower choir area as well as a higher one, over an ogival vault.

The funeral monument to Queen Elisenda is outstanding in the **interior**, with a stone sarcophagus borne by three stone lions. The images of Santiago el Mayor, San Francisco de Asís (St. Francis of Asisi), Santa Clara and a holy virgin appear in some of the upright supports. The **choir** is 15C. The **cloister**, which dates from the 14C, has an arcade with uniform column capitals. Both the Royal and the Montcada coats-of-arms can be spotted here, as well as squared columns from Gerona. In the southern corner of the cloister there is a large stone cistern and a small fountain decorated with a ceramic figurine of an angel, glazed white. The curb of the cistern is especially interesting. It was made in 1548 in the Plateresque style, but was modified in the 18C. The chapter house is older, dating to 1326. The stained glass of the rose and other windows, although restored, was first installed in 1419.

On the main wall of the apse there is a pictorial composition done in the middle of the 14C and depicting *Calvary, San Francisco de Asis* and *San Luis de Tolosa*; to the left are three figures, while on the right *Santa Clara* is represented.

The **Chapel of San Miguel**, actually the old cell of the Abbess Francisca Sa-Portella, is the most important niche in the entire monastery, owing to the **wall decorations** that enrich it. Over the door is the *Saviour and two angels with emblems of the Passion*, as well as two fortunate persons crowned by angels.

Gothic Quarter

The *Barrio Gótico*, once known as the *barrio* (neighbourhood) of the Cathedral, is an area marked by great Gothic edifices that are testimony to the apogee of the city and its culture in medieval times. It also contains the remains of ancient fortifications and palaces erected by the Romans on Monte Taber (Mount Taber). The quarter features vestiges of a temple dedicated to August; other Roman monuments next to the palace of the *Condes reyes* (Count Kings); the Cathedral itself; and other medieval structures.

The two government centres of the Generalitat de Cataluña (seat of the autonomous regional goverment) and the *Casa de la Ciudad* (City House) were built in the district later; both of them were begun during the reign of Peter III, the Ceremonious. The old Roman plan of the area, with two perpendicular streets dividing it into four quarters, has been preserved.

Hospitals and Institutes

Botanical Institute and Garden (*Instituto y Jardín Botánico*)
(Av Montayans). This curious place is well worth a visit. It is one of the most important centres for the study of botany in Spain. The flora of Catalonia, the Pyrenees and the rest of Spain is particularly well represented.

Hospital of San Pablo (*Hospital de San Pablo*)
(End of the Av Gaudí). This hospital was built between 1902 and 1910 thanks to the bequest left by Pablo Gil. It was designed by Domènech i Muntaner. The structure is clad in brick, ceramics and mosaics, and is graced with a painting by Labarta turned into a mosaic mural by Maragliano. A series of service and transportation innovations has been added.

Hospital of Santa Creu (*Hospital de Santa Creu*)
(c/ Hospital). In 1401, the four old hospitals of Barcelona united under the name of Santa Cruz y San Pablo. The hospital they built surrounds a patio with an 18C cross in the centre, and there are three naves with wooden coverings supported by pointed arches. A 16C Plateresque entrance is preserved, although the chapel was re-done in the 18C. It now contains a statue of Charity. The building also houses the Library of Catalonia.

Municipal History Institute (*Instituto Municipal de Historia*)
(c/ Santa Llucía, 1). The attractive building that houses the city's historical archives is the compendium of many centuries of construction. The oldest structure was part of the Roman city walls. During medieval times it was the residence of the Archdeacon of the Cathedral, and every new tenant of that office added new parts to the edifice.

The archives, created in the 13C, contain the official city records of Barcelona and records of various other public institutions as well. The building also houses a library with more than 140,000 volumes, the municipal newspaper library, a large photographic archive and other resources connected with the city.

Mansions, Palaces, Theatres, Centres and Foundations

Archdeacon's House (*Casa del Arcediano*)
(Pl de la Seu, s/n). This building was constructed in the 15C atop the ancient Roman walls of the city, as a residence for Archdeacon Desplá. It was Desplá who ordered the creation of the famous **Pietà**, which today can be seen in the Cathedral. The house is in the Plateresque style, although the sculptural details reflect Renaissance influences. Since 1919 this building has been the headquarters of the Municipal Institute of City History (*Instituto Municipal de Historia de la Ciudad*). A cloistered patio with a fountain and beautiful palm tree in the centre is one of the house's highlights.

The interior ornamentation of the original Roman wall can be appreciated from the ground floor. On the main living floor, among stately rooms hung with tapestries, the ***Salón de las Piñas*** is especially interesting. It gets its name from the decorative motif of its coffered ceiling.

Architects' College of Catalonia (*Colegio de Arquitectos de Cataluña*)
(Facing the Pl Nueva). Picasso designed the frieze of this building,

which hosts a series of activities and shows that are changed periodically. This institution also publishes a guide to architecture in the city —*Arquitectura de Barcelona*— that is a true jewel for experts and enthusiasts.

Batlló House *(Casa Batlló)*

(Paseo de Gracia, 43). When undertaking this project, the Barcelonan architect Antonio Gaudí was faced with the problem of reshaping the façade, stairway and main floor of a house flanked by two adjoining terraced houses. The undulating main façade is Baroque in its luxuriant detail, a prelude to Gaudí's later La Pedrera ▶ *page* 111. The balconies and rostrums, set on the sculptured waves of the polychromatic façade wall, seem to dissolve the distinction between inside and out. The sinuous form of the building's upper part, which recalls animal forms, tries to combine Gaudí's work with the shape of the pre-existing Amatller House by Puig i Cadafalch. The effect is fascinating.

As you walk into the building through an archway you will see a patio that is open to the very top of the building. This large shaft narrows toward the top; and the interior windows follow this pattern, getting smaller toward the top as well. The interior walls of the patio are of blue and white tiles of graduating intensity. All these changes are geared to the light that floods in from above, and they meet the chimneys and stairwell structures at the top.

The original interior decoration designed by Gaudí has been largely maintained. The main floor is the most interesting.

Catalan Music, Palace of (*Palacio de la Música Catalana*)

(c/ Amadeus Vives, 1). This building is the best known work of Domènech i Muntaner (1905-1908). Based on Gothic principles of construction, it resembles a great glass box, using natural light to its best advantage. There are allegorical sculptures by Pablo Gargallo of Clavé, Beethoven and the Valkyries. The suspended glass lamps are also noteworthy, as are the mosaics by Luis Bru and the sculptural motifs by Miguel Blay. All in all, it is a dazzling building.

Cervelló, Palace of (*Palacio de Cervelló*)

(c/ Montcada, 25). This structure dates from the 15C, 16C and 18C and presently lodges the Galeria Maeght. Besides visiting the patio or the exhibits being shown in the gallery, it is a good idea for those interested in contemporary art to take a look at the catalogue of wood engravings and etchings of the gallery. It includes works by Braque, Miró, Tapiès, Picasso, Arroyo and others.

Dalmases, Palace of (*Palacio de Dalmases*)

(c/ Montcada, 20). Built in the 18C, this mansion is notable for its staircase, a fine example of the delicacy and refinement of the sculpture of the 17C in the profusion of reliefs in the columns and the parapets. In the chapel there is a 15C relief decorating a vaulted ceiling.

Episcopal Palace (*Palacio Episcopal*)

(Pl Nueva). This palace was built at the end of the 12C and the beginning of the 13C. The present façade dates from 1784. Inside and on the main floor there is a spacious Romanesque gallery set with matching arches. The patio is adorned with 13C windows and a flamboyant Gothic window of the 14C. The **Throne Room** is very interesting, with walls decorated with tempera paintings and large Neoclassical Baroque compositions.

Past this palace on the right you will find the Pl San Felipe Neri, an enchanting square that may be one of the most poetic spots in the city. The church there is on the site of the old 17C *Oratorium*.

Batlló House, Gaudí

Excursions Centre of Catalonia (*Centro Excursionista de Cataluña*)

(c/ Parades, 10). This archaeological centre is in a building marked by its elegant tall windows and a patio with an outdoor staircase. Inside one can see entire columns from one of the corners of the Roman temple dedicated to August. Since the 19C, the centre has vigorously promoted the natural sciences and archaeology in Catalonia.

House of the Canons (*Casa de los Canónigos*)

(c/ Arzobispo Irurita, s/n). The so-called House of the Canons, a 14C Gothic structure located next to the apse of the Cathedral, was the residence of the canons, or local clergymen. There is an overpass that crosses c/ Obispo Irurita and gives access to the Generalitat Palace ▶ *page* 119, to which it now belongs. The building was changed a great deal during the 19C by the architect Mas Vila. He built a very large façade but kept many altered Gothic structures inside the building.

Joan Miró Foundation (*Fundación Joan Miró*)

(Montjuïc Park). Open daily from 11.00 a.m. until 8.00 p.m. and on holidays and Sundays from 11.00 a.m. until 2.30 p.m. Closed Mondays.

The foundation building was constructed to house all the art works donated by the famous painter Joan Miró, as well as the *Centre for Studies and Experimentation in the Plastic Arts*. The nucleus of the collection is formed by Miro's works; the visitor can trace them from 1914 to 1978. An extensive collection of works by contemporary painters complements the Miró collection. The foundation also mounts exhibits all year that focus on the art movements of this century. Fine posters also are sold.

The building is one of only two works that the architect Sert designed in Barcelona after the Spanish Civil War. The structure surrounds an interior patio which offers, from one end, magnificent panoramic views.

Main Royal Palace (*Palacio Real Mayor*)
(Pl del Rey). Originally the residence of the Counts of Barcelona, this palace has been much developed and enlarged since then. The 14C **Tinell Room** is an especially interesting salon. It was constructed at the behest of Peter the Ceremonious between 1359 and 1362 and occupies almost the entire southern end of the palace. Its name apparently derives from vats (*tinas*) of grain or from the furniture, the best in the palace, that was displayed in that chamber. Between 1372 and 1377 the *Cortes*, or Catalan Parliament, met in this room. In 1390 the legate of the Pope of Avignon asked for the aid of the Catalans in this salon. But perhaps most interesting, Columbus is believed to have presented himself for the first time to the Catholic Monarchs here in 1493, after his first voyage to the Americas. Clarist nuns converted the salon into a gloomy church with side chapels, but it was restored to its original situation between 1934 and 1936. Today it is the site of numerous exhibitions and other cultural events.

Marquises of Llió, Palace of the (*Palacio de los Marqueses de Llió*)
(c/ Montcada, 12). This mansion, which today houses the Textile and Clothing Museum, shows elements of both the 14C and the 18C. In the portico, there is a pleasant combination of the original Gothic structure and changes that were wrought during the 17C in the doors and windows and the roof terrace overhead.

Mies van der Rohe Pavilion (*Pabellón Mies van der Rohe*)
(Fairgrounds in Montjüic). The pavilion was designed by the German

Joan Miró Foundation

delegation to the International Exhibition of 1929. The work of Mies van der Rohe is considered a paradigm of modern architecture. A bronze copy of the sculpture by the German artist Georges Kolbe, which adorned the original building, has been installed in the same place. It was a gift of the government of the Federal Republic of Germany.

Milá House, or the Pedrera (*Casa Milá*)

(Paseo de Gracia, 92). It was in this building that Gaudí gave full range to his creative energies and intimate knowledge of construction techniques. He played with projections and ornamental designs in exciting new ways, referring in his sculptural details to vegetable and fruit shapes. The tops of chimneys became fantastic shapes, made of stone, iron and other materials. Gaudí took on the Mila House project immediately after finishing Batlló House ▶ *page* 108, so the striking relationship between the two should come as no surprise.

Gaudí's original project was much more ambitious that what was eventually built, and the architect made numerous changes during the course of the construction work. Nevertheless, he maintained to the end the same basic idea, with the only major modification being the elimination of a sculptural group dedicated to the Virgin of Grace. These large figures were to have crowned the façade and given the building as a whole the look of one massive stone sculpture.

The originality of the Pedrera is not limited to its lavishly sculptured façade, but extends to the building as a whole. The most glaring difference with respect to other residential buildings of the area was the absence of a common staircase, so that the living quarters could only be reached by way of an elevator or the service stairs. Thanks to this arrangement, Gaudí was able to incorportate two large patios, open to the sky. The location of the stables in the building basement, to which access is by means of helicoidal ramps, was another innovation.

Gaudí designed a very free interior plan for the building, allowing him to arrange a rich sequence of domestic and other spaces inside. This extraordinarily plastic situation culiminated in the attics, where sinuous profiles top the stepped but basically flat roof, which is populated by phantasmagorical chimneys, known as *espantabrujas* (witch-scarers).

Montaner i Simon Publishers (*Editor Montaner i Simon*)

This publishing house was built at the end of the 19C and was the work of Domènech i Muntaner. It is to be converted into the **Fundación Tapiès**, a foundation named after the famous Catalan painter, and will be a centre for modern art.

Opera Theatre (*Teatro del Liceo*)

(Rambla de Capuchinos). This theatre is closely linked to the romanticism of the Catalan *Renaixença*, and is the fruit of an initiative by the **Philharmonic and Dramatic Opera of Barcelona** (*Liceo Filarmónico y Dramático Barcelonés*).

The site it occupies was once an old convent of the Rambla. The first door was planned in 1845. The other is the work of Miguel Garriga i Roca, and was restored by the architect Mestres after a fire.

The paintings on the ceiling of the hall allude to the work of authors and playwrights of all periods, from Aristophanes to Lope de Vega. This is the first lyric theatre of Barcelona, and in Europe it is only outdone in terms of size by the Scala in Milan.

Pía Almonia House (*Casa de la Pía Almonia*)

(Av de la Catedral). This building was erected in the plaza of the Cathedral in the middle of the 15C to house various pious foundations under the control of the *Cabildo*, or local church chapter. It was expanded in 1453 following orders of bishop Berenguer. In the 18C various other changes were made.

Vicereine, Palace of the (*Palacio de la Virreina*)

See the Museum of Decorative Arts ▶ *page* 114, the Coin Museum of Catalonia ▶ *page* 114 and the Postal Museum ▶ *page* 117.

Monuments

Monument to Columbus (*Monumento a Colón*)

(Pl del Portal de la Pau). In the great esplanade that opens at the foot of the Ramblas there rises the monument to Christopher Columbus, commemorating the return of the European discoverer of America to the city of the Counts. The monument is the work of the engineer Buigas i Daulet. It was begun in 1882 but owing to economic ups and downs was not finished until 1888, when it was inaugurated along with the first Universal Exhibition. It is 60m high, with the statue itself accounting for 7m of that height.

Moored to the Moll der la Fusta (where you can take an unforgettable walk on a sunny day) there is a replica of the **Santa María**, the caravel that was Columbus' flagship.

Museums and Archives

Archaeological Museum (*Museo Arqueológico*)

This museum occupies the *Palace of Graphic Arts* built for the *1929 International Exhibition* in Montjuïc. It houses important collections of prehistoric Iberian artifacts and archaeological finds from all over the world. The outstanding collections are of Iberian, Greek, and Roman artifacts; the Roman collection includes mosaics, glass, ceramics, bronze, sculpture, arms and more. There are also very good collections from Ampurias and the Balearic Islands.

Archives of the Crown of Aragón (*Archivo de la Corona de Aragón*)

(Pl del Rey, s/n). Formerly the *Palacio del Lugarteniente*, or Deputy's Palace, this building is the work of the 16C architect Antonio Carbonell. It is typical of the late Gothic period, but shows some later, Renaissance elements. The palace is also known as the *Palacio de los Virreyes*, or Palace of the Viceroys. The archives contain fascinating documents of local and international relevance.

Art, Industry and Popular Traditions, Museum of (*Museo de Artes, Industrias y Tradiciones populares*)

This museum is located in the Pueblo Español in Montjüic, a *village* built in 1929 to display reproductions of local architecture from all parts of Spain. The museum occupies several buildings in the Pl Mayor and contains ethnographic collections from Catalonia, Valencia, the Balearic Islands, Aragón, La Rioja, Castile and León. At Pl Mayor, 6, you can visit an interesting *Pallaresa house*, a reproduction of the interior of a worker's home in the Pyrenean region of Pallara Jussá.

Art Museum of Catalonia (*Museo de Arte de Cataluña*)

(Montjuic Park). This museum is divided into three sections, the most important of which houses an unusual collection of Romanesque paintings, 11C to 13C, considered the most extensive and valuable in the world. Another section is devoted to Gothic art; it is one of the most complete of its genre. Finally, there is an area devoted to 16C to 18C art. It is fragmentary in character, though it has some great paintings of the Spanish, Italian and Flemish schools.

Atarazanas

(Pl Portal de la Pau, s/n). These medieval shipyards are remarkable for their size and excellent state of preservation. Their construction

Atarazanas, Maritime Museum

dates from different periods. The rear right section is 14C; the area around the entrance and the side that abuts the Paseo Marítimo date to the 17C; and the main central part is 18C.

The Maritime Museum, or *Museo Marítimo*, is lodged inside the old yards, and displays all kinds of objects related to navigation and the sea since the Middle Ages.

At the southern end of the yards a part of an ancient Gothic wall with square towers has been preserved. At the base of one of the towers the entrance door opens underneath an Ogive arch.

Automaton Museum of Tibidabo (*Museo de Autómatas del Tibidabo*)
(Amusement park in Tibidabo).

Book and Graphic Arts Museum (*Museo del Libro y de las Artes Gráficas*)

This museum occupies several buildings in the Pueblo Español replica village in Montjuic, next to the Pl Mayor. It displays all kinds of items related to graphics, letters, writing and images, as well as the technology for producing and mass-reproducing them.

Ceramics Museum (*Museo de Cerámica*)

Located in the **National Palace**, this museum has collections ranging from the 12C to the most modern work of today. There are also displays showing the changes and technical innovations in ceramics over the last 800 years.

Clará, Museum of (*Museo Clará*)

(c/ Calatrava, 27-29). The sculptor Josep Clará bequeathed to the city a very large collection of sculptures, drawings, watercolours and personal mementos, as well as the house where he lived and died and where his studio was located. It is in this studio, adapted as a museum, that one can see the most representative sample of his works.

Clariana-Padellás House (*Casa Clariana-Padellás*)

(Pl del Rey). This Gothic building used to be in c/ Mercaders. It was moved to its present location stone by stone and today it houses the City History Museum (*Museo de Historia de la Ciudad*). Remains of ancient Roman structures may be seen in the basement of this building. The place has the authentic flavour of a Catalan Gothic palace, although the decorative objects belong more to the Renaissance, which never reached full fruition in Catalonia.

City History Museum (*Museo de Historia de la Ciudad*)

(Pl del Rey). Located in a fine Catalan mansion characteristic of the 15C, the Padellás House. The museum consists of three floors and an interior patio with an open staircase. On the main floor there is a gallery with pointed arches. The basement contains important vestiges of the Roman city that continue on to the plaza of the Cathedral. The most outstanding Roman remains are those of the paleo-Christian basilica and the baptistry. The museum is divided into several main sections; rooms with frescoes of pre-Roman Barcelona, Jewish and Arab remains (11C to 14C) and various medieval elements. There are rooms containing other items important to the development of the city.

Coin Museum of Catalonia (*Gabinete Numismático de Cataluña*)

(La Rambla, 99, Palace of the Vicereine). When Catalonia recovered its autonomy this museum was moved from its former location in the Ciudadela Palace to make way for the Catalonian Parliament. Its exhibits were transferred to the Palace of the Vicereine.

Decorative Arts Museum (Museo de Artes Decorativas)

(La Rambla, 99). The museum occupies the main floor of the Palace of the Vicereine. It was built between 1772 and 1777 as a residence for Manuel d'Amat i de Junyent, Viceroy of Peru. It is an edifice of

Neoclassical lines and Baroque decorations. The museum contains a variety of decorative art collections; Catalan glass with some exceptional 16C pieces, Alcora porcelain, washbasins, watches, gold, silver, and enamelled objects and an excellent collection of Gothic and Renaissance boxes and small chests. The 16C to 19C furniture collection is also interesting.

Manuel Amat, the Viceroy of Peru, sent detailed plans from Lima for the construction of a house on the Rambla. But in the end, he died and it was his widow who got to enjoy the mansion; for this reason it became known popularly as the *Palace of the Vicereine.*

Ethnological Museum (*Museo Etnológico*)

This museum is in the Paseo de la Santa Madrona and was created in 1940. In 1973 a new building was inaugurated. It was planned as a museum, with hexagonal modules that allow optimal display of the pieces on show. The museum's collections contain pieces from all continents, most of them acquired by expeditions dispatched by the museum.

Experimental Physics, Museum of (*Museo de Física Experimental*)

(Ctra de Vallvidrera to the Tibidabo). A collection of scientific instruments basic to the physical sciences.

Federico Marés Museum

(c/ Comtes de Barcelona, 10). This museum is in the old **Palace of the Counts of Barcelona**. Its collections are of two types: sculpture ranging from classical Rome to the Baroque, condidered one of the most important sculpture exhibitions on the peninsula; and sumptuary art, known here as *Sentimental*, that is of great interest.

Footwear Museum (*Museo de Calzado*)

(c/ Santa Llucía, s/n).

Gallery of Illustrious Catalans (*Galeria de Catalanes Ilustres*)

(c/ del Bisbe Cassador, 3). The gallery is installed in the headquarters of the *Academia de las Buenas Letras*, in the Royal Palace ▶ *page* 18. The palace is a beautiful Gothic structure near the old Roman wall. The gallery was created in 1840 and contains portraits of 47 illustrious Catalans who lived between the 10C and 20C.

Gaudí Museum (*Museo Gaudí*)

(c/ Olot, s/n. Güell Park) ▶ *page* 37.

Geology, Museum of (*Museo de Geología*)

(Ciudadela Park). This is the oldest museum in Barcelona. It was constructed in 1878 to keep the scientific collections brought to the city by Francesc Martorell i Peña. They include the most important mineral collection in Spain.

Military Museum (*Museo Militar*)

The Military Museum is in Montjuïc, in the castle-fortress that was built mainly in the 18C, according to the French model known as the Vauban. The rooms of the castle were remodelled as museum halls to hold collections of arms from the Spanish army and a number of displays from smaller cities.

Modern Art, Museum of (*Museo de Arte Moderno*)

(Ciudadela Park). This museum takes up part of the *Palacio de la Ciudadela*, or Ciudadela Palace, the building which also houses the Parliament of Catalonia. It was built in the 18C and formed part of the city's defences, in part by being its arsenal. It was subsequently rehabilitated as a royal residence and later still, at the beginning of the 20C, it was turned into a museum. It now contains paintings, sculptures, drawings, engravings and decorative arts, dating from the beginning of this century to the present. Most of the artists represented are Catalan. They include Fortuny, Martí Alsina, Vayreda, Casas, Rusiñol, Nonell, Mir, Gimeno, Sunyer, Llimona and Gargallo.

Music Museum (*Museo de la Música*)

(Av Diagonal, 373). The museum was set up in a Modernist building constructed in 1902 by the architect Puig i Cadafalch for the Baron of Quadras. It holds diverse collections of musical instruments, including one of the most complete **collections of guitars** in Europe.

Pedralbes Palace Museum (*Museo Palacio de Pedralbes*)

(Av Diagonal, 686). Like the Royal Palace, this museum was conceived when a pavilion belonging to the counts of Güell was expanded in 1925. It contains collections of decorative art, furniture and some interesting paintings. The palace is surrounded by splendid gardens with ornamental statues and small fountains. At one end of the garden you will find the **Carriage Museum** (*Museo de las Carrozas*).

Performing Arts, Museum of (*Museo de Artes del Espectáculo*)

(c/ Nou de la Rambla, 3 and 5). The **Güell Palace** is one of the masterpieces of the great architect Antonio Gaudí, and it contains a collection of all kinds of things related to the performing arts. Miniature theatres, scene props, backdrops, written memoirs of the Catalan Renaissance literary giants and other documents related to actors and singers. The collections of posters and puppet theatre programmes are especially interesting.

The Güell Palace marked the beginning of Gaudí's real creative flowering. You can see the architect's tastes —predominantly Gothic, interspersed with elements showing Arab influences— in the sober stone exterior façade and inside the building as well. The palace is visually striking, with the relationship of horizontal planes and vertical lines creating a very complex and fluid inner space. That space seems to converge on the main hall, which is open to the top of the building, where it is capped with a perforated cupola. The cupola emerges from the centre of a flat roof as a cone shape. It is covered with broken pieces of *azulejo* ceramic tiles topped by a wierd and wonderful landscape of capricious crennels, balustrades and multiform chimneys.

Perfume Museum (*Museo del Perfume*)

(Paseo de Gracia, 39).

● **Picasso Museum** (*Museo Picasso*)

(c/ Montcada, 15-17). Although you can find many vestiges of the 13C and 14C in the **Berenguer d'Aguilar Palace**, where this museum is located, its present appearance is due principally to the rehabilitation undertaken by the noble Joan Berenguer d'Aguilar in the 15C. It is believed that Marc Safont, who designed the façade of the Generalitat Palace ▶ *page* 17, may have had a hand in it as well. It is to the 15C that the central patio, marked off by an ogival arcade resting upon consoles, belongs. Like other houses along c/ Montcada, this mansion has suffered numerous changes and mutilations during the course of its life.

The museum includes works donated before the Spanish Civil War and others deriving from legacies and acquisitions that were in the custody of the Museum of Modern Art until 1960. When Jaume Sabartés donated more works, a separate building, the actual one, was adapted to lodge Picasso's work. It was inaugurated in 1963. Five years after the inauguration, Picasso himself donated the series called **Las Meninas**, in memory of his friend Sabartés, who had died the same year. In 1970 Picasso donated an extremely important group of works from his youth that had been kept by his family. Later the museum received numerous contributions from individuals. Particularly noteworthy are the 41 pieces of ceramic donated by Jacqueline Picasso in 1981.

Postal Museum (*Gabinete Postal*)

(La Rambla, 99, Palace of the Vicereine). The postal museum has an extensive collection of everything having to do with the mail.

Science, Museum of (*Museo de la Ciencia*)

(c/ Teodoro Roviralta, 35). The Science Museum is lodged in a structure built at the beginning of this century by the architect Domènech Estapa, and offers four permanent exhibitions on optics, space, perception and mechanics. There are two halls used for temporary exhibitions on all kinds of scientific topics.

Seminary Museum (*Museo del Seminario*)

(c/ Diputación, 231).

Textile and Clothing Museum (*Museo Textil y de la Indumentaria*)

(c/ Montcada, 12-14). This museum is in the **Marques de Llió and Nadal Palaces**, Gothic buildings begun in the 13C. It has collections of ancient articles (Egyptian and Hispano-Arabic) and textiles that range from the Gothic period up to the 20C. There are embroidered pieces and a good collection of liturgical garments, the oldest of them dating from the 13C. The collection of civilian clothing was donated by Manuel Rocamora i Vidal, and it features clothes and accessories from the 16C up to 1930.

Verdaguer House Museum (*Casa Museo Verdaguer*)

(Villa Joana, in Valvidrera). In the *Villa Joana*, where Mossen Jacint Verdaguer died, there is a collection of things the great Catalan poet held dear.

Wax Museum (*Museo de Cera*)

(Rambla, 4-6). This museum is lodged in a building that was constructed in the middle of the 19C and has maintained its original rich decorations. There are more than 300 wax figures on show in the museum.

Zoological Museum (*Museo de Zoología*)

The museum is in a modernistic building in Ciudadela Park, the work of the architect Domènech i Muntaner. It was constructed for the Universal Exhibition of 1888, and now contains a collection of stuffed animals.

Parks

Escorxador Park (*Parque del Escorxador*)

This park was inaugurated some time ago but is still in the final stages of completion. It is an enormous space presided over by an elevated esplanade. In the centre of the esplanade there is an ornamental lake with a sculpture by Joan Miró in the middle entitled *Dona i ocell*.

Güell Park (*Parque Güell*) ʘʘ

The problem faced by the great architect Antonio Gaudí consisted of combining a park with a housing development. At the entrance, Gaudí designed a plaza, a staircase and several pavilions that, together, represent one of the most capricious and imaginative combinations of architectural elements known. Natural and architectural aspects are combined artistically, with porticoes, terraces and a ceramic park bench —said to be the longest in the world— made with ceramics from Jujol. In order to ensure that these works did not conflict with the rocky and hilly landscape around them, stone from the area was used in a number of ways. The stone, of a brownish yellow colour, made a covering that in some cases was a smooth surface, but in others was a rough sheathing for columns and the undersides of vaulted ceilings. The place is impressive and is, really, more a geological formation than an architectural construction.

Industrial Spain Park (*Parque de la España Industrial*)

Next to the Pl de los Países Catalanes, this park was designed by Luis Peña Ganchegui. The park was conceived as a group of *modern Roman hot springs*, with a navigable lake as its central element.

Public Buildings

City Hall (*Casa de la Ciudad* or *Ayuntamiento*)

(Pl de San Jaime). This building was first constructed at the end of the 14C and since then has never stopped changing. The present-day look of the building is the result of endless renovations aimed at keeping the seat of the city government and administration up to date and in fashion.

City government took form in Barcelona during the 13C, when King James I granted the city an important privilege: town councillors, up to then appointed directly by the king, could choose their successors and name their advisers. These new rights led to the formation of the *Consejo de los Cien Jurados*, or Council of 100 Jurors (*Consell de Cent* in Catalan). The new council, with no quarters of its own, met at first in the Convent of Santa Catalina and later in the one of San Francisco.

The *Casa de la Ciudad* has a Neoclassical façade, a magnificent patio and staircase, the 15C ***Salón de Ciento*** (Room of the Hundred Jurors) and the ***Salón de las Cronicas*** (Room of the Chronicles), which was decorated by the architect Josep María Sert with black marble.

The paintings which hang on the walls of the building refer to the expeditions of the Catalans to the east in the 14C. The Trentenario door and the main meeting room of the building are singularly beautiful. The façade that faces the c/ Ciudad is part of the old medieval section, and is marked by its flamboyant Gothic style.

The statues that flank the main door, on the plaza, are of King James I, on the left, and the adviser Fivaller, on the right. It is worth going inside the building to take a look at the marble staircase, where you can see the early coat-of-arms of the city carved on the pillar of the banisters. This staircase was built in 1929 and is decorated with murals by Miquel Viladrich. In the vestibule, at the end of the stairs, is Josep Viladomat's sculpture, *Maternidad* (Motherhood).

The central portion of the main floor is taken up by the ***Salón de Ciento***, the meeting chamber of the Council of the Hundred Jurors. It was built in three well-differentiated stages: the Gothic work between 1369-1407, with some additions up to 1525; the Baroque portions, dating to 1628-1684; and modern renovations that were begun in 1848 and finished in 1929.

The room is rectangular in shape and the beamed ceiling is divided into three sections by two stone arches with exterior buttresses. In the 17C a very ornamental Baroque decorative composition was superimposed on the original Gothic designs. But the new decoration did not last long; with the war of the Succession in 1714, the municipal body and all its privileges disappeared. A bombardment in 1842 destroyed a large part of the roof of this salon and it had to be extensively restored. It was at this point that the chamber was enlarged with the addition of two more sections. The decoration you see in the hall today was done in 1925. The designers tried to keep a Gothic flavour in their work. They built a presidential podium and, at one end of the room, installed an alabaster sculpture. It is made in the manner of a retable and bears the city's coat-of-arms and images of the Virgin, Santa Eulalia and San Andrés.

Generalitat Palace (*Palacio de la Generalitat*)

(Pl de San Jaime). The first thing you see of this centre of the autonomous Catalan government is a very large patio with an open air staircase and a double gallery of arches, all finely wrought in the Gothic style. The palace is connected by a modern bridge to the old Casa de los Canonigos, or house of the canons. The building was begun during the reign of James II, when the Catalan Parliament was inaugurated. Take special note of the Chapel of San Jorge (St George), in the flamboyant Gothic style, a work whose construction was directed by Marc Safont between 1432 and 1435. In 1620, the interior of the chapel was remodelled and enlarged with the addition of vaults and a cupola with hanging capitals. Among the most valuable works here is the 15C figurine of **San Jorge** (St George).

The rear part of the building features the **Patio of the Orange Trees**, the construction of which began in 1532. The patio floor was originally made of blue and white *azulejos*, or ceramic tiles, but is now of Carrara marble. Looking up and to the left, one can see the belfry, where popular, old melodies are played at noon on a carillon. The Gothic façade, which faces the c/ Bisbe Irurita, is graced with the 15C medallion of St George. Other pieces worthy of mention include the ***Salón de San Jorge***, a room with a Renaissance door, and the ***Salón Dorado***, or Gilded Room, where the Proclamation of the Republic was signed. The main façade is in a Greco-Roman style and recalls the *Farnese Palace* in Rome. In the middle of the façade there is an equestrian statute of St. George (*Sant Jordi* in Catalan) by the sculptor Aleu.

La Lonja

(Paseo de Isabel II). This building is today the home of the Bourse (*Bolsa*), or Stock Exchange, of Barcelona. It has a central patio with allegorical statues but the real interest here lies in the site of the original Gothic parts, the room now known as the *Salón de Contrataciones*. To reach it go up the left part of the main staircase.

Post Office (*Correos*)

The architects Torres and Goday designed this building, which was constructed between 1919 and 1927. There are interesting *noucentisme* paintings exhibited in the central lobby, including works by Obiols, Galí and Canyelles.

Streets, Plazas and Markets

Berenguer el Grande, Plaza of (*Plaza de Berenguer el Grande*)

This plaza, lavishly and splendidly lit at night, contains a bronze statue of Ramón Berenguer III, by the sculptor José Llimona, surrounded by a garden of cypresses.

Boquería, Plaza of the (*Plaza de la Boquería*)

It was in this area during the 18C that the development of the Ramblas began with the decision to allow building on the walls of the area. Today it is paved with designs by Joan Miró. It has a neo-classical fountain and the Quadra building, by Vilaseca, decorated according to the tastes of the end of the last century.

Borne Market (*Mercado del Borne*)

(Paseo del Borne). The iron structure of this marketplace, characteristic of the 19C, is the work of Josep Fontseré. The old market is now a centre for cultural activities and public celebrations.

If you walk through the arches along the Paseo del Borne into the narrow streets that run off it, you will find many old neighbourhood institutions: the tinsmith's workshop, a home candy factory, the cider shop, bread ovens like those used long ago, coffee shops and more.

Carrer de Montcada

This street, lined with an array of stately palaces, was the centre of Barcelonan life from the 14C until the 18C. Its entire length was declared of historic interest in 1947.

Países Catalanes, Plaza of the (*Plaza de los Países Catalanes*)

Facing Sants station, this space was conceived according to the most modern standards, and has been visited by many international city planners as a result. An innovative and provocative meeting place, it was the first plaza to be built without gardens or other visual relief; instead it is wholly constructed of stone.

Real, Plaza of (*Plaza Real*)

Like many of the works of the 19C, the present plaza was built in part, by the Capuchins. A block of symmetrical buildings and arcades is decorated with ceramic motifs, representations of the sea, navigation and the American conquests. Recently remodelled, the plaza is one of the most picturesque spots in Barcelona, although there is a problem of delinquency in the area, especially at night. It is an ideal spot to have an aperitif and enjoy the Barcelonan sun after a walking tour of the curious shops under the arcades. Especially interesting are the *Herbolario del Rey*, a herbalist's shop, the Museum of Natural Sciences and the *Bacardí Passage*, a narrow street. The street lamps were designed by Gaudí and refurbished during the restoration of the plaza.

Rey, Plaza of (*Plaza del Rey*)

This is the finest plaza of old Barcelona. During one of the excavations of this site a **cemetery** dating from the early Christian era was discovered.

The present plaza and the site occupied by the Deputy's Palace (*Palacio del Lugarteniente*) once formed part of the courtyard facing the palace. Despite belonging to the **Royal Palace**, this plaza was for three centuries a commercial site where forage and straw were sold.

San Antonio Market (*Mercado San Antonio*)

(Ronda de San Pablo/Ronda de San Antonio). The outside galleries of this market are filled with a colourful array of practically everything imaginable, while inside there is a spectacular market of provisions. On Sundays the market becomes a centre for buying all kinds of goods.

San Jaime, Plaza of (*Plaza de San Jaime*)

This plaza constitutes the political heart of the city. Its present layout dates from 1823, when it was enlarged with the opening of Fernando and Jaime I streets and the building of a new façade for the City Hall, or *Casa de la Ciudad*. The Casa de la Ciudad faces the Generalitat Palace ▶ *page* 119, seat of the autonomous government of Catalonia. The shape of the plaza corresponds to the perpendicular intersection of the two Roman roads that gave birth to the city, and where the forum and market were in Roman times.

San José Market, or La Boquería (*Mercado de San José*)

(Rambla de San José). This building, which has just celebrated its 150th birthday, is one of the real landmarks of the Ramblas. It occupies the spot where a convent of the same name, since destroyed, stood long ago. It is a fine example of ironwork architecture and has ornamental façades.

Walls and Porticoes

Porticoes of Xifre (*Porticos de Xifre*)

In the area facing the Lonja, there are two blocks of neo-classical arcades that have been recently restored. The terracota medallions that adorn the façade are the work of Campeny. This is one of the most characteristic spots in the waterfront area.

The Walls (*Las Murallas*)

(Next to the Pl Nueva). The walled areas that still remain were built in the years 270 and 310. The perimeter of the walls was 1,270m, following a rectangular course, with the corners bevelled. They were situated so that the fortress faced the sea.

The protection offered by the old walls was reinforced by towers of a rectangular shape. The exceptions were those on the corners of the wall and those flanking city gates; they were polygonal or circular. The arrangement of the gates and other clues has allowed archaeologists to theorize that the interior of the city could have been organized as a *castrum*. The growth of the city over the 11C and 12C gave rise to the formation of settlements outside it called *bóries*, or *vilanoves*. They sprung up along roads leading out of the city, thus reducing the defensive military value of the walls. In the 13C, King James I allowed the old walls to be opened up to the countryside to facilitate new building.

POLICE AND SECURITY

The **police emergency number is 091**. The police are at your service: do not hesitate to ask for their help if you need it.

Public order in Spain is the responsibility of three different police groups, and they are all available to help the visitor ▶ *page* 154. The ***Polícia Municipal*** (municipal police) is principally responsible for traffic problems within the cities. This city police corps usually wears blue uniforms and white caps. The ***Policía Nacional*** (national police) wear brown. They protect public buildings and patrol urban areas. Their *comisarías*, or police stations, are seen in all major cities and provincial towns with populations of more than 20,000. The ***Guardia Civil*** (civil guard) polices rural areas, the coasts and customs, and is in charge of traffic surveillance and highway assistance. Their uniform is green with a visored cap of the same colour —or they will be wearing the traditional and celebrated tri-cornered, black patent-leather hat.

Never lose sight of your personal belongings; you could lose them. Do not leave anything of value lying about in your car, and lock the vehicle carefully when you leave it. Be especially careful with purses and handbags in cities and other built-up areas. Take care with car stereos as well: most Spaniards either cover them or have removable car radio cassettes that they take out of the car when they leave it unattended. Be equally careful with your luggage; in the event of any problem contact your consulate or the police. It is wise to have the number and date of issue of your passport noted down separately; this information is useful in speeding up the resolution of several problems.

It is accepted and quite normal to go **topless** on Spanish beaches, but that is not true in the interior. Be courteous and attentive to local sensibilities and you will avoid embarrassing situations. Most Spanish coastal cities have nudist beaches.

It is legal in Spain to possess up to 8g of **hashish**, or what the Spanish commonly call *chocolate* or *costo*. But having more than that can get you into serious trouble.

Hitch-hiking is not illegal in Spain, but it is quite rare except among some young people. It you do try hitch-hiking be sure to position yourself so that you do not interfere with traffic and so that anyone stopping can do so without danger to you or other traffic. Avoid the highways and, in general, hitch-hiking at night. A woman is strongly advised to hitch-hike only with a friend of the opposite sex.

RESTAURANTS

Barcelona offers as wide a choice of quality restaurants as one could ask of any large city. A total of more than 80 restaurants that will meet the most exacting gourmet's requirements guarantee Barcelona a place on any list of the world's best-fed cities. Consequently, a huge variety of foods from other countries is available, and the city is endowed with genuine examples of the many forms of Spanish cuisine. Furthermore, Barcelona is a permanent backdrop for the delights of Catalan cooking, which owes its excellence to the fine quality of its basic ingredients ▶ *page* 25 combined with the long and rich culinary tradition of the region.

Catalans, and Barcelonans in particular, are known for their demanding palate. They are also great sticklers for quality service. You will soon discover that the restaurants of the region display a personality of their own, much of it the result of their customers' taste and demanding nature.

All the establishments listed in the following section should meet the requirements of the traveller in terms both of culinary quality and of aesthetic and social attributes. The selection can only serve as a guide, however, among the hundreds of worthwhile restaurants that the city has to offer. New restaurants appear daily while older, established ones change hands or chefs, so no listing can hope to be complete.

Balsa, La

☆☆☆☆ c/ Infante Isabel, 4 ✉ 08022 ☎ 211 50 48 $$$$.
In summer, a midday buffet is served with a variety of salads. Dining on the *terraza*, or terrace, is especially pleasurable here. The clientele is chic. The dishes offered are as original as the establishment. A very pleasant ambience.

Gran Café, El

☆☆☆☆ (Closes on Sundays) c/ Avinyó, 9 ☎ 318 79 86 $ to $$.
French cuisine and Catalan specialities such as *magret* of duck and chickpeas with mushrooms or *moixernons*. Lovely, modern decoration in what used to be an old sewing machine establishment.

Orotava

☆☆☆☆ (Closes on Sunday and during lunch hours) c/ Consejo de Ciento, 335 ☎ 302 31 28 All major credit cards accepted $$$.
French cuisine. High quality food, luxurious atmosphere, and prices to match. Specializes in game dishes.

Reno

☆☆☆☆ (Open 1/1-31/7 and 1/9-31/12) c/ Tuset, 27 ✉ 08006 ☎ 200 91 29 $$$$.

Classic Spanish cuisine, cooked and served with elegance. One of the best restaurants in Spain.

Aitor

☆☆☆ (Closes on Sundays, Easter Week, 15/8-15/9 and on Christmas) c/ Carbonell, 5 ☎ 319 94 88 V $$.

This is the ideal place for trying traditional Basque dishes like *marmitako* or *lomos de merluza con salsa de chipirones* (hake with squid sauce). Excellent Rioja wines.

Amaya

☆☆☆ (Open 1/1-31/12) c/ Ramblas, 20-24 ✉ 08002 ☎ 302 10 37 $$$.

Solid cuisine. Very good Catalan beans and sea bream cooked in the oven or in the *donostiarra*, or San Sebastián, style.

Azulete

☆☆☆ Vía Augusta, 281 ✉ 08017 ☎ 203 59 43 $$$$.

The cooking is irregular but always stylish and distinctive. A very pleasant terrace, long wine list and ample parking space. Although it is located some distance from downtown Barcelona and the night life districts, it is a popular gathering spot for the fashionable.

Botafumeiro

☆☆☆ (Open 1/1-31/7 and 1/8-31/12), c/ Mayor de Gracia, 81 ✉ 08017 ☎ 217 96 42 $$$$.

Tasty Galician meat pies and croquettes. Excellent shellfish in what may be Barcelona's best shellfish restaurant. The hurried visitor may want to try the oysters at the bar, along with some Ribeiro or Alvarinho Galician wine.

Can Culleretes

☆☆☆ c/ Quintana, 5 ✉ 08002 ☎ 317 64 85 $$$.

The doyen of Barcelonan restaurants, with two centuries of tradition behind it. A temple of Catalan cooking whose daily specials are the most interesting dishes to try.

Caracoles, Los

☆☆☆ c/ Escudellers, 14 ✉ 08002 ☎ 302 31 85 $$$.

Paellas, exquisite mussels and chicken *al ast* are the most popular dishes at this very busy restraurant.

Casa Isidre

☆☆☆ (Closes in August) c/ Flores, 12 ✉ 08001 ☎ 241 11 39 $$$$.

A small and nicely decorated place, it is a prestigious and traditional spot for Catalan food. Excellent game dishes. Very good meat and mushrooms in season.

Dorada, La

☆☆☆ c/ Travesera de Gracia, 44-46 ✉ 08006 ☎ 200 63 22 $$$$.

A great spot for Andalusian cuisine. Small fried fish, shellfish and stews are especially good. Fresh ingredients.

Gran Duca

☆☆☆ (Closes in August) Paseo Nuestra Señora del Coll, 16 ✉ 08023 ☎ 210 32 05 $$$.

The best imaginative Italian cooking. Dishes are constantly being changed and varied.

Finisterre

☆☆☆ Av Diagonal, 469 ☎ 239 55 76 DC, MC, V $$$$$.

A gastronomic institution. It serves both Catalan and continental dishes.

Flash-Flash

☆☆☆ (Closes in August) c/ La Granada, 25 ✉ 08005 ☎ 237 09 90 $$$.

An almost infinite variety of *tortillas*, or cold omelettes, and excellent fresh salads. Agreeable ambience. A gathering place for well-known Barcelonans.

Florian

☆☆☆ (Open 1/1-31/7 and 1/9-31/12) c/ Bertrand i Serra, 20 ✉ 08022 ☎ 212 46 27 $$$$.

An ideal establishment to try Catalan mushrooms when they are in season. Nevertheless, it also has an excellent range of bull-meat stews and Italian salads, along with traditional Catalan and Spanish dishes. A fine wine list.

Giardinetto Notto

☆☆☆ (Closes in August) c/ La Granada, 22 ✉ 08005 ☎ 218 75 36 $$$$.

A suitable place to dine after midnight in a *chic* environment.

Guría

☆☆☆ (Closes two weeks in August) c/ Casanova, 97-99 ☎ 253 63 25 AE, DC, MC, V $$$.

The most classic and luxurious of good Basque restaurants in Barcelona. The menu offers and exquisite *txangurro*, garnished king crab in its shell, or green peppers stuffed with squid. Excellent wine list.

Lagunak

☆☆☆ (Closes in August) c/ Berlín, 19-21 ☎ 322 12 56 Ⓟ ✱ EC, MC, V $$$$$.

Basque-Navarran cuisine. Excellent quality ingredients which are painstakingly prepared into delicious dishes.

Mascaró de Proa, El

☆☆☆ (Closes on Sunday nights and Mondays) c/ Doctor Dou, 2, Carmen, 40 ☎ 317 06 99 MC, V $$.

If you ask for braised fish, such as sea bass stuffed with oysters and Norway lobster, you can expect a wonderful meal. Green vegetables are also excellent.

Olivé, L'

☆☆☆ c/ Muntaner, 171 ✉ 08036 ☎ 230 90 27 $$$$.

Family cooking and traditional Catalan dishes served in a simple, small and pleasant dining room that is always full. The terrace is a pleasure during the summer.

Puñalada, La

☆☆☆ Paseo de Gracia, 104 ✉ 08008 ☎ 218 47 91 $$$$.

Popular and traditional restaurant whose name literally means the stabbing. Catalan dishes are much in demand here, especially chickpeas and broad beans and *butifarras amb monxetes*, a dish based on Catalan sausages.

Quo Vadis

☆☆☆ (Closes on Sundays) c/ Carmen, 7 ☎ 317 74 47 AE, DC, MC, V $$.

High quality dishes made from excellent foodstuffs. The sea bass with fennel is one of their incomparable specialities.

Recó de l'Arnau, El

☆☆☆ (Closes on Sundays) c/ Tapias, 21 (Paralelo) ☎ 329 81 53 AE, EC, MC, V $.

Seasonal tasty home-made cooking. The restaurant enjoys a regular clientele of theatre personalities among others. An old and pleasant dining room. The stuffed squid and the cream of tender garlic are marvellous.

Solera Gallega

☆☆☆ c/ París, 176 ✉ 08036 ☎ 322 91 40 $$$.

Good Galician specialities, especially the turbot, *rodaballo*, that is served in a number of ways. The somewhat cloudy house wine is quite good.

Tramonti

☆☆☆ (Closes in August) Av Diagonal, 501 ☎ 250 15 35 AE, MC, V $.

This establishment's cuisine derives from the Italian region of Liguria, but it is not limited to pastas. The basil sauces are very good. The wines are also Ligurian. Some of the better dishes are *filetto in scatola*, Ligurian *panzerotti* and marvellous *arrosto di vitello*. Very good ice cream as well.

Tritón

☆☆☆ (Closes on Sundays, holidays and Easter) c/ Alfambra, 16 ☎ 203 30 85 MC, V $$.

The kitchen's food is not easily classified, but its dishes are magnificent. Basque and Catalan dishes, as well as popular and traditional local foods are offered. In season, game dishes are also good.

Túnel de Muntaner, El

☆☆☆ (Closes in August) c/ San Mario, 32 ☎ 212 60 74 Ⓟ ✱ AE, MC, EC, 6.000, V $$$$$.

Good Catalan cuisine and wine list.

Venta, La

☆☆☆ (Closes on Sundays) Pl Doctor Andreu, s/n (Tibidabo) ☎ 212 64 55.

Attractive restaurant due to its three open air terraces, its privileged location on the slopes of the Tibidabo and its *nouvelle cuisine* featuring good fresh fish and fine desserts.

Vía Veneto

☆☆☆ (Closes in August) c/ Gauduxer, 10-12 ✉ 08021 ☎ 200 70 24 All major credit cards accepted $$$$.

This restaurant, one of the most elegant places in the city, boasts a very imaginative cuisine. Good atmosphere and truly great service. Try the excellent cod and the black rice.

Agut

☆☆ (Closes in July) c/ Gignas, 16 ✉ 08002 ☎ 218 42 30 $$$.

Simple and authentic Catalan food served. Popular ambience.

Agut d'Avignon

☆☆ c/ Trinitar, 3 ☎ 302 60 34 AE, DC, MC, V $$$.

A classic Barcelonan restaurant for some time now, it offers Basque, Catalan and Provençal cuisine.

Alt Berlín

☆☆ c/ Sabino de Arana, 54 ☎ 339 01 66 AE, DC, MC, 6000, V $$.

Excellent representative of German cuisine. Solid and nutritious dishes.

Antigua Casa Solé

☆☆ (Closes 1/2-15/2 and 1/9-15/9) c/ San Carlos, 4 ☎ 319 50 12 ✱ $$$.

An establishment that has been functioning for nearly 90 years, this restaurant has always dedicated itself to the products of the sea.

Años Locos, Los
☆☆ (Closes 15/8-31/8) c/ Mariano Cubí, 85 ✉ 08006 ☎ 209 69 15 $$$.
Excellent Argentinian cuisine.

Ara-Cata
☆☆ (Closes on Saturdays and holiday nights, August and Easter) c/ Dr. Ferrán 33 ☎ 204 10 53 AE, DC, MC, 6000, V $$.
Catalan cooking is combined with French specialities. Excellent desserts.

Asador Zure-Etxea Casa Alcalde
☆☆ (Closes in August) c/ Jorge Girona Salgado, 10 ☎ 203 83 90 ✱ V $$$$.
Basque cuisine specializing in fish and meat.

Bali
☆☆ (Closes Mondays at midday) located next to the amusement park in Montjuïc ☎ 241 36 09 and 241 30 84 AE, DC, MC, V $$.
Indonesian cooking and aphrodisiac cocktails.

El Barkito, El Pescadito Frito
☆☆ (Closes on Mondays and 7/8-21/8) c/ Córcega, 225 ☎ 230 51 60 EC, MC, V $$.
Good Andalusian food based on small fried or grilled fish. Cooking is done within sight of the customers. Pleasant terrace.

Braserie Flo
☆☆ c/ Junqueras, 10 ☎ 317 80 37 V $.
A very varied menu ranging from *sauerkraut* to *bouillabaisse* and game dishes. Late dining.

Cal Pinxo
☆☆ (Open 1/1-31/12) Playa San Miguel, s/n, Barceloneta ✉ 08003 ☎ 310 45 13 $$$.
Home cooking with fresh produce. Surprisingly good rice dishes. The *cazuela*, a type of casserole, is one of its specialities and is always good.

Can Juanito
☆☆ (Closes in August) c/ Ramón y Cajal, 3 ✉ 08012 ☎ 213 30 43 $$$.
Whatever you eat here, have it with *pan amb tomaquet*, or bread with tomato.

Can Majó
☆☆ (Closes in August) c/ Almirante Aixada, 23 ☎ 310 14 55 ✱ DC, MC, V $$$$.
One of the best restaurants in Barceloneta. Good shellfish.

Can Massana
☆☆ (Closed Wednesdays and Sunday nights) Pl del Camp, 6 ☎ 417 06 74 No credit cards $.
A truly popular restaurant where Catalan dishes are cooked in a traditional style: *sanfaina* accompanies a variety of dishes. Rabbit and cod fish are some of the most popular meals offered here.

Casa Agustín
☆☆ c/ Vergara and Balmes, s/n ✉ 08002 $$$.
Very good Catalan cuisine. Delicious milk-fed lamb, good wines and cordial service.

Casa Costa
☆☆ c/ Baluarte, 124 ☎ 319 50 28 AE, DC, MC, 6000, V $$$$.
One of the most famous establishments in Barceloneta. Good fish and shellfish.

Casa Jacinto
☆☆ (Closes 7/8-31/8) Av Carlos III, 29-31 ☏ 339 00 23 $$$$.
Basque and Navarran Cooking. Good sea food.

Casa Leopoldo
☆☆ (Closes on Sunday nights, Mondays, Easter and in August) c/ San Rafael, 24 ☏ 241 30 14 AE, MC, 6000, V $$.
Almost 60 years ago this simple and unpretentious place was a winery. Today it offers excellent fish and other foods cooked with great simplicity. One of the specialities is the Catalan tripe dish known as *Callos a la catalana.*

Centollo, El
☆☆ (Open 1/1-31/12) c/ Mosellón, 204 ✉ 08008 ☏ 215 83 67 $$$.
This restaurant offers anything from oysters and crabs to Andalusian eggs in vinaigrette sauce. Incomparable Galician house wine. Outstanding are the warming Galician soups and the Santiago cake.

Chicoa
☆☆ c/ Aribau, 71-73 ✉ 08036 ☏ 253 11 23 $$$.
Catalan cooking. Try the tender onions, the famous spring *calçot*, the shrimps in garlic or the codfish prepared in a number of different ways. Pleasant atmosphere and decoration.

Ciboulette, La
☆☆ (Closes on Sundays and Monday afternoons) c/ Camp, 63 ☏ 417 21 22 V $$.
In fashion for its novelty and the style of its decoration. Classic French cooking and some novel dishes of its own. Excellent desserts.

Dida, La
☆☆ c/ Roger de Flor, 230 ☏ 207 20 04 Ⓟ ✱ AE, DC, MC, V $$$$.
Good Catalan cuisine.

Eldorado Petit
☆☆ (Open 1/1-30/7 and 1/9-31/12) c/ Dolors Montserdá, 51 ✉ 08017 ☏ 204 51 53 $$$$.
Nouvelle cuisine is offered along with traditional fare. Palamós shrimps are served in an original dish that is superb. Other highly recommended dishes include *pimientos del piquillo rellenos de centollo* (stuffed green peppers), *calamares salteados* (lightly sautéed squid), and the fish *suquet* that is served in the Costa Brava style. Good wine list and splendid service. Very attractive garden and terrace, easy parking. One of the best restaurants in Spain.

Equus
☆☆ c/ Travesera de Gracia, 86 ☏ 237 51 33 ✱ DC, MC, V $$$$.

Estevet
☆☆ (Closes on Sundays) c/ Valldonzella, 46 ☏ 302 41 86 V $.
An interesting establishment offering popular dishes in a simple menu. It nevertheless includes such exquisite dishes as *buñuelos con bacalao* (fritters with cod), *fricandó* and a vegetable omelette with *allioli* sauce.

Garduña, La
☆☆ (Closes on Sundays) c/ Morera, 19 ☏ 302 43 23 All major credit cards accepted $.
Located in the La Boquería market, this restaurant uses fine fresh products in its cuisine. Closes late at night. The ham hock and the fish *zarzuela* are very attractive.

Gargantúa y Pantagruel
☆☆ (Closes on Sundays) c/ Aragón, 214 ☎ 253 20 20 All major credit cards accepted $.
Good, Lérida-style cuisine in an unpretentious establishment. Snails are cooked in a thousand different ways here.

Gorria
☆☆ (Closes on Sundays and 1/8-31/8) c/ Diputación, 421 ☎ 245 11 64 AE, DC, MC, 6000, V $$.
A great restaurant featuring Navarran and Basque cooking based on first rate products.

Govinda
☆☆ Pl Villa de Madrid, 4 and 5 ☎ 318 77 29 $$$.
Indian restaurant specializing in Tandoori chicken. Pleasant atmosphere and good service.

Hoy
☆☆ c/ Travesera de las Corts, 281 ☎ 230 00 79 ✱ $$$.
Very good quality Chinese cooking. Service is agreeable and attentive. Frequented by the Chinese residents of the city.

Indret, L'
☆☆ c/ Ganduxer, 31 08021 ☎ 201 65 08 $$$.
A restaurant-café-charcuterie and tea room, this modern spot offers unforgettable ham (*virutas de jamón*) and exquisite smoked salmon accompanied by good cava wines. You can eat in the dining room or at the bar.

Jaume de Provença
☆☆ (Open 1/1-31/7 and 1/9-31/12) c/ Provença, 88 08029 ☎ 230 00 29 $$$$.
Imagination and products of excellent quality combine to offer the diner impeccable cuisine. Pleasant atmosphere.

Mató de Pedralbes, El
☆☆ c/ Obispo Catalá, 19 ☎ 204 79 62 Ⓟ ✱ $$$.
Good traditional Catalan cuisine.

Neichel
☆☆ (Closed on Sundays, holidays, Easter, August and Christmas) Av Pedralbes, 16, bis ☎ 203 84 08 AE, DC, MC, V $$$.
Select French cuisine with a large number of unusual dishes bearing extremely long names, such as *cazuelita de pastas frescas, bogavante y cigalas gratinada*, but which are explained there. The food is excellent, as are the desserts. It is considered one of the best restaurants in the city.

Odisea, La
☆☆ (Closes on Sundays, during Easter and August) c/ Copons, 7 ☎ 302 36 92 AE, V $$.
Refined and imaginative cuisine. Some examples are the sea bass with oysters and black olives or the camembert cheese coated in a tomato paste.

Perols de l'Empordá, Els
☆☆ (Closes 15/8-31/8) c/ Villaroel, 88 08011 ☎ 323 10 33 $$$.
Masterly presentation of the cuisine of l'Empordá. Very good *butifarra* sausages.

Ponsa
☆☆ (Closes 15/7-15/8) c/ Enrique Granados, 89 ☎ 253 10 37 $$$$.
Open since the beginning of this century, this establishment offers Catalan home cooking.

Rey del Pescadito, El

☆☆ (Closes in July) c/ Valencia and c/ Aribau, s/n ✉ 08008 $$.
All sorts of fried fish and marinated dogfish.

Roig Robí

☆☆ (Closes 15/8-31/8) c/ Séneca, 20 ✉ 08006 ☎ 218 92 22 $$$.
Catalan cuisine. It is a true delight to eat on this restaurant's terrace during the summer. Try whatever the special of the day is, along with one of the specialties which the cooks are so proud of, for example, the *arros negré* (black rice), *fideus rossos* (a noodle dish) and the incredible Roig Robí hake, perhaps the most original dish in all Barcelona. Good wines and good service in a stylish and modern decor.

Rosa del Desierto, La

☆☆ (Closes on Sundays and holidays) Pl Narcís Oller, 7 ☎ 237 45 90 AE, DC, MC, V $.
One of the oldest Arab restaurants in Barcelona. Its speciality is Moroccan cooking, with such characteristic dishes as *tajine*, *cous cous real* and a range of desserts based on almonds, honey and puff pastry.

Sant Jordi

☆☆ (Closes in August) c/ Travesera de Dalt, 123 ☎ 213 10 37 AE, DC, MC, V $$$$.
Catalan dishes. Good value for money. Game dishes are especially good during the hunting season.

Satélite

☆☆ (Closes on Sundays and holiday nights, Saturdays from 30/6-30/9 and Easter) Av Sarriá, 10 ☎ 321 34 31 AE, MC, 6000, V $$.
High quality Catalan cuisine. Well prepared dishes and pleasant service in a hospitable environment. Hake with caviar is one of its specialities.

Senyor Parellada

☆☆ (Open 1/1-31/7 and 1/9-31/12) c/ Argentería (Platería), 37 ✉ 08003 ☎ 315 40 10 $$$.
Customers here are extremely fond of the house's game stews and fish. Among the latter the *guti*, hake combined with pig's feet and reserved for those with a taste for strong food, stands out. The house wine is acceptable; the wine list is somewhat short, but it includes a good selection of sparkling cava wines at good prices. Original desserts. Parking at the corner.

Siete Puertas

☆☆ (Open 1/1-31/12) c/ Isabel II, 14 ✉ 08003 ☎ 319 30 33 $$$$.
This charming restaurant, over 150 years old, is extremely popular and prestigious. Its menu is restricted to Catalan dishes prepared with carefully selected ingredients. The portions are generous and the rice dishes are perfect.

Soupe a l'Oignon, La

☆☆ c/ Padúa, 60 ☎ 212 77 42 MC, V $$$.
Some of the best classic French dishes in Barcelona.

Swan

☆☆ (Closes on Sunday nights) c/ Diputación, 269, Paseo de Gracia, 32 ☎ 302 61 29 All major credit cards accepted $$.
Quality Cantonese cuisine.

Taj Mahal
☆☆ (Closes on Mondays) c/ Londres, 89 ☏ 322 32 33 AE, DC, MC, V $.
This was the first indian restaurant in Barcelona. The mild and aromatic cooking is from the north of India. All dishes are prepared in a clay oven fed with coal. Specializes in *Tandoori* dishes. Lamb and chicken prepared in a thousand ways.

Tiró Mimet
☆☆ (Closes in August) c/ Ros de Olano, 11 ✉ 08012 ☏ 237 75 37 $$$.
Everything in this restaurant centres around duck.

Troballa, La
☆☆ (Closes in August) c/ Riera San Miguel, 69 ✉ 08006 ☏ 217 34 52 $$.
Simple and unpretentious menu. The terrace is a delight in the summer. It is wise to make table reservations for dinner.

Túnel
☆☆ (Closes on Sunday nights and Mondays) c/ Ample, 33-35 ☏ 315 27 59 No credit cards $$.
In this restaurant the diner may taste what many believe are the best *cannelonni* in Barcelona. They come in recipes as incredible as that which includes a cream of truffles. The fried fish, especially the red mullet, are very good. Simple but perfect cooking, based on extraordinarily good ingredients.

Yamadori
☆☆ c/ Aribau, 68 ✉ 08008 ☏ 263 92 64 $$$.
Japanese restaurant with a refined and exclusive tone. You should not leave without trying their *shashimi*, or raw fish. There is a private dining room for eating at low tables with chopsticks.

Cal Pep
☆ (Closed in August) c/ Espadería, 9 ✉ 08003 ☏ 319 17 27 $$.
Very fresh sea food.

Can Buj
☆ (Closes 15/8-15/9) c/ Provenza, 73 ☏ 250 13 14 MC, V $$$$.
Catalan dishes at good prices.

Egipto
☆ c/ Jerusalén, 12 ✉ 08001 ☏ 317 74 80 $$.
Catalan seasonal dishes in a somewhat Bohemian environment.

Raco d'en Jaume
☆ (Closes in August) c/ Provenza, 98 ☏ 239 78 61 ✱ $$$.
Catalan home cooking.

Vegetariano
☆ (Open 1/1-31/12) c/ Santa Anna, 11-13 ✉ 08002 $$.
Economical and high quality self-service restaurant.

SHOPPING

If there is one temptation you won't be able to resist in Barcelona it is shopping. This creative city, rich in fashion and design, offers just about every imaginable thing for sale. Take your time; put on a comfortable pair of shoes, stroll the streets of the city and take advantage of the marvellous bargains here —in virtually every case, you will find the prices here far lower than in any other Western European metropolis. No one will rush you; on the contrary, you will find that the shopkeepers are friendly and full of useful tips and information.

Barcelonans are famous for jealously protecting the traditional, but at the same time accepting without fuss all that is new and interesting. The multi-faceted but prudent qualities of Catalan commerce are based on a cosmopolitan and open-minded attitude to the most contemporary fashions and ideas. The liveliness and variety of the shops here will surprise even the most seasoned traveller.

The oldest and most traditional objects are sold just a few metres away from the places that offer the boldest, most modern items. Shops featuring the newest fashions and the most sophisticated designs sit side-by-side with those where the most classic and traditional clothes are for sale. To shop in Barcelona, then, is to explore an incredibly wide variety of tastes, styles and price ranges.

Near the port of Barcelona, facing the Post Office and before the Estación de Francia, there is an area of three or four blocks where the visitor will find the bazaar (*zoco*), a type of permanent Moroccan marketplace in Barcelona. Just about everything is sold here, but there is a particular abundance of electronic goods and gold and silver items. From the port to the Pl de Cataluña, the Ramblas is the exciting and world-famous artery of retail trade, a colourful thoroughfare replete with a variety of offerings —multi-coloured parrots squawking loudly in outdoor stalls, establishments specializing in making copies of antique arms, departament stores, and a beautiful old market selling food products that are no less attractive. Variety is the rule in the narrow little streets that run from the Ramblas to the Vía Layetana where, around the Pl de Cataluña and the Puerta del Angel, there are a number of large **department stores**.

But if you are looking for something a little more select, the best option is to walk out of the Pl de Cataluña by way of the **Paseo de Gracia**. This large avenue, from its beginning to where it meets Av Diagonal, is one continuous —and very smart— shop window. The displays here show the most elegant products in Barcelona: high **fashion for men and women, high-priced jewelry, beautifully made fur and leather products**, perfumes and cosmetics made by the best-known firms in the world —all this and more is found along this route. Walking further, into the streets that run perpendicular to the left side of Paseo de Gracia, you will find yourself in a different kind of shopping area. Here, one finds a variety of very **modern clothes, shoes, decorative objects** and more. Try looking, in particular, **between Aragón and Valencia streets**. This is where you will find the most *in* styles in all Barcelona.

Very reasonably-priced modern fashions will be found as you walk out into the **Rambla de Cataluña**; and alongside these stores is a wide selection of **galleries selling art works**. The stretch of **Av Diagonal between Paseo de Gracia and Pl Francesc Macià**, and the small streets to the north, are a similar kind of shopping district, offering modern, high-quality goods. It is an area of boutiques and fashion shops, jewelry, hairdressing salons and design stores. Along with the upper part of **c/ Muntaner**, this is the main centre for shops selling modem fashions, a place where good taste prevails.

As a counterpoint, the narrow and animated plazas of the Gracia neighbourhood offer a traditional but varied kind of shopping, far removed from the dictates of modernity but full of charm for those who like to walk city streets. And for the visitor who loves **antiques** or merely things that are old, Barcelona has a flea market known as ***Els Encants***. The market, located in an area around Pl de las Glorias, is a world of shops selling everything from second-hand clothes to handicrafts. The place is teeming with humanity on Mondays, Wednesdays, Fridays and Saturdays. Nearby is an area that specializes in furniture. One word of warning: haggling is not just a ritual in this flea market, it is a virtual necessity.

Stamp and coin collectors will find a stamp and coin market in the Pl Real on Sunday mornings. The area is full of bars and the visitor should not miss the opportunity to try out some of their tasty snacks. Also on Sunday mornings, next to the San Antonio market, there is a smaller market for books and old magazines. It's not unusual to find rare **old editions** of both types of publications here. A few metres away, on the corner of c/ Urgel, there is a bar with what many Barcelonans say are the best clams and anchovies in the city.

The visitor looking for do-it-yourself home decorations and furnishings will find a true supermarket of such goods in Barcelona, selling all the materials and tools needed. It is located at c/ Aragón, 270, near the corner of Paseo de Gracia ☎ 216 02 12.

Antiques

The so-called *Gothic Market* of antiques is held every Thursday in the Pl Nova. You can find interesting antiques in the streets of Call, the area around the Cathedral and in large parts of the Ensanche and the high part of Barcelona. On the Rambla de Cataluña, at the top of c/ Provença, there is a gallery with very well preserved objects and other items that have been restored.

Antigüedades Barón, c/ Banys Nous, 18. Furniture, ceiling lamps, paintings, chairs and statues.

Centro de Anticuarios, Paseo de Gracia, 55. There are 73 professional antique establishments here. They buy, sell and give valuations.

Gothsland, c/ Consell de Cent, 331, between c/ Balmes and Rambla de Catalunya. This was the first European gallery to specialize in Modernism. Sculptures by Clara, Llimona and others, console tables, chairs, tables and umbrella stands. Paintings by Ramón Casas, Urgell, Masriera, Gimeno and others.

Gremi d'Antiquaris de Catalunya, c/ Roselló, 233 ☎ 237 96 56.

Las Dos Coronas c/ Aragón, 511. Paintings, furniture, clocks and bronzes.

Las Ninfas, Paseo de Gracia, 55, shop 13. Shop specializing in Modernism, Art Nouveau and Art Deco.

Pasaje, c/ Mallorca, 237 bis. English furniture, bronze items, paintings and rugs. Also an art gallery.

Santiago Martí, c/ Provença, 243. Besides a collection of antiques, there is interesting art work and jewelry.

Trallero y Sitjas, c/ Aragón, 530. Interesting sculpture and furniture acquired from old, well-to-do Catalan families.

Verd-House, c/ Mallorca, 243. English-style furniture and pieces with cane-work predominate here.

Auction houses specializing in antiques and artistic objects include *Balcli's*, c/ Rosellón, 227; *Subarna*, c/ Provenza, 257, *Master's*, c/ Córcega, 299 and *Prestige*, c/ Valencia, 272.

Art Galleries

There are approximately 50 art galleries in Barcelona. The largest concentration of them is found around c/ Consejo de Ciento, between c/ Balmes and the Rambla de Cataluña. Numerous artists and art enthusiasts frequent the area between 7.00 and 9.00 p.m. Some gallery names enjoy international prestige —for example those of *Maeght, Pares, René Metras, Gaspar, Joan Prats, Dau al Set and Theo.* You will find complete listings and notices of art shows in the *Guía del Ocio* weekly, the *El País* newspaper and other local publications ▶ *page* 96.

Commercial Galleries

There is a commercial formula that has been much exploited in recent years in Spain: the grouping of shops selling similar styles in a small area. They enjoy a privileged location and have become favourite meeting places for Barcelona residents.

Besides the Galerías Maldá, a number of these shopping centres are located in different parts of the city. But the best known and busiest centres are the Avenida Centre, which only recently opened, the Boulevard Rosa, Diagonal Centre, Halley Centre, Urgell Centre and, recently, the Turo Centre.

Boulevard Rosa, Paseo de Gracia, 55. This establishment takes its name from the old Salon Rosa, a tea salon with outlets on the Rambla, c/ Aragón and c/ Valencia. It consists of shops like *Torrens, Succeso* and *Barbas* for men; and highly specialized shops like *Tokio,* a shop that specializes in stockings and bikinis, the *Pepa Paper* stationer's, the *Spleen* costume jewelry shop, the *Marcel* hairdressing salon and *Efectos Especiales,* which many think sells the finest hats in Barcelona. The display of shoes is exemplary —among others, try *Zambo* for women, *Ruis* for children and *Tascon* for men.

Diagonal Center, Av Diagonal, 584. A pioneer of this commercial formula, it features shops for men like *Paul Newman*; shoe shops like *Vermont*; children clothing shops like *Confetti*; items for women are concentrated in *Bambú, Raena* (bathing suits), *Le Sac* (handbags) and *Tentación* (corsets and underwear).

Galerías Avenida, Rambla de Cataluña, 121. It features shops for women like *Choses Bis, Marta Luque, Francisco Valiente, Cocktail, Barcelona Línea, Nola Zoo, Black Jack, Olga Martínez* and *La Blusa*; men's fashion in *Newman, Balil, Epta 7* and *Barbas*; unisex shops like *St. Trop* and *Benetton*; linen shops with finely worked goods like *Campos de Ibiza* (specializing in bathrobes) and fur and leather shops like *Isabel Canal.* There is also a well-attended bar-restaurant for the customers' convenience.

Costumes and Disguises

Capistros, c/ Mallorca, 246. Open only in the morning.

El Carnaval, c/ Diputación, 100. ☎ 325 07 12. All types of masks and articles for parties. Children's costumes.

El Ingenio, c/ Rauric, 8 ☎ 317 71 38. Costumes for hire.

Estapé, c/ Aribau, 188 ☎ 209 95 69. Articles for *fiestas* and disguises.

Jover, c/ Cardenal Casañas, 14 ☎ 317 89 93. Jewelry, feathers and other accessories for costumes.

Menkes, c/ Gran Vía, 646 ☎ 318 86 47. All kinds of costumes.

Peris, c/ Junta de Comercio, 19 ☎ 301 27 48. Items for rent. Tailoring for theatre and movie costumes.

Wileme, c/ Casanova, 29 ☎ 254 51 20. Regional costumes and disguises for children.

Department stores

El Corte Inglés, Pl de Catalunya, 14 ☎ 301 32 56; c/ Ausías March, 38 and 40; c/ Bolivia, 234; Av Catedral, 17; Av Diagonal, 617 and

Gran Vía de les Cortes Catalanes, 613. El Corte Inglés forms part of the small elite of major department stores of London, New York, Paris and Tokyo. Extremely popular in Spain, its many branch stores offer an enormous selection of goods, from the cheapest pen to high international fashion, from records and books to the most complex stereo equipment and computers. It has restaurants and cafés and it is an excellent place to go food shopping. It also offers a wide gamut of services like a travel agency, mailing of purchases to the customer's home and, if the customer is a foreigner, tax exemption for any item bought that will be taken out of the country.

Galerías Jorba Preciados, Av Diagonal, 471; Av Mare Deu Montserrat, 39; Av Meridiana, 352; Av Portal l'Angel, 19 and c/ Valencia, 527. This is the other major Spanish department store. With similar characteristics to those of its competitor, Galerías Preciados' new owners are undertaking a major rehabilitation following the store's decline some years back.

Design

B.D. Ediciones de Diseño, c/ Mallorca, 291. An exceptional shop, and not only because of the modern building by architect Domenech i Muntaner in which it is located. It offers the finest quality design furniture, comparable with the best products of Spain and the world.

Dos i Una, c/ Rosellón, 275. Objects for daily use, imaginatively designed in the most up-to-date styles.

Insòlit, Av Diagonal, 353. It is not unusual for the browser to find rare objects here. Imagination and the most *avant garde* designs are the norm in this shop.

Roche Bobois, c/ Muntaner, 266.

Everything on fashion (a Tony Miró design)

Fashion

Adolfo Domínguez, Paseo de Gracia, 89 and c/ Valencia, 245 (shop 14). The best-known new Spanish designer in the world.

Andrés Andreu, c/ Córcega, 261.

Aramis, Rambla de Cataluña, 183.

Avioneta, Paseo de Gracia, 55, Boulevard Rosa.

Bebelín, Paseo de Gracia, 39; c/ Consejo de Ciento, 298 and c/ Tenor Viñas, 5.

Bis and *Bis de Bis,* Paseo de Gracia, 55, Boulevard Rosa. Women's shoes and clothes by Teresa Ramallal.

Boa, c/ Ros de Olano, 8 (Gracia). Clothes and modern accessories.

Boogie-boogie, c/ Riera Baixa, 17. Clothes and accessories for rock 'n' roll enthusiasts.

Bolero, c/ Artesa de Segre, 7.

Cacharel, c/ General Mitre, 139.

Canadá, c/ Gran Vía, 441 and c/ Muntaner, 392. Few Barcelonans with modern tastes have not been into this establishment.

Carlos Torrents, Paseo de Gracia, 95; c/ Pau Casals, 6; Pasaje de la Concepción, 2 and c/ Portaferrisa, 34. Original men's clothing.

Chemisse, Rambla de Cataluña, 117. The most modern kinds of shirts for men and women, at very fair prices.

Choses, Paseo de Gracia, 97.

Christian Dior, c/ Pau Casals, 7.

Coco, Vía Wagner, s/n.

Cláusula, Paseo de Gracia, 62.

Conti, Av Diagonal, 512; Rambla de Cataluña, 78; c/ Tuset, 30 and c/ Pau Casals, 7. High quality clothing for many years. A classic in Barcelona.

Danzel-la, c/ Muntaner, 323 and Paseo de Gracia, 55.

Denver, c/ Travesera de Gracia, 80-82.

Don Algodón, c/ Ganduxer, 22. Part of the national chain launched by a very young businessman. Informal clothes for young people at reasonable prices.

Don Algodoncito, Rambla de Cataluña, 102. Like Don Algodón, but for children.

E4G, Av Diagonal, 490 and c/ Mallorca, 275. Modern and stylish.

Efectos Especiales, Paseo de Gracia, 55. Very fashionable clothing accessories.

Estanislao Furest, Paseo de Gracia, 12; c/ Pau Casals, 3 and Av Diagonal, 468. Originally opened in 1898 on the Pl Real as a store specializing in men's and women's clothing, this was the company that started fashion shows in Barcelona. Today its merchandise retains a high quality level.

Fancy, Av Diagonal, 461 and 463.

Fellini, Av Puerta del Angel, 24.

Ferreras, Paseo de Gracia, 79; Av Diagonal, 586; c/ Dr. Ferrán, 2 and c/ Ronda Sant Pere, 15.

Fiorucci, c/ Sant Gervasi, 79. Cheerful, pretty designs are sold by this well-known Italian store.

Franela, Galerías Turó.

Gales, Paseo de Gracia, 32; Pl Francesc Maciá, s/n and Gran Vía de les Cortes Catalans, 629. A classic shirt shop and tailor for men. Good taste backed by 40 years' experience.

Gazlo, c/ Taquígrafo Garrida, 125.

Globe, Paseo de Gracia, 55 and Rambla de Cataluña, 121.

Gonzalo Comella, Av Diagonal, 478; Vía Augusta, 2 and Paseo de Gracia, 6. This shop began selling underclothes in 1924. Today it has become one of the most prestigious stores in all Barcelona.

○ *Groc*, Rambla de Cataluña, 100. Clothes designed by Tony Miró and jewelry designed by Chelo Sastre.

Hard Rock Shop, c/ Del Rec, 65. Clothes sold by designers who are not yet well known to the general public.

Informe de Modos y Modas, c/ Carme, 90. Clothes, records and cassette tapes. Accessories made by craftsmen in limited editions.

Jordi Cuesta, c/ Muntaner, 402. One of the essential shops for those with today's tastes.

José Tomás, c/ Mallorca, 242.

○ *Loewe*, Paseo de Gracia, 35 and Av Diagonal, 570. Leather jackets, overcoats, gloves, suitcases, clothes for men and women. Prestigious fashion. The perfume *Aire*, one of the leading scents of Europe, is sold here.

Lupe, Av de Sarriá, 146.

Mad, Rambla de Cataluña, 107.

María Shop, Urquinaona Centre.

Massimo Dutti, Via Augusta, 33 and Av Diagonal, 602. Specializes in shirts at very reasonable prices.

Matrícula, c/ Pau Casals, 24; c/ Tenor Viñas, 12 and c/ Rector Ubach, 48.

Mayffred, c/ Valencia, 241; Urgel Centre and Vía Wagner.

Neon, c/ Travesera de Gracia, 15.

○ *Pedro Morago*, Av Diagonal, 518. Clothes designed by one of the most daring and modern designers in Spain.

Regent's Diagonal, Av Diagonal, 598.

Saint Laurent, Av Diagonal, 606.

Santa Eulalia, Paseo de Gracia, 60 and 91. Established in 1843, this shop is the symbol of high fashion in Barcelona.

Shikara, Rambla Cataluña, 68.

Simorra, c/ Canuda 45-47; Vía Augusta, 14-16; Boulevard Rosa (shop 28); c/ Tenor Viñas, 7 and Galerías Turó.

Sir, c/ Mandrí, 42 and c/ Consejo de Ciento, 317.

Spleen, c/ Paseo de Gracia, 55, Boulevard Rosa. Bold costume jewelry shop.

Swim, c/ Castanyer, 40. Specially made clothes for rock 'n' roll enthusiasts.

○ *Teresa Ramallal*, c/ Maestro Nicolau, 17. Women's clothing, shoes and accessories by this new designer, who manages to combine elegance and modernity in a stylish way.

Tienda de Olga, c/ General Mitre, 179.

Tiza, Galerías Malda.

Torrens, Paseo de Gracia, 12-14; c/ Pau Casals, 3; Av Diagonal and Gran Vía, 630. Elegant and original clothes designs.

Trau, c/ Valencia, 260. *Prêt-a-porter* clothing.

Tres Siete Ocho, c/ Muntaner, 378. This place is considered *de rigueur* in Barcelona among those who are seeking style and modernity.

Trip Difusión, c/ Provenza, 259 and c/ Flassaders, 23. This popular shop sells clothes for young people. Good taste.

Vehils, c/ Puerta del Angel, 32.

Vidosa, c/ Balmes 339-341.

Zas, c/ Mallorca, 275.

Zona, Paseo de Gracia, 55 (shop 18) and c/ Monistrol, 2.

1701, c/ Casanovas, 197.

Food

Barcelona is a real paradise for the food-buyer, with its markets crammed with products from the *huerta* (irrigated plains of the region) and from the sea, a feast for the eye as well as the palate. There are wine stores, bakeries, confectioneries and places that sell ready-made meals to take away.

Baixas, c/ Calaf, 14 ☎ 209 21 20. Pork products, quality cheeses and homemade dishes to take away.

Celler de Gélida, c/ Vallespir, 65. A wide variety of Spanish wines and sparkling cava wines, as well as foreign labels. A true discovery here is the selection of wines from Penedés and Ampurdán. Reasonable prices.

Colmado Quílez, Rambla de Cataluña, 63. Foodstuffs from five continents, wines, liquors, coffees, teas and so on, all at good prices.

Fleca Balmes, c/ Balmes, 156. One of the oldest bakeries in the city. Every type of bread is sold here, and the place is well-known for its *pan de payés* (country bread) recipe. Garlic, cheese and whole grain breads are some of the range.

Mauri, Rambla de Cataluña, 102 ☎ 215 44 65. A good tea shop that offers exquisite candies and chocolates.

Merce's, Av Diagonal, 539 ☎ 239 44 82. High quality homemade dishes. It may be helpful to order in advance.

Semon, c/ Ganduxer, 31. Elegant and sophisticated establishment with a carefully selected range: salmon, cheese, sausages, liquors, biscuits, and so on, both Spanish and foreign-made. Good pre-made dishes. You can also eat in the shop. One of the best food shops in Barcelona.

Footwear

Alvarez, c/ Mariano Cubí, 3. A classic shop for women.

Bis de Bis, Paseo de Gracia, 55 (Boulevard Rosa). Stylish and modern products for women.

Camper, c/ Muntaner, 248 and c/ Valencia, 249. Young and informal.

Gales, Paseo de Gracia, 32. A classic shoe shop in Barcelona, for men.

Patricia, Av Diagonal, 466. Also sells leather goods.

Paulí Vila, Pl Francesc Macià, 1. International brands.

Stéphane Kelian, c/ Rosellón, 218. Chic and international.

Torrens, Gran Vía, 630. Custom-made shoes.

Canvas shoes

Francesc Tasies i Ginestà, c/ Avinyó, 7. Also known as *Manual Alpargatera,* this shop has done much to bring old traditional models up to date with new colors and shapes.

Nuria Roig, Placeta del Carme, 1. Authentic traditional canvas shoes.

Fur and Leather Goods

Bolsos Ribe, c/ Muntaner, 250.

Gala, c/ Muntaner, 323 and Vía Augusta, 29. Fashionable and well-made handbags.

Loewe, Paseo de Gracia, 35. Elegant and sophisticated products sold the world over.

Sara Navarro, Av Diagonal, 598. Very individual designs created by the propietor.

Vogue, Rambla de Cataluña, 33.

Handicrafts

Artespaña, Rambla de Cataluña, 75. Carefully selected range of native Spanish handicrafts, ranging from simple pottery to furntiture.

Eloi Abat, c/ Romans, 30. Its pieces are seen all over the world.

Joan Martí i Roig, c/ Martí, 36. Engraved plates and gift objects. Orders accepted.

Joaquim Sanchez i García, c/ Pintor Fortuny, 21 , second floor. Located near the Ramblas, this workshop is the one that each year designs the Condes de Godo tennis trophy.

Xavier Roca i Coll, c/ Sant Pere mes baix, 24. Belongs to a family with a long silversmithing tradition. They make silver reproductions of various buildings of the city.

Fine Lace

Carolina Curriu i Caral, c/ Duquessa d'Orleans, 2.

Montserrat Coll, c/ Pelayo, 48, fifth floor, 1A. Disciple, like the preceding shop owner, of the grand masters of lacemaking, Antonia and Monserrat Raventos. Very delicate and original work.

Roser Abelló i Francolí, Passatge Torastre, 2, second floor, 2. The porprietor is director of the school of fine lace of the Palace of the Vicereine.

Glass and Crystal Engravers

Boulevard Rosa, Paseo de Gracia, 55.

Joan Sans i Colom, c/ Nuestra Senyora dels Desemparats, 28.

Joaquim Aguiló, c/ Aulestia i Pijoan, 8.

Pere Serra i Casas, c/ Pintos Pahizza, 35.

Ramón Purçals, c/ Diputación, 32.

For other handcrafted items, you may wish to consult the official guide published by the city of Barcelona. It is put out by the *Departamento de Relaciones Ciudadanas*, City Hall.

On the ground floor of the *Boulevard Rosa*, Paseo de Gracia, 55, there is a permanent exhibition of crafts put on by the Departament of Industry and Energy of the Generalitat, or regional government. The items displayed for sale are regularly rotated.

Jewelry

With more than 3,000 years of experience in jewelry-making, Barcelona offers a magnificent repertoire, from the most advanced designs of Joaquín Berao and Chelo Sastre to the world of classic stones and gold.

Bagues, Paseo de Gracia, 41. A city classic.

Capdevila, c/ Pau Claris, 129. A classic in Barcelona.

Cartier, Av Diagonal, 622.

Cubic, Paseo de Gracia, 49. Lovers of stones, as well as the curious visitor, should not miss this place.

Felix Riera i Busquets, c/ Mare de Déu dels Reis, 8.

Groc, Rambla de Cataluña, 100. This shop sells fashionable clothes. But in addition to the textile work of Tony Miro, there are also very interesting jewelry designs by Chelo Sastre.

Joaquín Berao, c/ Rosellón, 277. Modern designs executed in traditional materials like silver and newer metals like titanium and a number of alloys. It is no surprise this designer has had such success in New York City. The shop itself is of a spectacular design, more interesting even than the best that Madrid has to offer. Prices, keeping in mind that these are original designs, are very competitive. Berao's jewelry may also be purchased in *Cubic*.

Jordi Lara, c/ Sales i Ferer, 2 bis. A prestigious shop with 130 years of tradition behind it.

Josep Oriol i Novelles, Paseo de Gracia, 7. A family of jewelers for four generations.

Josep Real i Ruiz, c/ Loreto, 17. Specializing in silver jewelry.

Lluis Conill i Pujol, c/ Diputació, 154.

Masriera y Carreras, Paseo de Gracia, 29. Tradition and prestige.

Puig Doria, Av Diagonal, 580. This jewelry store has always enjoyed the patronage of Barcelona's middle classes. Now, its products are making major inroads in the United States.

Roca, Paseo de Gracia, 18.

Rosa Bisbe, c/ Ganduxer, 20. A well-known Barcelona jeweler's.

Salvador Espriu i Pujol, c/ Mozart, 23. A fine craftsman, Salvador will be retiring soon with no one to succeed him.

Vasari, Paseo de Gracia, 73. A world of gold and jewels, with prices according to the value of the expensive materials used.

Markets

Cucu, c/ Cucurulla, 3. Colourful, amusing clothes for young people.

El Bronx, c/ Portaferrisa, 6. Clothes for all tastes.

El Mercadillo, c/ Portaferrisa, 17. Clothes for all tastes.

Musical instruments

Gabriel y Francesc Fleta, c/ de los Angeles, 4. Stringed instruments, instrument-making and repair.

Joan Estruch i Pipo, c/ Ample, 30. Operating since 1880, this is one of the city's oldest music shops, featuring many interesting instruments.

Lluis Camps, c/ Martínez de la Rosa, 58. This establishment has been repairing and restoring pianos since 1890. This is the shop that maintains the old pianos kept in the city's museums.

Paper Shops, Assorted Gifts and Others

Artesanía Eva, c/ Conde de Salvatierra, 10. Hand-painted, canvas shoes. Also sells hand-painted T-shirts, pants and key rings.

IXIS, c/ Provença, 270. Nightclothes and bathroom wear. Original clocks. Stationer's.

Pepa Paper, Paseo de Gracia, 55. Located in the shopping centre of Boulevard Rosa, this stationer's is an institution in Barcelona. A sister shop is located at c/ Paris, 167.

Perchas, c/ Pino, 4. Every type of clothes hanger in every size, including hangers for necklaces, bracelets, belts, ties and suits. Also sells classic night suit stands.

Spleen, Paseo de Gracia, 55, Boulevard Rosa. Surprisingly modern costume jewelry.

Torrent, Rambla de Cataluña, 122. All kinds of stockings and socks. Torrent produces the *taleguillas* (silk stockings lined with cotton) of Spain's bullfighters, as well as the sashes worn by generals.

Vinçon, Paseo de Gracia, 96. This establishment is difficult to describe due to the fact that it is constantly being imaginatively renovated. It is hard to leave this Barcelona institution, without buying something. Always filled with customers.

SPANISH WAY OF LIFE: INFORMATION FOR FOREIGNERS

Spain is in many ways the most easygoing country in the western hemisphere. Its extraordinary **youthfulness** reflects, in part, the fact that Spain is demographically young. In addition many are surprised by the extent to which the country's key professional, business and political posts are held by people who are barely 45 years old. As an unhassled, young society, Spain is **hospitable** toward strangers. Pride in the recent recognition of his country as both newly democratic and European —and the determination to keep it that way— has given the Spaniard a special respect for the differences and peculiarities of foreigners.

The first thing to remember is that Spain is a patchwork of **very different lands and peoples**. The second is to forget the clichés and commonplaces of the past: a profound and rapid process of change has modernized this country, even while traditional life probably remains more alive in Spain than in any other European country. The Spaniard is cultured, hardworking and efficient, but he nonetheless retains his personality, his *joie de vivre* or *alegría*.

Freedom Spanish-style extends to shopping hours and to ways and rhythms of living. This unhurried life, together with the ingrained youthfulness of its contemporary society, makes Spain a particularly easy place to visit. The foreigner can choose from among a host of lifestyles the one that suits him best.

Bars, Wine Bars, Taverns and Cafeterias

Alcoholic beverages can be bought in virtually any grocery store; furthermore, they can be legally consumed almost anywhere, the street included. Wine bars, taverns, bars and cafeterias offer their drink according to their peculiar grading system. The **wine bar** or *bodega* usually sells wine from small barrels, more often than not purchased from local vineyards; draught beer served as a *caña*, a fifth of a litre serving that takes its name from the cane-shaped glasses it usually comes in; and low-grade brandies and anisettes. **Taverns** or *tabernas* serve cheap bottled wine and beers and soft drinks. In both *bodegas* and *tabernas* drinks are often accompanied by small servings of tinned goods such as mussels or smaller shellfish with bread. **Bars**, which usually offer sandwiches (*bocadillos*), cigarettes and, nearly always, coffee and tea, specialize in that wonderful Spanish creation, the *tapa* —a small plate containing one of an enormous variety of appetizers. Among the usual fare are stews, sausages (*embutidos*), cheeses, conserves and fried foods: tuna, almonds, salads and nuts, cheese, salami or ham, clams in red sauce, grilled shrimp, cold omelette with potatoes (*tortilla*), small fish *boquerones* that come fried or in vinegar, skewered marinated meat, octopus and snails. In some places, the fare includes *garbanzos guisados*, or stewed chick peas, tripe and offal and *paella* —the seafood, saffron flavoured rice dish for which Spain is justly famous. *Raciones* are simply somewhat larger orders of *tapas*. A very Spanish way of eating lightly and informally is simply to order *raciones*; better yet, if you're in a group, the best thing to do is order a variety of these appetizers and share them around.

The *tapa* is a sensible gastronomic institution in Spain, derived from the lightness of the morning meal: usually a simple *café con leche* (coffee with hot milk) with toast, or the traditional *churros*, fried dough normally accompanied by thick drinking chocolate. The *tapa* also supports the Spanish habit of drinking before the day's first major meal, which is eaten in the afternoon. A tradition of socializing has grown up around the *tapa*, and the name *tapeo* has been given to a series of drinks which are each consumed with their proper *tapa*. This custom has made its way as far as New York City.

The **cafeteria** is subtly different from the bar. It is more modern in conception, adding a range of services, milk products, sweets and other foods to its offerings. You can generally eat and drink either at the bar of sitting at a table. Service is fast.

The Spanish **eating and drinking schedule** is full of surprises. Bars and cafeterias usually serve breakfast until 11.00 or noon, when they begin offering *tapas* and aperitifs (wine and wine spritzes made with a sweet soda pop or soda water, beer, vermouth, *vino fino* and other varieties of sherry); this continues until the lunch hour, which in Spain is generally between 2.00 and 4.00 p.m. After lunch, the diner usually has a coffee, normally *solo* (without milk), and a glass of brandy or anisette, often accompanied by a cigar. Round about 4.30 is the traditional *siesta*, but this is pretty much a relic of the past except during vacations and weekends. Towards 6.30 or 7.00 p.m. many Spaniards have a snack, or *merienda*. This is usually *café con leche* or a chocolate drink, and those most often seen taking it are women finishing up their afternoon chores and meeting their friends. After about 8 o'clock, the bars and cafeterias begin to fill up again with a mixed crowd, who will continue drinking and eating until 10.00 or 10.30, when the dinner hour —finally— arrives. The evening meal can last until midnight or later, although most restaurants close at that time. Specialized eateries such as hamburger bars, pizza parlours and other late-closing restaurants often remain open after midnight, particularly in the big cities.

Beverages

Aside from cheap and excellent wines (see 'Wines'), Spain also produces soft drinks and a great deal of **beer**, both draught and bottled. Some of the better-known bottled brands include *Aguila, San Miguel, Mahou and Cruzcampo*. Among the **fizzy non-alcoholic beverages** are *Coca-Cola, Trinaranjus, Kas and Pepsi-Cola*. An enormously popular brand of *gaseosa* —a sweetened bubbly water— is *La Casera*, so much so that its name has become interchangeable with *gaseosa* as a generic term. *La Casera* is often mixed with wine.

Spanish **coffee** is very good, and is normally served as an Espresso-type beverage rather than the lighter, American-style drink. It comes *solo* (without milk), *con leche* (with milk) or *cortado* (only a small amount of milk is added). *Irish coffee* is very popular, especially among the middle and upper classes; another variant, *carajillo*, or black coffee served with brandy, is more popular with the less affluent. **Tea** and other quality infusions are usually prepared with tea bags.

The Spanish drink best known to the world is almost without doubt ***sangría***, made with red wine, lemon, brandy, slices of orange and peach, and some sugar and cinnamon. A purely alcoholic drink, strictly for the seasoned drinker, is the *sol y sombra*, which combines anisette and brandy. On the other hand, **fresh, non-alcoholic drinks** are varied, from *horchatas*, which are milk-like cold drinks, made of earth almonds, to *granizados*, sherbet drinks that come in flavours of lemon, orange, and coffee. Also available are the *aguas de cebada* or *de arroz*, literally barley and rice water.

Bullfighting

Summer afternoon is the time of the **bullfight**, or *corrida de toros*, that festival of light and death in which animal is measured against man for bravery, astuteness and skill. The fight usually begins at 7 o'clock sharp, lasting between 90 and 120 minutes and consisting of a *lidia* of six bulls.

Much like a play, each of the six bullfights is divided into three *tercios*, or acts: first come the *picadors*, who, mounted on a horse, jab the bull with a long lance; second are the *banderilleros*, men who scamper in front of the bull and plant brightly coloured barbed darts (*banderillas*) in the nape of his neck; and finally the *matador*, the master bullfighter who passes the animal with his cape before delivering the death stroke with his sword. *Novilladas* are fights featuring apprentice matadors and young animals (between two and three years old). *Rejoneadores* are bullfighters who pass and kill the bull while mounted on a horse.

The bullfighting season runs from the end of March through October; it is somewhat longer in the south. The principal rings are the *plazas* of Madrid and Seville. Matadors like *Joselito, Belmonte, Manolete* and *El Cordobés* make up the legend of Spanish bullfighting. Today, *Manzanares* and *Espartaco* are among the better known fighters. Every season, however, new bullfighters make their names.

Customs and Courtesy

Pressures of formality and convention are scarcely felt in Spain outside the workplace. Most people dress in sports wear, much of it manufactured by Spain's well-developed fashion industry. In any case, the spirit of living together that characterizes the country means that conventional dress takes its place alongside the more bizarre clothes worn by those people the Spaniards call *new-look postmodern* or *punkie*. The variety of clothes is even wider in the cities and the popular summer resorts. The establishments that require formal dress are few, most of them casinos and very expensive restaurants. These latter often stock a whole wardrobe of their own ties to lend to the improperly attired customer.

Spanish men normally greet one another with a handshake; women, and very often teenagers of both sexes, normally kiss each other once on either cheek. The formal mode of conversational address is *Usted* but among young and middle-age people, even those who do not know each other, the more familiar *tú* is more usual. Very often what may be taken for arrogance is simply a reserved way of showing respect. The Spaniard is proud of his nationality. He is sharply critical of his own country; but he does not like to hear others criticize it so freely.

It is general practice in Spain to heap courtesies on women, opening doors and the like; the rule applies also to senior citizens and guests. Queuing, on the other hand, is not a Spanish virtue and is not widely practised.

Electricity

Electricity in Spain is normally alternating current at 220v, although many hotels have a special 110-120v plug so that travellers may use electric razors without danger to the appliance. The plugs are generally of the universal two-pronged, round-shaped variety.

Gambling

For those who are interested in **games of chance**, there are many to sample in Spain. These include the *Lotería Nacional*, or National Lottery, the popular *Loto*, or *Lotería Primitiva* which has weekly draws and the *Cupón de los ciegos*, a lottery run by the organization for the blind, ONCE, which has daily draws. There are also football pools and horse racing punts both known as *quinielas*. In the vast majority of bars and many other establishments as well, you will find electronic gambling machines. Lastly, casinos abound in major tourist sites.

Mailing Addresses

To address mail in Spain, or to Spain, you should write out the envelope like this (the *c/* stands for *calle*):

D. Manuel Pelaez
c/ Velasco, 3
28043 Madrid

Pharmacies

Pharmacies in most cities have a rotating system whereby one is always open round the clock; a listing may be found in local newspapers. In this same list, the opening and closing times of others are given. Pharmacies in Spain sell many drugs over the counter that require prescriptions elsewhere. An example is antibiotics. Contraceptives are available without much difficulty.

Public Washrooms

The apparent scarcity of public washrooms should not cause panic to the stranger: there is an informal network of public services in bars, cafeterias and other eating and drinking establishments. Most owners will not mind non-customers walking in off the street.

Some of the rest rooms in bars, restaurants and railway stations are not models of cleanliness. For that reason, the visitor may prefer to stick to better eating and drinking establishments, hotels, museums and so on. If there is an attendant, a small tip is customary.

The Spaniards' Schedule

The conventional image of Spain is that of a country that stays up late —true in terms of meals, shows and bedtimes, but far less so in other areas of life. Factories start work at 8.00 and offices open at 9.00, just as in any industrialized country. Nevertheless, lunch is not until 2.00 and dinner until 10.00 p.m.: evening sessions of cinemas and theatres generally start at 10.30 p.m., and it is unusual to go to bed —on a working day— before midnight.

Spain's **banking schedule** is quite strict, normally running from 9.00 a.m. until 2.00 p.m. or 9.00 until 1.00 on Saturdays. The **schedule for other establishments**, especially shops and boutiques, varies more widely, according to both locality and season. Generally, establishments of all kinds are open from 10.00 until 1.30 or 2.00, and again from 4.00 or 5.00 until 8.00 p.m. The department stores or *grandes almacenes*, do not usually close during lunch hour and many are open all day Saturday and even Sunday. Of course, there are also many places of all types that remain open longer hours in cities and tourist centres.

The normal thing in the evening is to walk the streets, taking the air, socializing, perhaps indulging in a little flirtation. Spain, after all, is known for its **tradition of night life**.

Taxis

A taxi is usually identified by a horizontal or diagonal stripe on the body and a sign marking it as a taxi on the roof or behind the windshield. As a general rule, the rates charged are set by local authorities. In the cities, at least, the rate schedule is posted where the traveller can easily read it. There are many taxi ranks, marked by signs in blue that carry the letter T or the word taxi. There are also a good many radio-dispatched taxi companies that you can reach by telephone. And of course you can pick one up in the street. Unoccupied taxis carry a card in their windshield marked *libre* in the day; at night, they are marked by a green roof light.

Telephone

Spain has a good telephone communications system that has a fully automated national and international network. International telephone calls may be made easily and without the help of an operator to most countries (see the instructions and list of prefixes below). Apart from the many **telephone booths** along the streets, the majority of restaurants, bars and cafeterias have **public telephones** that work with coins. You insert the coins, listen for the dial tone and then dial. You can make local, national and international calls on these phones. It is advisable to use these rather than hotel phones in general —hotels often charge more than 25% extra. If you are planning a longer international call you should either provide yourself with a good supply of coins or find a phone marked **international**. Better yet, go to the local **public office** of the utility CTNE, better known as *Telefónica* (*Compañía Telefónica Nacional de España*), where you can pay with bills after making your call. Rates are substantially lower at night and on holidays.

When you dial a number, the sound of the ringing phone will be long intermittent tones. A busy signal is more rapid.

All Spanish **provincial prefixes** begin with **9**, followed by the number in the province. These prefixes must always be used when calling from another Spanish province. Within a province they are dropped. When calling Spain from another country the provincial 9 prefix is also dropped.

To make **automatic calls from Spain to another country** —calls without the assistance of the operator— you need to dial **07**, followed by the country code for where you are calling (see the list of international prefixes below), the area (dropping the zero if there is one), and finally, the number of the party you wish to reach. If you do not know the area code, or need the help of an operator for another reason, dial **008** (Europe) and **005** (the rest of the world) if you are calling from Madrid; dial **9198** (Europe) or **9191** (the rest of the world) if you are in any other province of Spain. Remember that Spanish time usually runs an hour ahead of Greenwich Mean Time (GMT).

International Prefixes

Algeria: 213
Andorra: territorial code 9738
(do not dial 07)
Argentina: 54
Australia: 61
Austria: 43

Bahrein: 973
Belgium: 32
Bolivia: 591
Brazil: 55
Cameroon: 237
Canada: 1
Chile: 56
Colombia: 57
Costa Rica: 506
Cyprus: 357
Czechoslovakia: 42
Denmark: 45
Dominican Republic: 508
Ecuador: 593
Egypt: 20
El Salvador: 503
Federal Republic of Germany: 49
Finland: 358
Formosa: 886
France: 33
Gabon: 241
German Democratic Republic: 37
Greece: 30
Guatemala: 502
Haiti: 509
Honduras: 504
Hong Kong: 852
Hungary: 36
India: 91
Indonesia: 62
Iran: 98
Ireland: 353
Israel: 972
Italy: 39
Ivory Coast: 225
Japan: 81
Jordan: 962
Kenya: 254
Kuwait: 965
Liechtenstein: (first dial Swiss prefix 41) 75
Luxemburg: 352
Mexico: 52
Monaco: (first dial French prefix 33) 93
Morocco: 212
Netherlands: 31
New Zealand: 64
Nicaragua: 505
Nigeria: 234
Norway: 47
Panama: 507
Paraguay: 595
Peru: 51
Philippines: 63
Poland: 48
Portugal: 351
Puerto Rico (USA): 80
Rumania: 40
San Marino: (first dial Italian prefix 39) 541
Saudi Arabia: 966
Senegal: 221
Singapore: 65
South Africa: 27
South Korea: 82
Sweden: 46
Switzerland: 41
Thailand: 66
Tunisia: 216
Turkey: 90
United Arab Emirates: 971
United Kingdom: 44
United States of America: 1
Uruguay: 598
Vatican City: (first dial Italian prefix 39) 6
Venezuela: 58
Yugoslavia: 38

Tipping

Tips generally do not need to be more than 5% to 10%, depending on the size of the bill: the larger the bill, the smaller the percentage. Bills for many services already include a service charge of 5%. Some establishments do not permit individual tipping, and instead use a common tin, or *bote*, for all tips. For those cases where a service charge isn't included in your bill, here is a general guide to some key services: a hotel porter might normally get a tip of between 100 and 150 pesetas; a taxi driver usually gets about 5% over what shows on the meter; parking lot attendants, 15 to 25 pesetas above the cost of the ticket; 25 to 100 pesetas to a cloakroom attendant. Of course the size of the tip depends on the type of place and how expensive it is. And it is always up to the customer to decide how well he has been served and what he wants to leave.

SPORTS

Barcelona, host to the **1992 Olympic Games**, has more than 1,200 sports clubs and associations, 1,300 installations and 250 areas for informal sports, in addition to the jogging and walking trails that are threaded through the city's many parks. Thus, the city's sports infrastructure is already geared to the Olympics. There is hardly a sport —from mountain skiing to water skiing— that is not practised in Barcelona or its environs.

This wide variety is due, in part, to the peculiar situation of the area. The sea is always nearby, and thus sailing is a popular local sport. The mountains are also close, giving rise to the frequently practised sports of mountaineering and hiking. The Pyrenees have spawned a well developed ski industry, while the widė green areas have produced a large number of golf courses.

The local sports guide, *Guia de l'Esport en Barcelona*, carries information and listings grouped by city districts.

Archery, Olympic Shooting and Pigeon Shooting

Federación de Tiro con Arco (the local Archery Association), Fossar del Castell de Montjuïc. Shooting range with 20 bulls-eye targets.
Federación Local de Tiro Olímpico (the local Olympic Shooting Association), Ctra Castell de Montjuïc ☎ 241 43 62. It has 4 shooting pits and 2 shooting galleries.
Tiro de Pichón (the local Pigeon Shooting Association), Ctra Castell Montjuïc ☎ 241 49 84. Shooting field of Barcelona's Pigeon Shooting association.
F.C. Beisbol, c/ Tres Pins, s/n ☎ 224 02 25. Baseball field.
Maritim Fútbol (C.N. Barceloneta), Passeig Maritim, s/n ☎ 319 30 06. Football field.

Golf

Club de Golf de Llavaneras, c/ San Andrés de Llavaneras, s/n ☎ 792 60 50. This golf club is reached via Ctra A19, 34km from Barcelona. Sixty-six strokes is par for the course, which is narrow and hemmed in by off-limits areas. It is 4,298m overall, said to be the shortest golf course in Spain. Hotels in nearby Mataró, Arenys de Mar and San Pol de Mar, as well as Barcelona. Open daily all year except Mondays.
Club de Golf de Pals, Playa de Pals (Gerona) ☎ 63 30 06. Located 7km from Bagur on the Costa Brava, 40km from the Gerona airport and 135km from Barcelona, it is easily accessible by car via Ctra A17 which joins Barcelona with La Junquera. The course has 18 holes —a 73-stroke par— and measures 6,204m in all. There are hotels nearby in Bagur, Tamariu, Llanfranch, Calella, Palamós, Playa de Aro, S'Agaró, San Feliú de Guixols and Estartit. Open daily all year except Tuesdays.
Club de Golf de San Cugat, San Cugat del Vallés, Barcelona ☎ 674 39 08. This course is located 20km from Barcelona in San Cugat del Vallés. It has 18 holes and a par of 70 strokes. Open daily all year except Mondays.
Club de Golf Terramar, P.O. Box 6, Sitges, Barcelona ☎ 894 05 80. Located in Sitges, 37km from Barcelona and 60km from Tarragona, this course —with 18 holes and a par of 70 strokes— is set

attractively by the sea. The closest hotels are in Sitges, Vilanova i la Geltrú, Castelldefels and Barcelona. Open all year.

Club de Golf Vallromanas, P.O. Box 43, Montornes del Vallés ☎ 568 03 62. Located on the Ctra Masnou-Granollers, the easiest access to this course is via Ctra A19 from Barcelona to Mataró, taking the exit at km7.5 in Masnou. The first 9 holes are quite flat, and the greens are separated by stands of pine. For the next 3 holes there is an incline. The greens, generally flat and surrounded by bunkers, are the hardest part of the course. Open daily all year except Tuesdays.

Green Place, c/ Infanta Carlota, 145 ☎ 321 41 31. Training course.

Real Club de Golf del Prat, Prat de Llobregat ☎ 379 02 78. This is the closest golf course to Barcelona. It is a flat and easy course. The golf club is characterized by its good facilities, including 2 restaurants, cloakrooms, sports shop, 3 swimming pools (one for children), paddle-tennis court, babysitting service, trams, and others.

Horseback Riding and Equestrian Sports

Campo de Hípica, Av Montanys, s/n, Montjuïc ☎ 301 16 18 and 224 73 07.

Club Hípico Llavaneras, Finca La Baya in San Andrés de Llavaneras ☎ 792 73 61.

Real Club de Polo de Barcelona, Av Diagonal, s/n ☎ 249 29 70 and Av Dr. Marañón, 17-31 ☎ 334 92 11.

In some cases you have to be a club member or the guest of one in order to practise the sport. Starting in the spring, a large number of equestrian contests are held in Barcelona. For information contact the Catalonian Equestrian Federation ☎ 230 90 53.

Hunting

The area that offers **game hunting**, while remaining convenient to Barcelona, is the Pirineo de Lérida. The most abundant game animals found there are wild boar, chamois, and wild goat. The hunting season of this species runs from the second week of September until the third week in February, with some variations. Any kind of hunting or trapping is forbidden for the rest of the year. For further hunting information, contact: *Sección del Medio Natural*, c/ Sabino Arana, 22 ☎ 330 93 97, 330 90 27 and 330 92 07.

Small game hunting is one of the most popular sporting activities in Spain. In the province of Lérida, bordering that of Barcelona, there is plenty of such small game —especially pigeons, starlings, thrush and turtle doves. The legal hunting season runs from August to March, generally speaking, although there are variations for some animals.

Ice Skating

Pista de Gel del F.C. Barcelona, c/ Aristides Maillol, s/n.
Skating, c/ Roger de Flor, 168 ☎ 245 28 00.

Marinas and Sports Ports

Catalonia has more than 35 marinas and other harbours pleasure boats. Together they offer more than 11,000 berths for private craft. More than 23,000 private boats leave Catalan ports on sporting expeditions of one kind or another every year and an additional 11,000 yachts visit this coast annually. Besides its own port, the closest ports to Barcelona are those of Arenys de Mar, El Balis, Premià de Mar, El Masnou, Garraf and Aiguadolç (in Sitges) and Vilanova i la Geltrú.

Aiguadolç. Administration: Port of Aiguadolç-Sitges ☎ 894 12 30. A 30 to 40 minute ride from Barcelona in good traffic along a winding highway. There are 671 berths. Water, electricity, garbage collection, bar, restaurant, showers, bathrooms, a pharmacy, gas-oil and petrol, launching ramps, repair shops and a waiting area for boats.

Arenys de Mar. Location: 41 34'5"N - 2 35'5"E. Administration: Club Naútico de Arenys de Mar ☎ 792 08 96. There are 294 berths. Water, electricity, garbage collection, a social building, bar, restaurant, showers, bathrooms, a pharmacy, gas-oil and petrol, radio weather information, a launching ramp, crane and repair shop. It is 30 minutes away from Barcelona in light traffic.

Barcelona. Location: 41 20'N - 2 10'E. Administration: Real Club Marítimo de Barcelona; Real Club Naútico de Barcelona ☎ 315 00 07 and 315 11 61. There are 278 berths. Water, electricity, garbage collection, a social building, bar, restaurant, showers, bathrooms, pharmacy, telephone, mail service, radio weather information, gas-oil and petrol.

El Balis. Location: 41 33'5"B - 2 30'5"E. Administration: Club-Nautic El Balis ☎ 792 69 47. Depth: 6m at the mouth; 4m in the outer port: 3m in the yacht basin. It has 400 berths. Water, electricity, garbage collection, a social building, bar, restaurant, showers, bathrooms, swimming pool, pharmacy, telephone, mail, radio weather information, gas-oil and petrol, crane and repair shop, and waiting area for boats. A 40 minute ride from Barcelona.

El Masnou. Location: 41 28'5"N - 2 18'6"E. Administration: Promociones Portuarias S.A., Port ☎ 555 30 00. There are 483 berths. Water, electricity, garbage collection, a social building, bar, restaurant, showers, bathrooms, swimming pool, pharmacy, telephone, postal service, radio weather information, gas-oil and petrol, crane, repair shop and a waiting area for boats. It is 25 minutes from Barcelona by a good highway.

Garraf. Location: 41 15'N - 1 54'E. Administration: Club Nautic Garraf. It has 60 berths. Water, electricity, a social building, bar, restaurant, showers, bathrooms, pharmacy, repairs shop. There is no gas-oil or petrol, Tourism office: Sitges ☎ 894 12 30. 25 minutes from Barcelona by a much-traveled highway.

Premià de Mar. Location 41 29'5"N - 2 21'5"E. Administration: Club Nautic, Port ☎ 751 14 45. There are 274 berths. Water, electricity, garbage collection, a social building, bar, restaurant, showers, bathrooms, swimming pool, pharmacy, telephone, radio and repair shop. There is no gas-oil or petrol. It is 30 minutes away from Barcelona.

Vilanova i la Geltrú. Location: 41 12'5"N - 1 43'6"E. Administration: Club Nautic de Vilanova, Port ☎ 893 07 58. It has 400 berths. Water, electricity, garbage collection, a social building, bar, restaurant, showers, bathrooms, pharmacy, telephone, radio, gas-oil and gasoline.

Skiing

Baqueira Beret. Located some 300km from Barcelona, Baqueira stands 1,500m above sea level, while Beret is somewhat higher at 1,800m.

The resort area does not only have good runs, lovely landscapes and very fine accommodation, but it also has a lively social life of its own. The Spanish Royal Family is often seen skiing down its slopes. From Beret to the famous ski trails of Luis Arias and Escornocrabes, everything is organized to take advantage of the possibilities the snow offers. If you want to get to the upper slopes of Aneto, then you have to take a helicopter from Baqueira. The entire Baqueira Beret complex offers *nearly 200ha of well marked trails*: 6 of them are ranked as beginners trails, 29 of them as intermediate runs and 4 of them are reserved entirely for competitions and expert skiers. The highest point is 2,500m above sea level, while the lowest is 1,500m above sea level. It is possible to ski *4,459m of slope* from top to bottom. There are *18 ski lifts*, among them 9 chair lifts, 8 regular ski lifts and 1 telebaby lift. Altogether, these lifts can carry 13,000 skiers per hour. In order to *obtain information* about lodging, reservations, state of the trails and weather forecasts, you should contact the Tourism Office of Baqueira Beret, P.O. Box 60, Viella (Lleida) Lérida ☎ (973) 64 50 50 and 64 50 25.

La Molina. The grand old lady of the winter season, to this day La Molina gets more than 170,000 skiers to visit her slopes every year. It is set on forested slopes and is blessed with sunny weather. Parking space is available for 3,000 cars. There are *40km of ski trails* —2 for experts, 14 for intermediate skiers and 6 for beginners. The resort also offers 3 ski jumps, 6 competition-only trails and 2 stadiums. *18 lifts* carry skiers up the mountain, 11 of them being regular lifts and 6 of them being chair lifts. *Information* can be obtained at Paseo de Gracia 45, second floor ☎ 215 61 08.

Llesui. An alternative to Baqueira Beret, Llesui is set into a very similar kind of landscape in the centre of the Pallars Sobirá region, an area that is also ideal for a bit of gastronomic tourism. It has a total of *30km of trails* that descend *3,600m*. There are *9 lifts* —6 regular lifts, 1 chair lift and 2 telebabies. *Information* can be obtained at Paseo de Gracia, 83 ☎ 215 81 80 and 215 83 22.

Port del Comte. This is the closest ski resort to Barcelona. Its slopes are very varied, and traversed by *15 lifts* —3 chair lifts, 11 normal lifts and a telebaby— for a total capacity of almost 10,000 people an hour. As at Baqueira, there are medical and X-ray teams available.

Vallter 2.000. Located in the Ter Valley (Gerona), at the very eastern end of the Pyrenees, Vallter 2.000 can be easily reached via the N152 highway, 150km from Barcelona. The trails are well-groomed, broad and treeless. The slopes are very varied, although most of them face NW. One trail is lit for night-skiing. It has *7 lifts*: 1 chair lift, 1 telebaby and 5 regular lifts. For further *information* contact Vallter, S.A., c/ Valencia, 1, Campodrón (Gerona) ☎ (972) 74 03 53.

Various Types of Information. To check the condition of the trails, call ☎ 302 70 40 (answering machine). For information on tourist resorts and winter sports in general, contact the *Asociación Catalana de Estaciones de Montaña*, Paseo de Gracia, 83 ☎ 215 81 80 or the *Federación Catalana de Deportes de Invierno* at ☎ 318 60 28.

Sports Centres

Can Carelleu, c/ Esports, s/n ☎ 203 78 74. Football field, indoor swimming pool, outdoor swimming pool, fronton court, indoor football court and four artificial turf tennis courts.

Circumvalació, Passeig Circunvalació, 1. Multipurpose court.
Corts, Travesera de Les Corts, Pasaje Gerard Piera, s/n ☎ 239 41 78. Outdoor swimming pool, outdoor basketball and other courts.
Escola Industrial, c/ Urgell, 187 ☎ 230 92 00. Football field, gymnasium and basketball court.
Folch i Torres, Pl Folch i Torres, s/n ☎ 241 01 22. Three swimming pools, gymnasium and fronton court.
Llars Mundet, Passeig de la Vall de Hebrón, s/n ☎ 229 16 00. Football field, indoor football court, hockey field, athletics track, volleyball court, indoor and outdoor swimming pools.
Maritim Piscina, Passeig Maritim, s/n ☎ 319 30 06. Two swimming pools, indoor gymnasium and outdoor fronton court.
Pau Negre, c/ Ramiro de Maeztu, s/n ☎ 213 43 44. Two indoor pools, fronton court and an indoor gymnasium.
Poeta Bosca, Pl Poeta Bosca, s/n ☎ 310 05 46. Outdoor multipurpose court.
Real Club de Polo, Av Diagonal, s/n. Only for members. Outdoor swimming pool. Public invited to some equestrian events. Polo games are private. Tennis.
Real Club de Tenis Pompeya, c/ Simón Bolivar, s/n ☎ 224 79 26. Seven tennis courts, outdoor fronton court and outdoor swimming pool.
Sant Pau, c/ Sant Pau, 97. Multipurpose outdoor court.

Squash Courts, Saunas and Gymnasiums

Can Melich Club, Av 11 de Septiembre, s/n, San Just Desvern. It has 20 squash courts, two of them with tier seats for more than 200 spectators and portable seating for 500; a gymnasium, 10 tennis courts, swimming pool, sauna, solarium, artificial sun, jazz dancing and aerobics. Open daily from 8.00 a.m. until midnight.
Club Gimnasio Cambridge, c/ Obispo Catalá, 52 ☎ 207 00 49. Men only. Squash, heated swimming pool, sauna, massage, artificial sun and solarium. Open Monday to Saturday from 8.00 a.m. to 10.30 p.m.; Sundays from 8.00 a.m. to 1.30 p.m.
Club Squash Tibidabo, c/ la Granada, 25 ☎ 237 02 78. It has 8 squash courts, gymnasium, aerobics, sauna, water massage, artificial sun, swimming pool and solarium. Open daily from 8.00 a.m. to 8.00 p.m.
Squash Barcelona, c/ Doctor Gregorio Marañón, 17 ☎ 334 02 58. It has 12 squash courts, 2 fronton courts, a football field, and artificial sun. Open long hours, from 8.00 a.m.to 1.00 a.m. daily.
Squash Club Barcelona, Av Roma, 2 (Cataluña Tower) ☎ 325 81 00. Squash, fronton court, gymnasium, sauna, swimming pool, solarium and personal defence classes. For women, gymnastics, aerobics, jazz dancing, a tennis court, covered swimming pool, Finnish sauna and table tennis. Body and facial treatments as well as artificial sun. Open Monday to Friday from 7.00 a.m. to 10.00 p.m.; Saturdays from 8.00 a.m. to 2.00 p.m.; Sundays from 9.00 a.m. to midday.
Squash Club Sant Cugat, c/ Sant Jordi, 33, ☎ 674 98 62 in Sant Cugat del Vallés. With easy access to the Rabassada highway and the A7 motorway. It has 8 squash courts, gymnasium, aerobics, saunas, water massage and swimming pool. Open daily from 9.00 a.m. to midnight.
Squash Diagonal, c/ Roger de Flor, 193 ☎ 258 08 09. It has 8

squash courts, swimming pool, sauna and gymnasium. Open daily from 8.00 a.m. to midnight.

Sport Dyr, c/ Castillejos, 388 ☎ 255 49 49. Heated swimming pool, 16 squash courts, 4 gymnasiums, weights, a mini-basketball court, skating rink, table tennis, sauna and massage, artificial sun and solarium. Open Monday to Friday from 7.00 a.m. until midnight; holidays from 8.00 a.m. to 10.00 p.m.

Swimming

Club Hispano-Francés, c/ Camí St. Cebrián, s/n ☎ 229 10 29. Outdoor pool. Tennis.

Club Natación Barcelona, c/ Escullera Llevant, s/n ☎ 319 46 00. One indoor, one outdoor pool.

Escoles Pies Sant Antoni, c/ Ronda Sant Pau, 72 ☎ 241 06 05. Indoor swimming pool.

Piscina Can Caralleu, c/ Esports, s/n ☎ 203 78 74. The covered pool is open all year except August; the outdoor pool is open from June 1 to September 15. Open daily from 9.00 a.m. to 4.00 p.m.

Piscina Les Corts, c/ Gerardo Piera (Travesía de Gran Vía de Les Corts Catalanes between Vallespir and Numancia). Open from June 1 until September 15 from 8.00 a.m. to midnight.

Piscina Montjuïc, Av Miramar, s/n ☎ 241 35 04. Open from June 1 to September 10, from 9.00 a.m. to 3.00 p.m.

Piscina Pau Negre, c/ Ramiro de Maeztu, s/n ☎ 213 43 44. Two indoor pools open all year. Non-club members may only swim during the mornings.

Piscina Poble Nou, c/ Llull with c/ Espronceda ☎ 307 10 04. Indoor pool, open all year except August, from 7.00 a.m. to 8.00 p.m.

Piscina Sant Jordi, c/ París, 114 ☎ 250 91 55. Open all year, except August, from Monday to Friday, 7.00 a.m. to 6.00 p.m. Indoor pool.

Pisicnas y Deportes, Av Sarriá, 96 ☎ 201 23 42. Open from June 1 to September 15, from 10.00 a.m. to 6.00 p.m.

Real Club Maritim, c/ Moll d'Espanya, s/n ☎ 315 00 07. Outdoor pool.

Tennis

Club de Tenis Barcino, Pasaje Forasté, 33 ☎ 417 08 05.

Club de Tenis La Salud, c/ Mare Deu Salut, 75 ☎ 213 56 98.

Real Club de Tenis Barcelona, Av Diagonal, s/n ☎ 240 92 44 and 249 43 54; c/ Bosch i Gimpera, s/n ☎ 203 77 58.

Real Club de Tenis del Turó, Av Diagonal, 673 ☎ 203 80 12.

USEFUL ADDRESSES

Airlines

Iberia, Pl España, s/n, 08004 Barcelona ☎ 325 12 02 and 325 69 00. Telex 54767. Reservations: ☎ 325 15 15. Fares: ☎ 325 43 04.

Lufthansa, International Airport of El Prat de Llobregat ☎ 379 37 66 and 379 43 67.

Pan Am, Paseo de Gracia, 15, 08007 Barcelona ☎ 301 72 49 and 301 75 90.

Royal Air Maroc, c/ Gran Vía Corts Catalanes, 634 ☎ 301 84 74.

Scandinavian Airlines, c/ Mallorca, 277 ☎ 215 32 44.
Schuler R., c/ Castelitersol, 24 ☎ 219 46 00.
Societé Tunisienne de l'Air, c/ Consell Cent, 308 ☎ 317 16 95 and 302 44 47.
South African Airways, c/ Gran Vía Corts Catalanes, 634 ☎ 318 07 97.
Sudamérica, Paseo de Gracia, 83 ☎ 215 95 10 and 215 95 53.
Swissair, Paseo de Gracia, 44 ☎ 215 91 00 and 215 91 16.
Trans World Airlines, c/ Gran Vía Corts Catalanes, 634 ☎ 318 00 31 and 301 50 36.
Varig, c/ Gran Vía Corts Catalanes, 634, 08007 Barcelona ☎ 301 60 70. Telex 97549.
Venezolana Internacional de Aviación, c/ Pau Claris, 177 ☎ 318 34 82 and 318 88 08.

Airport

International Airport of El Prat de Llobregat, located 14km from Barcelona ☎ 370 10 11 and 325 43 04. Tourist information ☎ 325 58 29. Train to the airport ☎ 379 00 24.

Automobile Rental

Atesa, c/ Balmes, 141 ☎ 237 81 40.
Avis, c/ Casanova, 209 ☎ 209 95 33.
Europcar c/ Consell de Cent, 363 ☎ 239 84 03.
Hertz, c/ Tuset, 10 ☎ 237 37 37 and in the airport ☎ 241 13 81.
Ital, Travesera de Gracia, 71 ☎ 321 51 41.
Regente Car, c/ Aragón, 382 ☎ 245 24 02.
Tot Car, Av Infanta Carlota, 93 ☎ 321 37 58.
Vanguard, c/ Londres, 31 ☎ 259 13 25 and 259 13 25.
Vip, c/ Tuset, 19 ☎ 201 36 59.

With Multilingual Drivers

International Limousine System, c/ Cardenal Sentmenat, 35, 08017 Barcelona ☎ 253 96 94 and 229 13 88. 24-hours service: ☎ 358 05 98. Telex 52739.
Vip Car Service, c/ Tuset, 19, 08006 Barcelona ☎ 201 36 59. Saturdays and holidays: ☎ 253 45 61 and 662 68 29.

Credit Cards

American Express ☎ 217 00 70. The American Express service office is located at the El Prat Airport, in the international terminal ☎ 379 30 62.
Diners Club ☎ 302 14 28.
Master Charge ☎ 315 25 12.
Visa ☎ 302 32 00.

Emergencies

Ambulances (24 hours) ☎ 300 04 22.
Clinic Hospital ☎ 254 25 80.
Emergency Medical Aid ☎ 212 85 85.
Health Information Service (a city service) ☎ 310 50 50.
Hospital of Santa Cruz y San Pablo ☎ 235 55 55.
Red Cross ☎ 235 93 00.

Tourist Information Offices

City Hall, P! San Jaume, ☎ 318 25 25. Open Mondays to Fridays from 9.00 a.m. to 9.00 p.m. Saturdays from 9.00 a.m. to 2.00 p.m.
El Prat Airport ☎ 325 58 29. Open Mondays to Fridays from 8.00 a.m. to 8.00 p.m. On holidays, from 8.00 a.m. to 3.00 p.m.
Francia-Término Station ☎ 319 27 91. Open Mondays to Saturdays from 8.00 a.m. to 8.00 p.m.
Generalitat de Catalunya, Gran Vía de les Corts Catalanes, 658 ☎ 301 74 43. Open Monday to Friday from 9.00 a.m. to 1.30 p.m. and from 4.30 to 8:30 p.m.
Municipal Tourism Office, Sants Central Station ☎ 250 25 94. Open daily from 7.30 a.m. to 10.30 p.m.
Pablo Neruda Plaza, Av Diagonal-c/ Aragón, at the entrance to the highway ☎ 245 76 21. Open daily between March 15 and October 15 from 8.30 a.m. to 8.30 p.m.
Puerto Porta de la Pau, facing the Columbus Monument. Open every day except Monday from 10.00 a.m. to 8.00 p.m.

Various Other Useful Telephone Numbers

Barcelona Information ☎ 010.
City Hall ☎ 302 42 00.
City Traffic ☎ 325 03 00.
Court on Duty ☎ 309 91 46.
Firemen ☎ 080.
Generalitat ☎ 302 47 00.
Generalitat Trains ☎ 205 15 15.
Highway Information ☎ 204 22 47.
Highway Traffic Accidents ☎ 352 61 61.
International Maritime Station ☎ 301 25 98.
Lost and Found Objects ☎ 301 39 23.
Municipal Police ☎ 092.
National Police ☎ 091.
Olympics Office ☎ 432 19 92.
Port of Barcelona ☎ 318 87 50.
Post Office (main branch) ☎ 318 38 31.
Radio-Taxi ☎ 330 08 50.
RENFE (the Railroad Company) ☎ 322 41 42.
Telephone Information ☎ 003.
Weather Information ☎ 094 212 56 66 and 212 58 16.

Youth Information

Area de Joventut del Ayuntamiento (City Youth Area), c/ Avinyo, 7 ☎ 301 12 21.
Dirección General de Joventut (General Youth Department), c/ Sant Honorat, 11 ☎301 92 49.

WINES

Spanish wines are a mosaic of different tastes and types, but they are singular both for their **high quality** —under the control of the Institute of Officially Regulated Wine Regions, *Instituto Regulador de Denominación de Origen*, whose mark appears on the back of the bottle— and for their **genuinely low prices**, which compare very favourably with European and American wines.

The most famous Spanish wine, with the longest tradition and the highest prestige, is **sherry** (in Spanish *Jerez*, after the southern city of that name). Sherry is a tasteful wine, strong, as one might expect of the hot climate of the south of Spain. It is drunk, generally, before meals, with hors d'oeuvres, during a *tapeo*, that is a round of appetizers or with desserts. From the more temperate north come a variety of wines: **Rioja**, which competes in quality and taste with French table wines; Catalan table wines of many types, including **cavas**, bubbly wines that are similar to French champagnes; and white wines, young-tasting and made from grapes grown in humid Galicia, in the northwest, that are commonly drunk with Galician dishes and with shellfish. The robust table wines produced in central Spain are quite varied, from those carrying the **Ribera del Duero** label, very good wine with strong body, to the many varieties of **Valdepeñas**, produced in vast quantities and very popular in Spain as a table wine.

Catalonia

Catalonia is the area with the widest variety of wines, from sparkling wines like the **cavas** to still wines. **Alella** mainly produces whites that are pale, young and fruity, with a distinctive bouquet and flavour; they are good with shellfish, white-fleshed fish and mild cheeses. *Marqués de Alella (82)* is a good example. The most characteristic wines from **Ampurdán** are rosés that are cherry-coloured, fruity-tasting and aromatic. They go well with fish, light meat, pastas and other foods. A very good, young white is *Blanc Pescador (83)*. The reds are robust and full-bodied, best suited for expert drinkers.

Penedés may be the Catalonian wine best known to the rest of the world, with the sparkling **cava** wines the most important in the province. Still, Torres, for one, has worked to produce several lesser-known whites of very high quality. The **cava** wines are one type of many sparkling wines, a very well regarded beverage elaborated and aged in the same bottle —that is to say in the same way as champagne is made. The cavas are relatively cheap and quite good, and so they have made a major impact on the international markets. The *brut* and *seco* varieties are good for any occasion, while the *dulces* (sweets) and *semisecos* (semi-dry) are well-suited to desserts. Sant Sadurní d'Anoia is home to Codorniú, Freixenet —the two best wineries—, Castellblanch, Conde Caralt, Juve and Camps, Segura Viudas, Marqués de Monistrol and others.

Miguel Torres, in Villafranca del Penedés, is one of the most famous of Spanish wineries. Its non-sparkling wines are excellent and include, among the whites, *Gran Viña Sol (83)* and *Viña Sol (83)*, and among the reds, *Gran Coronas Etiqueta Negra (77)* —described by a Paris jury as better than the mythical *Chateau Latour*. Rene Barbier produces excellent whites such as *Kraliner (83)*.

Central Spain

From La Mancha come the ubiquitous **Valdepeñas** wines, at the moment the most popular and best-selling type of wine in Spain. *Clarets* are the variety seen most often; they are light-coloured and light-bodied, not very alcoholic, and can be drunk on all occasions and with all kinds of food. They are frequently served in bars and taverns.

A wide range of wines is produced in Castile and León, from the strong reds of **Toro** or **Cebreros** to the delicate whites of **Rueda** —like the excellent *Cuatro Rayas (83)* of La Seca— and the clarets of **Cigales**. **Ribera del Duero** is the nomenclature of some of the greatest and most famous Spanish reds, the *vega-Sicilia* wines, and of the excellent *Valbuena (80)*.

Galicia

Albariño wines —whites of great delicacy, a yellow-straw colour, acidic and young, producing a tickling sensation in the mouth— are made with grapes from high vines. They have a relatively low alcoholic content and go well with shellfish and fish. **Ribeiro** offers several whites, good with fish and shellfish, and reds that are well-suited to such local specialties as octopus, hake and others dishes.

Rioja and Related Wines

Riojas have a tradition of high quality —only Bordeaux and Burgundy come out ahead, and that may be in name only. Although the Rioja tradition in the area may go back to pre-Roman times, today's principal wineries date to the 19C. They include Bodegas Bilbaínas, Martínez Lacuesta, Muga, CVNE, Paternina, López de Heredia, Berberana, Marqués de Cáceres, AGE, Lan, Franco-Española and Marqués de Murrieta. All these wineries are good, and they produce wines up to Rioja Alta, literally High Rioja. Most Riojas are red —although both white and fruity Riojas have been made for several years now—, light-bodied, with a light aroma and a noticeable taste of oak, deriving from the barrels in which they are made. **Excellent** years were 1964, 1970, 1978, 1981 and 1983. **Very bad** years were 1972, 1977 and 1980.

Among others, some of the excellent red wines produced after 1970 are *Marqués Villamagna (70), Viña Cumbrero (78), Prado Enea (76), Viña Albina (73), Imperial Gran Reserva (73), Viña Vial (78), Viña Ardanza (76), Marqués de Murrieta Reserva (70)* and *Viña Tondonia (sixth year)*. Among the rosés we can include *Cerro Añon (73)*, and among the whites, *Monopole (81)* and *Marqués de Cáceres*.

The young white wines go well with grilled fish and shellfish, while older whites are better suited to fish with sauces. Rosés are usually drunk with egg dishes, pastas, rice and so on. Young reds go well with dark-fleshed fish and light meats. The better, older reds, according to their age, make an excellent accompaniment to a variety of foods including non-red meats, fish with sauces, game and similar dishes.

Navarre produces heavy-bodied red wines of great character, aromatic and sweet rosés, and clarets. Its best wines are similar to those made in neighbouring Rioja. Notable Navarran reds include the excellent *Gran Vino Señorío de Sarriá (73)*.

Sherry and Andalusia

Sherry is known to date back to before the Middle Ages. Sherrymakers of today can trace their lineage back, in many cases, to the 18C. Some examples are Terry, Duff Gordon, Garvey, González Byass (19C), Agustín Blázquez, Osborne, Domecq, Sandeman, and Williams/Humbert (19C). Under the all-embracing name of *Jerez*, however, there is a rainbow of sherries. The most important are the ***finos***, sherries that are dry and

Codorniú Cellars, Sant Sadurníu d'Anoia

light, straw-coloured, pale, and marked by a distinctive aroma, both pungent and delicate. They are graded between 15.5° and 17°. *Tío Pepe, La Ina, Carta Blanca, San Patricio, Perla, Quinta* and *Tío Mateo* are some of the most famous names. The ***manzanilla*** wines from Sanlúcar de Barrameda are similar to the *finos*, but there is a subtle difference, perhaps owing to the fact that they come from an area closer to the sea. *La Guita* is one of the popular *manzanilla* labels, but there are many more. The ***amontillado*** wines are amber-coloured, smooth, with much body, a hazel tint and graded between 16° and 18°. Some well-known labels are *Coquinero, Don Zoilo* and *Etiqueta Blanca*. The ***olorosos***, the sweet-smelling, or odorous, ones, are dark, very aromatic, dry and heavy-bodied and graded between 18° and 20°. *Río Viejo* and *Dry Sack* are among the better-known olorosos. ***Palo cortado*** wines lie midway between the *olorosos* and the *amontillados*. Finally, there are the **sweet wines**: *Moscatel, Pedro Ximénez* and *Cream*.

The *fino* sherries are drunk chilled and, like the *amontillados*, are an ideal wine served with hors d'oeuvres; both are excellent with fried or grilled fish or serrano ham. The *olorosos* and *palo cortados* go well with nuts, serrano ham and sausages. The sweet wines are usually drunk as dessert accompaniments.

Famous Córdoba wines include **Montilla-Moriles**, which is similar to sherry, and wineries like Alvear, Crismona, Navarro; some popular labels are *C.B., Moriles* and *Montilla*, all finos, and *Oloroso Viejo*. **Málaga** is known for its sweet wines, notably the *moscatels* and *Pedro Ximénez*, made to go with sweets and pastries.

STREET INDEX

Aldana II-5B-5A
Ample XIII-6A-6B-5C, XIV-5A
Angel, Pza. de L' XIV-2B-2C
Angels IV-3B-2B-2C-1C
Antoni López, Pza. d' XIV-6A-6B
Arc Cid XI-3C-4C
Arc de San Agustí IV-7A-6B
Arc del Triumf VIII-6C-5C
Ausias March VIII-1A-2A
Bailén VIII-1C-2C-3C
Barberá III-8C, IV-8A-8B-8C
Bisbe Urquinaona, Pza. VII-1A-1B-2A-2B
Blasco de Garay I-4A-4B-4C
Blai I-2B-3B-4B-5C-6C-7C-8C
Blesa IX-1C-2C-3C
Bonsuccés V-3A-3B
Boquería, Pza. de la V-7A
Born, Paseo de la XV-5B
Bruc VII-1C-2C
Cabanes IX-3C, X-3A-3B-2B-2C
Cabanyes I-6A-6B-6C, II-6A
Canaletas, Rambla de V-2C
Caputxins, Rambla dels IV-8C-7C, XII-1C-2C-3C
Carme III-3C, IV-3A-3B-4C, V-4A
Carrera X-6C, XI-6A-6B
Catalunya, Pza. de VI-1A
Catedral VI-7A-7B
Circumvalació, Paseo de XVI-7A-8A
Colom, Paseo de IX-8B-8C, X-7A-7B-7C, XI-7A-7B-7C, XII-7A-7B-7C, XIII-7A-7B-7C, XIV-7A
Comerç XV-6C-5C-4C-3C, XVI-1A-2A
Comerç, Pza. VIII-6C-6B
Comte Borrel II-3A-2A
Concordia I-2A-2B
Consolat XIV-6B-6C
Creu dels Molers I-3A-3B
Drassanes, Avda. de les XI-2C-3C-4C-5C
D'Ali VIII-4C-3C-3B
Egipciaques IV-5A-4A-3B
Elcano, d' I-1A-2A-3A-4A-5A-6B-7B
Estudi, Rambla dels V-3C-3B-4B
Ferran XIII-1A-1B-1C-2C
Fontanella VI-1B-1C
Fontrodona I-8C, II-7A
Fortuny IV-3C
Francesc Cambó, Avda. VII-7A-7B
Fusina XV-4C, XVI-4A
Fustería XIV-5A-6A
Girona VIII-1A-2A-3A
Hospital III-3C-4C, IV-4A-5A-5B-6B-6C-7C
Icària, Avda. d' XIV-8B-8C
Isabel II XIV-7B-6B-6C-7C
Jaume I XIV-2A-2B
Joaquim Costa III-1C-2C, IV-3A

Jonqueres **VII-2B-2A-3A**
Josep Anselm Claver **XII-6C-6B-6A**
Laietana, Vía **VI-8A-8C-7C-6C-5C-4C-3C-2C, VII-4A-3A-2A, XIV-2B-3B-4B-5B-6B**
Lluis Companys, Pza. **VIII-7C-8C**
Magalhaes **I-5A-6A-7A-8A**
Margarit **I-5A-5B-4C**
Marqués de l'Argentera, Avda. **XV-6A-7A-6B-6C, XVI-6A**
Marqués C. Sagrado **I-3C, II-3A-4A-4B**
Mercé, Pza. **XIII-6B**
Miramar, Avda. de **IX-4C-5C-7A-7B, X-5A-6A**
Montcada **XV-2B-3A-4A**
Montjuic, Passeig de **IX-1B-2B-3C, X-4A-5A-5B-6B-7B**
Nou de la Rambla **IX-1A-1B-1C, X-1A-1B, XI-2A-2B-2C, XII-2A-2B-2C**
Nova, Pza. **VI-6A**
Ortigosa **VII-3A-3B-3C**
Palau, Pza. del **XIV-7C, XV-6A-7A**
Palaudaries **X-4C-5C-5A**
Paralell, Avda. del **I-1B-2B-2C-3C-4C, II-4A-5A-6A-7A-7B-8B, XI-2A-3A-4A-5A-5B-6B-7B-7C**
Parlament **II-2C-2B-2A**
Pelai **V-1C**
Picasso, Paseo de **XVI-2A-3A-4A-5A-6A**
Piquer **X-2A-3A-4A**
Portaferrisa **V-5B-5C**
Portal de l'Angel, Avda. **VI-1B-2A-3A-4A-5A**
Portal de Santa Madrona **XI-4B-5B-5C, XII-5A**
Portal Nou **VIII-7B-7A-8A**
Princesa **XIV-2C, XV-2A-2B-3C**
Puig I Xoriguer **X-5C-5B, XI-5A**
Pujadas, Paseo de **XVI-2B-2C**
Radas **I-3A-2A-2B**
Reial, Pza. **XII-2C, XIII-2A**
Ribera **XV-5C, XVI-6A**
Roser **I-8A-7B-7C, II-7A**
Salvá **I-7A-7B-7C, II-6A**
San Antoni Abad **III-1A-2A-2B**
Sant Jaume, Pza. de **XIV-2A**
Sant Josep, Pza. de **IV-5C**
Santa Josep, Rambla de **V-5B-5A-6A**
Sant Miguel, Pza. de **XIII-2C-3C**
Sant Pau **II-7C-7B, III-7A-7B-7C, IV-7A-7B-7C, XI-1C, XII-1A-1B-1C**
Sant Pau, Ronda de **II-1C-2C-3C-4C-4B-5B-6B-7B**
Sant Pere, Ronda de **VII-2B-2C-3C, VIII-3A-3B-4B-4C**
Santa Mónica, Rambla **XII-4B-5B-5A-6A**
Tapioles **I-6A-5B-5C, II-5A**
Teatre, Pza. del **XII-3C-3B**
Trafalgar **VII-2B-3B-3C-4C, VIII-4A-4B-5B-5C**
Vila **II-7A-8A, X-1A-1B-2B-3B-4B-5B-6C-7C**
Viladomat **II-1A-2A, I-2C-3C**
Villa de Madrid, Pza. de **V-4C**

I
A
B
C
1
2
Avda.
Concordia
Radas
3
Creu dels Molers
del
Blai
4
Blasco de Garay
5
Margarit
d'Elcano
Magalhaes
Tapioles
6
Cabanyes
Blai
Cabanyes
Salvá
7
Salvá
Roser
Roser
Fontrodona
8
IX
A
B
C

A
B
C
1
2
3
4
5
6
7
8
Parlament
Comte Borrell
Marques C. Sagrado
Pau
Sant
Aldana
Ronda
Sant Pau
Paral.lel
Vilà
A
B
C

III
A
B
C
1
Joaquim
Costa
2
Sant Antoni Abad
3
4
II
5
6
7
Sant Pau
8
A
XI
B
C

A
B
C
IV
1
Angels
2
Fortuny
3
Carme
Egipciaques
4
Pza. Sant Josep
Hospital
5
6
Arc de Sant Agustí
7
Liceu
R. dels Caputxins
8
Barbera
A
B
C

A
B
C
1
2
3
4
5
6
7
8
Pelai
R. Canaletas
Bonsuccés
R. Estudis
Pza. Villa de Madrid
Carme
Portaferrisa
R. Sant Josep
Plza. la Boquería
A
B
C

A
B
C
VI
1
Plza. de Catalunya
Fontanella
2
3
Avda. del Portal de l'Angel
4
VII
5
Laietana
6
Pza. Nova
Catedral
Laietana
7
8
XIV
A
B
C

VII
A
B
C
1
2
3
4
5
6
7
8
Pza. Bisbe Urquinaona
Ronda
Bruc
de
Laietana
Jonqueres
Trafalgar
Ortigosa
VI
Françesc Cambó
XV
A
B
C

VIII
A
B
C
1
2
3
4
5
6
7
8
Ausias March
Girona
Bailén
Sant
Pere
d'Alí
Trafalgar
Arc del
Triomf
Plta. Comerç
Pza. Lluís Companys
Nou
Portal
XVI
A
B
C

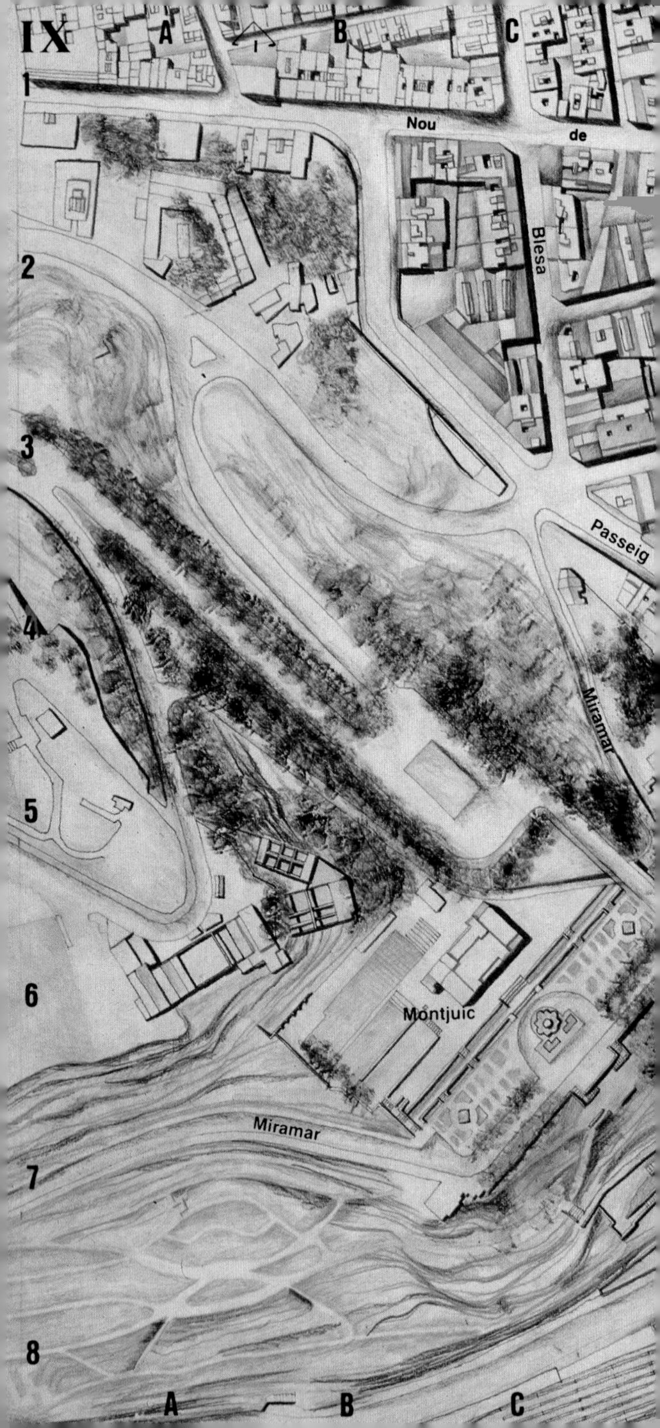
IX
A
B
C
1
Nou
de
Blesa
2
3
Passeig
4
Miramar
5
6
Montjuic
Miramar
7
8
A
B
C

A
B
C
X
II
1
la
Rambla
2
Cabanes
Vilá
3
Piquer
4
de
Paludaries
XI
5
Montjuic
Puig I. Xoriguer
Vilá
6
Carrera
7
Paseo de Colom
8
A
B
C

XI
A
B
C
III
1
2
3
4
5
6
7
8
Nou de la Rambla
Avda. de les Drassanes
Arc
Cid
Avda. del Paral.lel
Palandaries
Portal de Santa
Puig i Xiriguer
Carrera
Atarazanas
Paseo de Colom
A
B
C

A
B
C
XII
Sant Pau
1
R. del Caputxins
Plza. Reial
2
3
Plza. del Teatro
4
XIII
R. Santa Mónica
ona
5
Plza. del Portal de la Pau
Josep A. Claver
6
Monument a Colom
Paseo de Colom
7
8
A
B
C

XIII
A
B
C
1
Ferrán
2
Pza. Reial
Pza. Sant Miquel
3
4
XII
5
Ample
Ample
Pza. Mercé
6
Paseo
de
Colom
7
8
A
B
C

A
B
VI
C
XIV
1
eralitat
de
aume
Jaume I
Pza. de l'Angel
2
Princesa
3
Via Laietana
4
XV
5
Fusteria
Consolat
6
Pza. Antoni López
Isabel II
Pza. del Palau
7
Avda.
d'Icaria
8
A
B
C

XV
A
VII
B
C
1
2
Princesa
3
Comerç
4
Montcarda
XIV
Paseo de la Born
5
Ribera
6
Marqués de l'Argentera
Pza. del Palau
7
8
A
B
C

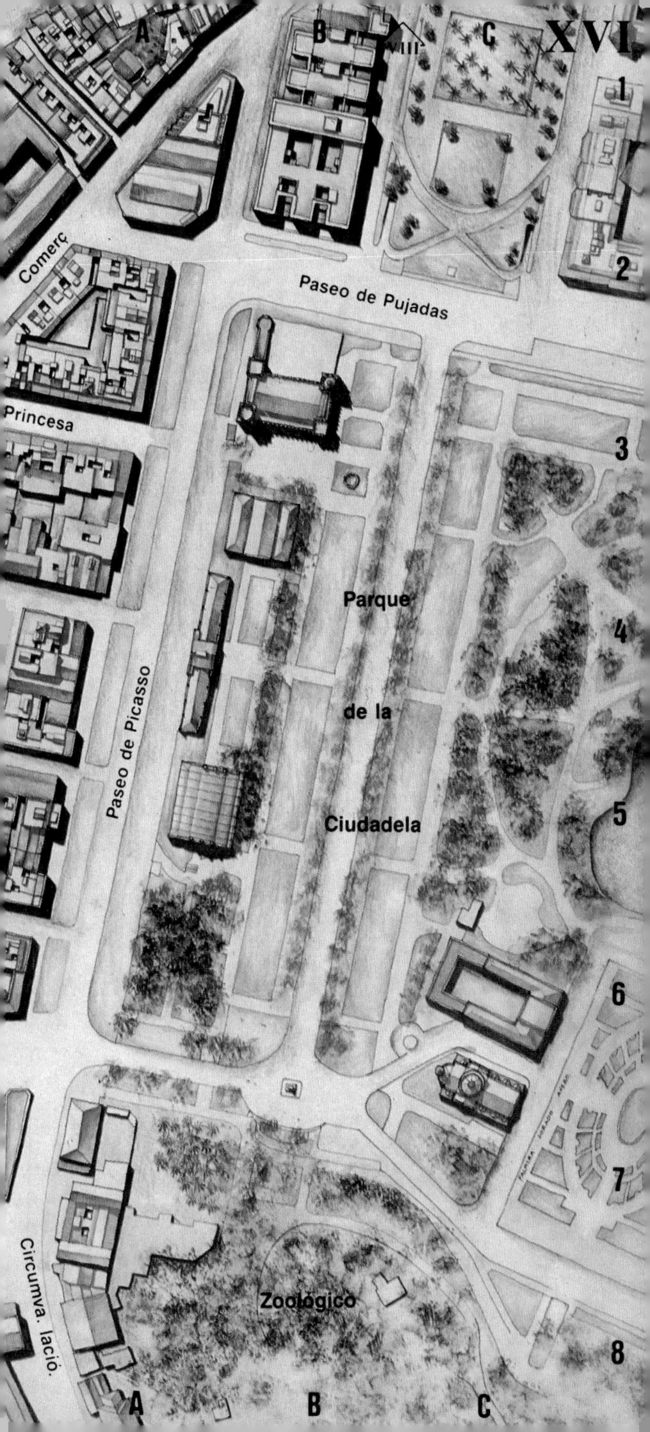
XVI
A
B
VIII
C
1
2
3
4
5
6
7
8
Comerç
Princesa
Paseo de Pujadas
Paseo de Picasso
Parque
de la
Ciudadela
Zoológico
Circumva. lació.
A
B
C

M
Metro
de Barcelona
a Terrassa
a Sabadell Rambla
Sant Cugat
Valldoreix
La Floresta
Les Planes
Baixador de Vallvidrera
Vallvidrera Superior
Peu del Funicular
Tibidabo
Peu del Funicular
Montbau
Vall d'Hebron
Penitents
Vallcarca
Lesseps
Fontana
Reina Elisenda
Sarrià
Les Tres Torres
La Bonanova
Muntaner
Sant Gervasi
Av. del Tibidabo
El Putxet
Pàdua
Plaça Molina
Gràcia
Zona Universitària
Palacio
Palau Reial
Maria Cristina
Les Corts
a Manresa i Igualada
Sant Boi
Gavarra
Sant Ildefons
Maladeta
Can Vidalet
Cornellà
Can Boixeres
Buxeres
Pubilla Cases
Collblanc
San Ramón
Badal
Cornellà
Torrassa
Mercat Nou
Plaça de Sants
Sants
Plaça del Centre
Entença
Hospital Clínic
Provença
Diagonal
Almeda
Santa Eulàlia
Sant Josep
L'Hospitalet
Sants-Estació
Roma-Est. RENFE
Tarragona
Hostafrancs
Rocafort
Urgell
Espanya
Universitat
Catalunya
Poble Sec
Parlamento
Liceu
Paral·lel
Pueblo Seco
Avinguda de Miramar
Canvi de tren
Castell
Drassanes
Atarazanas
Aeroport
Horta
Vilapicina
Llucmajor
Virrei Amat
Maragall
Roquetes
Trinitat Vella
Torras i Bages
Baró de Viver
Santa Coloma
Sant Andreu
Fabra i Puig
Alfons X
Guinardó
Congrés
Viviendas del Congreso
Joanic
Hospital de St. Pau
Dos de Mayo
Sagrera
Verdaguer
Sagrada Família
Camp de l'Arpa
Navas
Clot
Girona
Passeig de Gràcia
Aragón Gran Vía
Glòries
Urquinaona
Marina
Arc de Triomf
Jaume I
Barceloneta
Ciutadella
Ribera
Bogatell
Pere IV
Llacuna
Luchana
Poblenou
Selva de Mar
Besòs Mar
Besòs
La Pau
Verneda
Joan XXIII
Sant Roc
Gorg
Pep Ventura
N